Verbeck of Japan

By

William Elliot Griffis

Published by Forgotten Books 2012

Originally Published 1900

PIBN 1000435701

Verbeck of Japan

A Citizen of No Country

A Life Story of Foundation Work
Inaugurated by Guido Fridolin Verbeck

BY

WILLIAM ELLIOT GRIFFIS

Author of "The Mikado's Empire," " The Religions of Japan,"
" The American in Holland." etc.

NEW YORK   CHICAGO   TORONTO

Fleming H. Revell Company

Publishers of Evangelical Literature

THE CAXTON PRESS
NEW YORK.

DEDICATED

WITH SINCERE REGARD

TO

MARIA MANION VERBECK

THE " HELPMEET FOR HIM "

AND

THE MOTHER OF THE CHILDREN

Contents

List of Illustrations

Preface

At the direct and urgent request of the friends of the late Dr. Guido Fridolin Verbeck, "Verbeck of Japan," the greatest, under God, of the makers of the new Christian nation that is coming and even now is, I have written the story of his life, in my own way. I had no desire, nor was any desire expressed by others that I should paint in words the picture of an immaculate saint, or set forth a being of supernal powers. Neither have I the taste or the ability to enter into the minutiæ of ecclesiastical politics. Let others write of these, or do justice to his work as a churchman. I have told in outline the story of one of the "nursing fathers" of a nation, even of Christian Japan. I have striven to portray a faithful brother-man and a child of God, one whose tender love to his Father was shown in a life hid with Christ and a constant ministry of service to his fellow-men. I have wrought not for those who knew Verbeck, but for those who knew him not.

I knew Verbeck of Japan during four years of intimacy in the Mikado's empire. Thrice visiting his birthplace, Zeist in Holland, I learned many facts about his early life and his unconscious preparation for wonderful work in the Far East.

11

Preface

I have had access to the file of his letters, from 1860 to 1898, written home to the secretaries of the Board of Missions of the Reformed Church in America, and to many of those sent to his own relatives, as well as to his own diaries, note-books, and to other documents lent me by his daughter. Nevertheless, Verbeck was mightier in work than in word, and left relatively comparatively little writing of a personal nature. To all who have in any way aided me, I return sincere and hearty thanks.

The bulk of the book treats of what God gave Guido Verbeck to do, as quietly and as unseen as if he were leaven hid. Verbeck's work belongs less to the phenomenal than to the potent. It was just when men were asking "do missions in Japan pay?" and even when good people in the Reformed Church, almost weary in welldoing, were hinting at abandonment of their Japan Mission, that God by means of true servants wrought His most wonderful work of educating the Japanese for their new life.

Vigorously suppressing my own opinions and views of things ecclesiastical, I have let Dr. Verbeck tell his own story, and, also, show his own powers and limitations. With other things and persons, Japanese and foreign, I have been more free in comment and criticism. In the Introduction, I have sketched briefly Verbeck as a man of action, rather than of words. His was the life of one willing as bridge builder to toil in the caissons, unseen, as well as on the cables in view of all, to fight as a sailor in the turrets, not knowing how the battle went, as well as on deck or in the conning tower.

In my text and quotations, I have used the standard spelling of Japanese names and avoided as far as possible the use of Chinese forms.

May Christians and missionaries like Verbeck, ever faithful to Jesus the Christ abound, to confound and convince all those who ask " do missions pay ? "

W. E. G.

ITHACA, N. Y.

A STAR's serene radiance is better than a meteor's whizz and flash. The quiet forceful life of a missionary like Guido F. Verbeck makes contemptible the fame of a popular idol, admiral, or general, who may have caught the fancy of the public and the newspapers. Such a life, as unknown to general fame, as the leaven in the meal is out of sight, was that of Verbeck of Japan.

For nearly forty years he gave the best powers of mind and body for the making of the new state which we behold to-day and the Christian nation we see coming. He was a destroyer of that old hermit system in which barbarism, paganism, cruelty, intolerance, ignorance, sensualism, and all things detestable ran riot. He was a conserver of that "Everlasting Great Japan," which has in it, and, let us hope, always will have within it, so many things lovely and of good report. He was one of "the beginners of a better time," working for liberty of conscience, for righteousness, for brotherhood, and for the making of that new man in Christ Jesus which is yet to dominate the earth.

Guido Verbeck was willing to do his work, as God gave him to do it, in silence and shadow, even in secrecy if need be. He was a "Jesuit" of the right sort. Never for one moment concealing his identity, his character, his mission, protesting against persecution, oppression, and suppression, he stood for free thought, free speech, and the open Bible. He respected the individuality of every man from the Eta to the emperor. Ever modest and retiring, apparently shy and timid when giving his own advice, he was bold as a lion in doing what seemed right. Brave as the bravest conqueror of cities, he controlled himself and knew when to keep still. He feared the face of no man.

Surrounded often by spies and traitors, ruffians and assassins, living amid dangers and pestilence in the old days, he was never touched by malignant man or contagious disease. Never robust, he was able by care, exercise and temperance to preserve his splendid powers of mind and body to the last year of his life. Coming to Japan in the old days of the repression of truth and light, when the whole country was under the clamps of despotism, when the spy, the informer, and the liar were everywhere, Guido Verbeck seemed to the Japanese to be sheathed in light and to bear one invincible weapon, truth. Since he always told them just what he believed about them, and about their present and future, and the great realities of time and eternity, and since he always kept self in the background, they came to trust him implicitly and to believe him fully. The novelty of meeting a plain man of truth amid so many polished liars, had an effect on the Japanese of the early sixties, at once electric, tonic, self-revealing. Here was a man whom they likened to what in material form they prized so highly—the flawless crystal sphere, that seems first to gather and then to diffuse abroad the sunlight.

So it came to pass that almost from the moment of his landing in Japan, this "Americanized Dutchman," as he called himself, disarmed the old suspicions, winning new confidence. Becoming the servant of servants, as teacher and helper, he attracted to himself the humble and the great. In the days of their impressible youth, he taught those who were to be statesmen and councillors of the emperor and in their manhood he was their guide, philosopher, and friend. Men nearest the throne, yes, even the Mikado himself, in the most hopeful of Asiatic countries have acknowledged freely and gratefully their obligations to Guido Verbeck. A citizen of no country, they gave him a home and protection, awarding to the untitled missionary an honor unique in the history of the empire. When Verbeck of Japan lay " dead in his harness," titled statesmen and nobles came to pay unstinted honors to their friend who had helped to make Japan great. Japan's soldier veterans with their laurels won in continental Asia still fresh on their flags, by imperial order, escorted his body to the tomb. The emperor, who had already decorated the servant of his people, gladly paid the expenses of the funeral. The authorities of the city of Tokio deeded to his family the lot honored by his grave. Japanese friends, pupils, and admirers reared the granite shaft that marks the spot, beneath which his dust mingles with that of the land he loved so well, and to which he gave his best endeavor.

Yet Guido Verbeck loved truth more than he loved Japan, or the United States, or the Netherlands,—the countries in which his three homes were. He never flattered either Japanese or Americans or Dutchmen, no matter how much he loved them or was willing to serve, or work, or die for them. During his long life and in the shadow of death, he feared, indeed, to lessen his influence by rude and unnecessary criticism or by blurting out truths better told later. Yet even as " it is the glory of God to conceal a thing," so Verbeck was wise in withholding, while never afraid at the right time and place to utter his convictions. He spoke the truth in love. He knew what was in man and especially in Japanese man, genus, species, variety, and individual. Yet knowing, he did not despise. Sometimes he pitied, oftener he helped, admired, or encouraged. He saw possibilities and cheered on.

He told me once, in one of many confidences whose seals I feel now at liberty to break, that he thought he knew the individual Japanese better than he knew himself. He believed in Japan and in her possibilities. He did not, like so many men from abroad, think that he knew the Japanese people, because he was well acquainted and

A Glance in Perspective

even intimate with a few scholars and thinkers. On the contrary Verbeck knew the peasant as well as the prince, the outcast as well as the citizen, the people in the mass, as well as those who wear decorations and gold-embroidered coats. In his eyes all men were the children of the Father, and nobles were no more. When some thought that missionary effort should be directed more toward "the upper classes," Verbeck said, "It is the people we must reach, the people."

Hence, it was never possible, either in the craft or state, or church, by old politician or fresh missionary, by dogmatist or the polemic, wolf disguised in the sheep's clothing of "liberalism" so-called, to deceive this master of men and ideas. With him, names were nothing.

Verbeck of Japan had his limitations, which some of us knew well. He was not a business man and could not always see eye to eye with those trained in the canons of commerce. Inheriting from his father some old-fashioned prejudices regarding a mind bent only on pecuniary profits, and never having had the elements of practical business principles taught him, he sometimes offended when he meant to be generous. It would have been better, too, for his household, perhaps, had he given a little more attention to that "filthy lucre," a careful use of which so sweetens the relations of life and saves from undue anxiety. However, none more than himself grieved over this lack in his make-up. Had he been better trained commercially, he would not have been plundered so often by rascals, both pagan and pseudo-Christians. Generous to a fault, he was often imposed upon.

His humor was keen, sometimes to the point of cutting. After he had been in Japan some thirty years, one day he walked the platform at a country station, waiting for the train. A kilted, barelegged student eyed him for a time, then concluded he would patronize this innocent alien and air his English. With that superb assurance which is the unfailing endowment of Japanese schoolboys, this eighteen-year-old colt swaggered near and shouted: ''When did you come to our country?'' Dr. Verbeck adjusted his benevolent spectacles, and, after a calm survey, responded, in choice vernacular: '' A few years before you did, sir.'' It is said that the student retired.

In his character and service as a missionary, Verbeck possessed in a high degree the gift and power of mental initiative. He knew how to begin. There was no Macawber in him. He waited not when work called. He turned things up. I have often heard him glory even to exultation in the glorious freedom and the power of independent work possessed by a *pioneer* missionary. As a builder of the true church of Christ in Japan—the church of souls, of faith and of righteousness, rather than of corporations, names, and creed limitations, Verbeck was sometimes a trial to his own brethren. He was not only a cosmopolitan linguist and scholar, but his Christianity was more of a continental than of an in-

A Glance in Perspective

sular type. He was "at the call of any or all of his brethren of whatever Evangelical Mission." He saw things through and through,—the cosmic currents down in the deeps, rather than the "unnumbered laughings" on the surface,—in their issues rather than in their temporary relations. At the same time Verbeck was a conservative both in theology and organization, and here he had marked limitations. It will be generally agreed, I think, that he was the master missionary in evangelism and in the importation of light and life, a very Fuji Yama in the loftiness of his gifts and powers as teacher, preacher, prophet, and statesman.

Yet all this said, his abilities as actual organizer belong on a lower level. He did not possess, or apparently wish ever to gain, those gifts of manipulation and adjustment, or that organizing faculty which enables a man to turn his profound connections into institutions. He cannot be said to have left behind him pupils upon whom his mantle fell. He was innately sociable and his sociability increased with his years, yet he had no one very close intimate among his friends. God called him to do great and mighty work in the high places of the Spirit on Sinai, rather than in Canaan, and this work he did well.

The life of Guido Verbeck covers three periods. The first of childhood and youth covering twenty-two years, from 1830 to 1852, was spent at Zeist, in the Netherlands. His early manhood as civil engineer and theological student from 1852 to

1859 was passed in the United States, the former part in what was then "the West" and the latter in what was then "the East." The third period extended, with occasional brief intervals of absence, through nearly thirty-nine years, from 1859 to 1898.

In Dai Nippon, three distinct epochs of his life are also to be noted. The first decade, spent at Nagasaki, was as the toiling of a miner in the deep and dark places. The second decennium in the new capital, Tokio, was passed as educator and translator in the service of the Japanese government. Then followed nearly two decades of Bible translation and the direct preaching of the gospel, chiefly in evangelical tours. For over twenty years he supported himself and his family on his salary paid him by the Japanese government, so that he was during this time at his own charges, costing the Mission Board nothing. In later years, as a laborer under the Bible societies and Mission Board of the Reformed Church in America, he was worthy of his hire.

Guido Verbeck was a many-sided man. His intellectual and spiritual inheritances were great. He was engineer, teacher, linguist, preacher, educator, statesman, missionary, translator, scholar, gentleman, man of the world, child of his own age and of all the ages. Among those in Japan, who seemed to have the most confidence in and respect for him, were persons of rank and very old and very young people who are thoroughly conservative still as to habits and opinions. Among these were bigoted Buddhists and Shintoists, who knowing Verbeck to be an uncompromising Christian missionary, yet always honored and trusted him as a gentleman.

Guido Verbeck was also the father of a family of seven children, five sons and two daughters, six of whom, surviving to-day, do their country honor, serving abroad under the flag as soldier or as missionary, teacher, or at home as artist, or in business. Amid paganism, he represented Christ and Christendom to them.

One secret of his power among Japanese, high and low, was that he always regarded the self-respect of each individual with whom he came into contact. One of his traits of character was an extreme unwillingness to exercise his will in influencing the will of others. He respected the right of each individual to act independently too much to use undue influence over them. Consequently, as a missionary even, he would never try to force Christianity on a Japanese. With his own children even, he avoided, after they had reached a certain age, as much as possible, giving a direct command. " He would give advice to us," said one, " but rarely, even if needed, a command."

Verbeck's is one of those names honored both by foreigners and natives. Though he was a citizen of no state, three countries claim him as their son.

Verbeck was a man who believed with all his heart in the sufficiency of the gospel, the good news of God, proclaimed by Jesus Christ. He was too honest to explain it away. In him the historic spirit was too strong to dissipate it in vague theories, or put it on a level with anything which the ancient or ethnic teachers have expounded. He believed that twenty centuries had added nothing to what Jesus had taught of God and man, or in their relations one to the other. He did heartily believe that nineteen centuries, and especially his own century, had added vastly to the sum of man's knowledge in other subjects of inquiry and revelation. Denying himself otherwise many luxuries and personal enjoyment, he never hesitated to possess himself of the best works in philosophy, science, and language, so as to keep abreast with the best thought and real knowledge of the age.

Verbeck knew well the shams of the period. He had no use, in the transmission of his message from God, for what some men imagine to be necessary; such, for example, as a detailed knowledge of the method, manner, and results of what is so vulgarly misunderstood and also called the higher criticism, or of comparative religion, though he was a hearty believer in the legitimate use of both. He was a consummate master in the art of literary analysis and criticism. He was once engaged during many months in elaborate researches, with the idea of publishing a book upon literary or higher criticism. He was asked more than once by prominent American inquirers and scholars whether for successful missionary

A Glance in Perspective

work, especially in preaching, he did not feel it necessary to study thoroughly the native religions of Japan. His one answer was, that he had never considered it worth while to spend time in proving to the Japanese that two and two did not make five. He found it was more economical in time and labor, and ultimately far more effective, to demonstrate that two and two make four, and this he kept on doing for nearly forty years.

Yet Dr. Verbeck was very far from undervaluing native thought, history, customs, or beliefs. Indeed, one thing that made him a past master in the art of public discourse, able to hold his Japanese audiences spellbound for hours, and to keep their eyes, ears, yes, and even their mouths, wide open, and this often in one place night after night, was his profound knowledge of the heart and thought of his audience. He could use with tremendous effect their own proverbs, gems of speech, popular idioms, and the epigrams of their sages. Often he "carried them to Paradise on the stairways of surprise" by showing how their own great men had groped after the essential, even as he was leading them to the historic, Christ. He threw great floods of light on themes otherwise abstruse by opening the windows of illustration from their own national history. I once heard him praise glowingly Nicolai, the Russian archimandrite, (now bishop) for his effective use of Hideyoshi's gourd-banner in illustration of the magnetic power of the cross. Verbeck's method was like the sliding

back at daydawn of the *shoji*, (house-shutters) so
as to fill with glorious sunshine and perfumed air
the room of night and sleep.

Others might be content with mere fluency or
a superficial knowledge of things Japanese. Dr.
Verbeck always kept himself familiar with the
best native writing and the classic forms of
modern speech. While many others would be
enjoying social relaxation, or the newspapers,
Dr. Verbeck would have in hand, whether sitting
on the porch or walking in the garden, a copy of
some standard Japanese author, usually Kaibara,
reading it again and again in order to master
literary graces as well as lines of thought and argument. He knew the language well, both in
its ancient, mediæval, and modern form. He
loved it in its native purity, freshness and power,
even more than in its reinforcement and adorn-
ment, yes, even its weakening and degradation
by Chinese infusion and adulteration.

Hence his absolutely unique position as evangelist and preacher and, possibly, we may even
add, as translator. With emphasis the natives
called him Hakase, professor, or most learned
man. In his methods of turning the sublime
Hebrew and plastic Greek into a clear dignified
and enjoyable Japanese, he was like Luther and
Tyndale. These had in mind not only the
scholar but also the plowboy. Verbeck knew
the speech of the plain people as well as of those
who dwell in palaces. He could confound and
humble the Chinese pedants. Seeing them in his

A Glance in Perspective

audience, these lovers of "words of learned length and thundering sound," he usually made them wonder how "one small head could carry all he knew." Then after a little fun of this sort he preached the gospel in plain, clear, fluent, elegant language "understanded of the people." I remember once coming to Tokio, after a year's stay in Echizen, with ears well attuned and responsive to local lingo, and noting at once the easy, elegant, and dignified colloquial of the master.

Hence it is that above the ranges and table-land of the diction of the Bible in Japanese—one of the most successful missionary translations ever made—the work of Guido Verbeck on the Psalms, is like that of peerless Fuji. Other peaks are indeed noble, but reach not the highest of the "no two such."

Yet here again, we note human limitations. As Verbeck, always mightier in work than in word, wrote far fewer letters than his friends desired or even perhaps justly expected, so also he committed to writing few if any of those sermons, which, like the tempest or the soughing of the wind among the leaves of the forest, moved the hearts of men to righteousness. Did these but exist in print, how helpful would they be to those who admired his inimitable style, and hearing, despaired. Yet had they now the text to study and analyze, many might become what so few foreigners are, or can be, either fluent or eloquent preachers in Japanese.

Verbeck of Japan

Several times, when living in Boston, my genial neighbor and friend Dr. Edward Everett Hale, the author of " A Man Without a Country " honored me by calling to learn the latest news or earliest light upon the most interesting of Asiatic countries.   He was particularly eager to learn the secret of Japan's wonderful renascence, and to find out why her people showed such a liking for what we usually associate with " Anglo-Saxon " inheritances.   Possibly this sketch of Dr. Verbeck's life may help in solving the fascinating riddle.   At any rate, let us see how and why Verbeck of Japan, a man without a country, while receiving citizenship of none, was honored in three lands and by one uniquely.

II

THE name Verbeck, or, more properly Verbeek, is a contraction of Van der Beck, van der Beek, meaning, from the brook or rivulet. The name is essentially Dutch, the prefix *ver* being contracted from *van der*. In tracing the ancestry of the Verbecks we find them in both Holland and Germany. They moved back and forth, east and west, between the Dutch and the Deutsch. In one or two instances they married in the land of Luther, though belonging to the land of Erasmus.

The Verbeeks are found allied by wedlock with the Van Laer and Van der Vliet families. The latter furnished several ministers to the Reformed Church and at one time dwelt in Embden, where they had fled before Alva's persecution. On their tombstones in the church at Embden are the coats of arms of Cornelius and Samuel Van Laer, who died in 1654 and 1712 respectively.

The Van Laer family was strong in religious culture and character. Count Von Zinzendorf, leader of the Moravians, was the guest at the house of Jan Van Laer in Amsterdam during several of his visits. In 1773, when the Count would found a Moravian settlement in the

Verbeck of Japan

Netherlands, Cornelius Renatus Van Laer (1731–1792), who greatly favored the plan, bought Zeist from his wealthy cousin Schellinger, and generously assisted the Brethren.

The fact that Zeist with over two thousand acres of land and some hundreds of houses on it, was once in the possession of the Schellingers and later the Van Laers, shows the well-to-do conditions of the two families. Jacob Van Laer, born in 1663 was Burgomaster of Zwolle, the city of Thomas a Kempis, in which also " The Imitation of Christ" had been written. In 1725 he was Commissioner of the Admiralty in Amsterdam and in 1736 a member of the States-General. An older member of the family held the same office, and was director of one of the six sections of the mighty East India Company, whose huge buildings remain to this day at Delft, their seaport being Delfshaven, whence sailed the Pilgrim Fathers to found Massachusetts. The Verbeeks, were prominent and wealthy merchants in Amsterdam. Through their alliances with the Van Laers, they were drawn also to Zeist, where one of them built a house on the square. In later generations, some of the Verbeeks adhered to the Moravian Community, while others were Lutherans.

Zeist is a pretty little town of about six thousand inhabitants, of whom about thirty-five hundred are settled inside the village boundaries. It lies in the province of Utrecht, a few miles to the westward of the university city of the same

The Koppel

name, the village being reached from the larger city by both steam, and tram or horse cars. As early as A. D. 838, this village is known to have existed, being just on the western border of a large stretch of woodland. In 1667 "the house of Zeist" now called "the Castle," a "deftig gebouw" as the Dutch say, was built by William of Nassau, the lord of Odijk and Cortgene. This magnificent old mansion, still standing among lordly trees and with a superb park attached to it, was bought in 1746 by Mr. C. Schellinger and in 1767 by Marie Agnes, Countess of Zinzendorf and second daughter of the famous Count, who afterward married Maurice William, Count of Dohna. Since 1862, this lordly mansion has been possessed by the late Mr. C. B. Labouchere, and since 1891, many are my happy memories of the courtesy and bountiful hospitality of the host and hostess and their brilliant and accomplished sons and daughters, who move within the first circles of Holland's social life. Theirs was a typical home, rich in character, ability, and piety. Yet further down the avenue was once another home, more modest and less known to wealth and fame, which God made a storage battery of spiritual power for the re-vitalizing of a nation.

In 1776 the Moravian Community, which had been begun at Ijsselstein, was fixed at Zeist. To-day their houses, of the sisterhood on one side of the great wide avenue of planted trees and of the brotherhood on the other, form the chief feature of the place. In this community, besides the cultivation of pure and undefiled religion, industry is a striking characteristic.

The Verbeeks, as the older and proper form of the name and as chiselled on the tomb in Tokio, may be traced far back into Dutch history. Suffice it to say that when the Moravian settlement at Zeist was formed in 1776, the year of American independence, there were two brothers Jan and Pieter, sons of Jacob. The descendants of the latter are found in nearly all the Moravian congregations in Germany. Jan did not remain in such friendly feeling with Moravian church government and though he did not himself leave the community his children and grandchildren did. He went to Germany, but later the family returned to Holland, as we shall see.

Jan Verbeek (1709–1763) married Anthonia Van der Vliet (1709–1744). Their grandson Hendrik Jan Verbeek (1769–1817) living in Saxony with the Moravian Community, withdrew from it and married Dorothea Elizabeth Henning (1773–1848) of Celle, Hanover. The couple settled at Cholsdorf, where their older children, including Carl Heinrich Willem (1769–1864), father of Verbeck of Japan was born. Later they moved to Hamburg and obtained a livelihood from a vinegar factory, which in the siege of the city by Napoleon was destroyed. The parents then fearing to lose their son by military conscription, sent him to their relatives in Zeist. So Carl grew up in his father's sister's house in the Moravian Community.

The Koppel

At "the castle" then lived Anna Maria Jacomina Kellerman, the daughter of Coenraad Willem Kellerman, a famous Patriot. Carl Verbeek and Ann Kellerman, parents of Guido Verbeck were married in 1818, and lived at Rysenburg, a little village southeast of Zeist, of which the husband, Carl Verbeek was Burgomaster, and here four of their children were born. In 1827 they moved to Zeist, occupying the house called "the Koppel," in which four more of their offspring saw the light, the second one in this second group of four being Guido Herman Fridolin Verbeck, who was born January 23d, 1830.

From his father, a gentleman of fine feelings, diffident and retiring, the future maker of New Japan inherited his simplicity and modesty. To those who did not know his lion heart, these at times seemed to border on timidity. With both father and son, it was Jesus-like gentleness that made great. Guido's love of poetry and music came from his mother, a woman of refinement and culture. Besides the piano and organ, Guido Verbeck played well on the violin and guitar, often accompanying his sister on the harp. At the mother and the ancestral roots that nourished her being, let us look.

The Kellermans originated in Italy, where centuries ago they had borne the name of Paravium. Accepting early the doctrines of the Reformation, they were persecuted as heretics and fled for their lives. One of them, while being searched for by the inquisitors, hid during several days in a cellar at Strasburg. On emerging, to baffle his pursuers and secure greater safety, he secured asylum under the name of Kellerman, in the land in which he, the Anabaptists, the Pilgrim Fathers and the Huguenots, as well as Jews and Catholics had heard and found that "there was freedom of conscience for all men."

In 1788, at the time of the civil strife between "Patriots"[1] and "Prince-Adherents," Mr. Coenraad Willem Kellerman, one of the descendants of the Italian Bible Christians, was living in the castle at Zeist. Having taken the side of the Patriots or Anti-Orangists, he had to leave the Netherlands when the Prussians invaded the country. He went to England. He was twice wedded. From the second marriage with Maria Wilhelmina van der Vliet, was born Anna Maria Jacomina Kellerman, the mother of Guido F. Verbeck. Thus in the veins of the child destined to be "the foremost teacher of the Japanese" were blended Southern fire and Northern energy. The best inheritances of Latin and Germanic Christendom met in the man who gave the Japanese one of the types of Christianity in a life at once broad and deep. The ancestors of Verbeck of Japan were strenuous in that one common faith which is to win and hold Japan also.

The hardiness of the race is shown in Guido's Aunt Miesje (Cornelia Marie Kellerman), who lived to be nearly a century old. Though she

[1] See De Patriottentijd, by Dr. H. T. Colenbrander, Hague, 1899.

The Koppel

was very small in stature, her mind was bright and clear until the last. For more than thirty years she was the lady principal or inspectress of the Moravian Young Ladies' Boarding School in Zeist, beloved and respected by a host of friends, parents, scholars, and teachers. In her latter years though quite blind, she knitted many a stocking for those in need. When sight failed, touch was revived and she learned to read the Bible by the finger with the help of raised letters.

The youngest of the eight children and the only one now (in 1900) living, has furnished the biographer with reminiscences of the Koppel, the pretty little home, in which Guido Verbeck was trained for his life's noblest work. Another, and a young relative who has called it "a sort of El Dorado," has richly reinforced the notes gathered during several visits to Zeist, its community, and its castle. The Koppel stood on a gentle knoll well embowered among trees, with the characteristic canal and bridge not far away and with dumb domestic creatures generally in sight and feeding on the rich grass. A dovecote prominent in the foreground was of royal dimensions and contained seven hundred pigeons.

The word "Koppel" occurs in many places on Dutch maps. Besides Koppeldijk, Koppel- rust, and Koppelsteeg in the Netherlands, we have no fewer than eight towns or villages with the same name.

The word "Koppel" is the same as the English "couple." It means a brace. Two objects linked together in idea make a pair. There are two Koppels on a map of Utrecht and environs now before me, and also the Koppeldijk and Koppelvaart, the names being given because they connect two water or land paths. If there is a crossing of two canals, with different levels of water there must be a lock or sluice near by. This means waiting,—with patience also. Almost as a matter of course, there springs up in due time an inn for the boatmen or passengers, and for their accommodation and refreshment. The name "Koppel" is thus indicated for a sign. Did the house at Zeist take its name from the old inn on the dike, in times long gone, the name being much older than the house? Or, is "Koppel" the popular corruption of "Koepel," meaning a pavilion, kiosk or summerhouse in a garden? We incline to the former view.

To make their eight children as happy as possible on earth and to fit them for the largest usefulness in life, was the chief concern of the parents. After purchasing the Koppel, the next aim was to make it lovely. This with the aid of a most faithful serving man, true to his master during thirty-six years, they were able to do. The Creator and his servants wrought together to make beauty. The house and home, the Koppel and its surroundings, became very lovely to the eye. Besides the elm-trees reared for shade, forming a perfect bower, there were the choicest pear-trees and flower and vegetable

gardens, surrounded by a double hedge. Thus
there were fruit, vegetables and nuts in abun-
dance and in the large stable was the hay loft.
Although their place was not a farm, the Verbeeks, besides garden, orchard, and meadow
had two cows, two donkeys with cart and sad-
dles and a white mare, "Fatima," that carried
the father of the home and the Burgomaster of
Rysenburg to his daily tasks.

Guido's favorite pets were the two colts,
"Hector" and "Sylvan." He had also rabbits,
geese, ducks, chickens, and a most gorgeous
peacock and hen. Nor must the faithful watch-
dog "Castor," which on one occasion when
Guido was absent, went out and searched for
him two days and returned home disconsolate,
be forgotten. On one of the branches of the
large English walnut-tree there was a swing. In
the boathouse, which was roomy enough for all
the children to get into, there was a rowboat.
As a Dutch rural home would hardly be complete
without a stork, there was on the top of the two
high elms at the side of the house a stork's nest.
As sure as March returned, so did the storks,
heralds of summer. Eight times also did the
magic stork of fairy tale visit the home and fill
the cradle. The Verbeeks believed in the bless-
ings of Psalm cxxvii., and their quiver was full.

In this home of love and affection Guido Ver-
beck passed nearly twenty-two years of his life.
These were "the days of heaven upon earth."
Years afterward from Green Bay, Wisconsin, he

sent a letter to his youngest sister, giving a memory-picture in transfiguration of the Koppel. As he was very fond of putting down his thoughts in verse his epistle took the form of sixteen verses of eight lines each, a verse being devoted to father, mother, and to each of his sisters and brothers. In after years, as his eye of memory ranged along that perspective of the past which had its farthest end at the Koppel, he wrote, "We lived like Jacob did, in the free Temple of Nature, enjoying the garden, the fruit, the flowers, with joy, on green benches between green hedges. And after sunset when the stars were sparkling, then we brothers and sisters went lovingly arm in arm and passed our time in garden, wood, or quiet arbor enjoying each other's happiness and God's peace.

"The winter days we spent mostly on the ice, but toward evening in the cozy twilight we gathered around the warm stove, to enjoy with all our heart our Koppel happiness. Then father told us many a story, and we sang many good and favorite songs, after lamps were lit we all engaged in reading, ate apples, nuts, and pears."

Yet this was a home without luxury, most of the household work being done by the inmates themselves. It was plain but high living. Educated, as most Dutch boys in well-to-do families are, to use fluently and exactly the four languages, Dutch, English, French, and German, Guido Verbeck was able all his life long to use these freely. He chose one or the other, as he desired, for the particular purpose of conversation, business, devotion, or the expression of the heart's deepest feelings. For this last, he always employed German. In after life it was a puzzle to Guido Verbeck that some people with very little culture could put on great airs, because perchance they might have a little money or employ servants.

In after life one who knew Verbeck of Japan by daily intimacy wrote: "I have often heard Mr. Verbeck say that the Koppel spoilt him for his after life. In reading books of old-fashioned country life such as described by Jane Austen in her novels, and Mrs. Gaskell in Crawford, I have often heard him remark how much they reminded him of the social life in Zeist in his childhood.

" He had a sweet and gentle attractiveness that babies and all animals and birds found irresistible. He loved children and was happy in their company. He could entertain them with charming, old-fashioned little fables and stories he had heard in his boyhood. He condemned severely cruelty to animals, and said that in his family the children had been taught from infancy just how to handle and treat domestic animals. He often said when feeding a cat or a dog, 'We are as a god to these poor animals; they depend upon us and look up to us as we do to a deity.' His love of nature, and the beauties of nature, was strong. He loved to go out into Nature and commune with her, but he did not prefer a permanent abode in the country. As he grew older his sociability seemed to increase. He liked small companies of friends, but disliked large public gatherings or entertainments. He enjoyed games of all sorts in the evening. In his own family in boyhood he was accustomed to pleasant social gatherings and evening card parties. Passionately fond of music, he was a good critic of it too, and delighted in finished execution. He was a good chess-player. He did not care for riding on horseback, but was extremely fond of watching the motions of a fine horse, and of seeing trained horses perform. His father had been a good horseman, and in his youth he himself had had opportunities of riding a good deal."

The happy years sped on golden wings. Then parting, sickness, and death broke up the home. The Koppel passed into the hands of strangers. After some years the grounds were turned into ordinary meadow land. Nothing of house or home now remains except a few trees and a new pigeon house.

Such changes in Holland are less common than in a new country and the loss of his home was a great grief to Guido, especially, who had hoped to make it his own and keep his father in comfort all his life. He wrote in after years,—in a strain not to be interpreted too literally by those who know little or nothing of the Fifty-first Psalm or "conviction of sin," "I, oh I was full of hopeful expectations, how I did dream of great and noble deeds. To me life was all beauty, light, and goodness, and oh! what use did I make of these gifts? Until to-day, they only

The Koppel

brought to me sin and disappointment and cares to those I should have supported. But thanks to the Father, whose earnest voice still calls me to His love and truth."

So happy a childhood was not very eventful. Nevertheless, it is a chronic mystery how boys are reared. Is it not a wonder that any of them escape the consequences of their daring and ever come to mature life? Baby boy Guido had one hair-breadth escape. In Holland the landscape is marked off by ditches instead of fences, for here the earth is like a sponge. When only two years old, Guido fell into one of the many trenches on the Koppel, tumbling off the little bridge that led to the meadow, where his brother, with the donkey then was. Happily for Japan and humanity, the well-soused baby was picked up half frozen and almost drowned. Put to bed with his mother, he was warmed and fondled until the doctor arrived.

Though Guido Verbeck's father had been born in Germany, and he and many of his relations were Lutherans, yet there was no Lutheran church in Zeist. Attendance at worship was always with the Moravians among whom also were many relatives. The five elder Verbeck children, one after the other, were sent in due time to their uncle, a Lutheran minister in Amsterdam, to be instructed and confirmed, but Guido and his younger brother had the privilege of being confirmed together in the Moravian church at Zeist and there admitted to the holy communion. This was much more congenial to his taste, as from his infancy he had attended that church, literally imbibing from her bosom his missionary spirit.

To show how nobly committed to take Jesus seriously and obey His commands, the Moravians were and are, it was no unusual thing for pupils in the Zeist school to have their teacher suddenly receive a call to go to Labrador, or Greenland, or the West Indies. It was also as inspiring as it was interesting to see and meet the veteran missionaries returning from their distant fields, often bringing a dozen children from other missionaries with them to be taken to Germany to school. Thus they were to be separated from their parents for years. Such lives of self-denial made deep impressions upon the Verbeck children. Gutzlaff of China was especially inspiring to young Guido.

As soon as they were old enough to cross "the ten ditches" on their way to school, they were sent to the Moravian Institute to be taught. Very happy were those school days, during which Guido made rapid progress in all his studies, especially the three languages, Dutch, French, and German. As many of the boarding scholars, both boys and girls, were English, the Verbeek children picked up that language, before they began studying it in books and the English-speaking children were often guests at the Koppel. Guido took particular care with himself and younger sister to get a good pronunciation. One of his favorite sentences, oft re-

The Koppel

peated in order to train the tongue from slipping from the soft *th* to the hard *t* was this, which he made his sister also repeat over and over again: "I thrust the thistle in my side and the thorn in my thumb," or "Theophilus Thistle thrust three thousand thistles into the thick of his thumb." Hence it was that in after years in America, few people suspected that the brother and sister had been Hollanders.

The Koppel was a hospitable home and many were the guests, both friends and strangers, as well as relatives from Zeist and neighboring cities. There was always room for more at the large mahogany table indoors, through the nine months of cool weather, or around the green table set out under the large old English walnut-tree before the house, where in summer the morning and evening meals were enjoyed. Indeed, both the Koppel and the Koppel family were centres of popularity.

Every season had its attractions. The coming of the storks, the sweet smelling flowers, life under the trees, the delicious Dutch vegetables, the luscious berries, such as Holland only can produce, marked the spring and early summer. Then in summer and autumn, the ripening fruits, the baskets full of nuts, and the roasted pigeons, ducks, and geese were shared with city relations. In the outdoor games both young and old joined, while in the beautiful moonlight evenings the sweet Dutch and German songs and music made, with a wonderful variety of other

Verbeck of Japan

delights, a round of enjoyment such as only can be found in a large family.

The winters were no less attractive. From early childhood the children watched the weather vanes to see if the north wind would blow, so that they might have ice to skate on. If, after the ice was strong enough to hold them, the snow would fall to disappoint, how glad they were to see their faithful servant with his big broom clear off enough space to skate on. All in the family, except the mother, could glide over the ice on steel. They were taught and obliged to skate gracefully, as it was the father's motto, "whatsoever is worth doing at all, is worth doing well." In times of severe frost, when the rivers were frozen over, the young folks and sometimes the whole family would start out in the morning with friends and move gaily over many leagues of ice, returning in the evening "without ever being tired." It was the custom with the Verbeeks to celebrate with plenty of fun and gifts the birthday of each one in the family.

One of Guido's summer delights was in walking. When young city cousins were staying at the Koppel, he made quite long expeditions. About two hours' tramp from Zeist, there was a high mound which the soldiers of Napoleon had reared during the French occupation. The boy Guido proposed a stroll thither, in order to see the sunrise. The lads and lassies had to start very early, while it was yet dark, and the highway was not only very lonely, but the greater part of it lay through gloomy woods. Yet the more the mystery, the more the fun. To cheer up his companions and beguile the time, the young leader proposed telling stories. These, whether fairy tales or extemporaneous, were in harmony with the environment, so that as the woods grew thicker and darker, the lore became more sober and mysterious. This made the young folks draw all the closer to their guide and protector. At last the pyramid was in sight and after climbing to the top, these young dwellers in the flat land of the European Egypt, saw the sunrise in all its glory. Then after rest and refreshments, they reached home in time for breakfast, full of admiration for the courage of Guido.

Probably no body of Christians hold more beautiful and impressive, albeit simple services, appropriate to Passion Week, than the Moravians. At each recurring anniversary of the Saviour's rising, at Zeist as at Bethlehem in Pennsylvania, the early morning found them at break of day, first in the church and then in the cemetery. The young hearts of the children were filled with peculiar joy and expectation, when the Easter music burst upon the air as the sun greeted their vision.

The happiest day of the year was the day of the birth of the Son of Man. After the early Christmas Eve service, held especially for the children, each of whom received a lighted candle and sang Hosannas in response to the choir, they walked home full of expectations as to what they should find. They were never disappointed. There was the Christmas tree glorious with lights and pendant with glittering decorations. Beneath the tables were spread the many presents.

Although the Verbecks at Zeist, of the male line, had no German blood in them and were true Dutch people, using the vernacular fluently and correctly and, when away from home, writing to each other in Dutch, they always spoke German at home, for many of their relatives and most of the Moravian people at Zeist were German-speaking people. It was no smattering of language that the Verbecks received. Guido, the future translator of the Code Napoleon and of Bluntchli, as well as of the Book of books, mastered also the literature of each tongue. He was all his life especially fond of poetry. It is no wonder then that Guido called German his heart language. Yet it was conscientiously and with delight that the Verbeeks often sang:

> " Wien Neerlandsch bloed in de aderen vloeit,
> Van vreemde smetten vrij." [1]

Enough has already been made manifest, of Guido Verbeck's early home life, to show how therein he was grandly fitted for the amazing polyglot labors of nearly forty years in Japan, and to reveal the secret also of his resources of recuperation.

[1] Whose Netherlandish blood flows in his veins, free from alien stain.

The Koppel

Guido Verbeck was born in the year 1830, signalized by the construction of the first railway in Europe. This marked the beginning of a new era in mechanical engineering. "A few years later, when the time came for deciding upon a future profession for the boy Guido, a family council was called, and it was unanimously agreed that engineering was the 'coming profession' and the one for which he should be trained."

After graduating from the Moravian School, he entered the Polytechnic Institute of Utrecht, coming especially under the care of Professor Grotte. He had a short experience in the foundry at Zeist, for the production of bronze, brass, and artistic iron work. He made also some attempts at improving the methods of coffee roasting. Probably in his opinion, as in that of most Americans, the Dutch overdo the browning of the berry, even to blackness. Yet after all, Zeist seemed to the expanding ambition of the young Dutchman a pent-up Utica. America, the land of opportunity, beckoned and he saw and heeded.

III

IN THE LAND OF OPPORTUNITY

IT was through the suggestion and invitation of his brother-in-law, Rev. George Van Deurs, backed by the Rev. Otto Tank, son of a Scandinavian nobleman, who had been a Moravian missionary in the West Indies and who was living at Green Bay, Wisconsin, that Guido Verbeck set his face toward America. Mr. Tank having married a wealthy Dutch lady in Zeist [1] intended with his means and opportunities to establish near Fort Howard, across the Fox river, a model town. Being very benevolent, he hoped to do a great good by helping young Hollanders to larger opportunities of life.

Guido left Holland on the 2d of September, 1852, and was met on his arrival in New York by Mr. Tank who induced him, with two other promising countrymen of his, to go to Tanktown, near Green Bay, Wisconsin. They were to employ their talent in the foundry which Mr. Tank had set up with the idea of building machinery for steamboats to help in developing the West. Guido's letter in Dutch written to his

[1] The Tank Home for Missionary Children at Oberlin, Ohio, and the Tank Library of Dutch Literature at Madison, Wisconsin, take their name from Mrs. Tank.

In the Land of Opportunity

sister Aline from Fort Howard, opposite Green Bay, and dated January 19th, 1853, tells of his experiences.

"Passing through Auburn, N. Y., I spent a happy fortnight with Minna (his sister who lived there. She had left home a year before and was married to Mr. P. C. Van Laer.) On Saturday the first of November, I left Auburn for Buffalo, much admiring the country through which I passed. I was astonished to find a seaport a hundred miles inland, with many steamers and two- and three-masters."

Waiting until the 6th of November, the young Dutchman got on board a steamer for Green Bay. After a stormy day on Lake Erie, she had to return, starting again the following Monday, arriving at Cleveland on Thursday, leaving that same night, but getting into a gale that carried off the smoke stack and the rudder chains, leaving the vessel to drift helplessly during four days. With land only two miles away but without any possibility of reaching it, the passengers and officers were every moment on the lookout for help. To have crossed the Atlantic Ocean to be drowned upon a lake was a prospect that impressed Guido both solemnly and ludicrously. The errant steamer was finally taken in tow by an iron government warship and brought back to Cleveland. From this city, first by steamer and rail, and then by wagon and sleigh over the worst roads imaginable, the weather beaten voyager arrived on the 23d of November, very much

out of pocket, but with a warm welcome by
Mr. Tank.

He soon found, however, that Tanktown was
not the place for him to stay in always. He
writes: "I must see more of America and be
where I can improve myself. I am determined
to become a good Yankee." Thus early, he was
in process of becoming an "Americanized Dutchman," a product that often in sterling qualities,
excels the average original element in either
Holland or America.

This he further proved in one way, as thousands of Netherlanders and other Continental
Europeans in England in the sixteenth and seven-
teeth centuries did before him, and as thousands
do now in the United States. He made his name
quickly intelligible to American eyes as well as
ears. Tired of repeatedly pronouncing his name
in proper Dutch style, he changed the spelling
from Verbeek (which sounded as Verbake) and
made its orthography to suit English-speaking
people. "Verbeck" was the nearest in sound to
the original. So "Verbeck" he continued to
use, sacrificing history to convenience. It is certain that the Japanese were all the more able to
apprehend and pronounce his name because of
the modified orthography. It is Verbeek, that is
sculptured upon his monument in Tokio, but in
history it is Verbeck of Japan.

In other ways not a few, and almost invariably
for the better, Guido became "an Americanized
Dutchman."

In the Land of Opportunity

On November 1st, 1853, he came to Brooklyn where his sister Selma was living as the wife of Reverend George Van Deurs. He was in hopes of finding something in New York more congenial to his taste, but, shortly after, receiving an offer to go as an engineer to Helena, Arkansas, he accepted the offer. He went first with his brother-in-law to Philadelphia, spending a week there in seeing the wonders of that great city founded by the son of a Dutch mother.

His initial letter from Helena, Arkansas, written on the 4th of November, 1853, shows him busily engaged in drawing plans of bridges and in making maps and various kinds of engineering calculations. When he saw the poor slaves, working in the cotton fields all day and even on Sundays, his growing Americanism received a chill. He longed for more food for the soul, hungered for good preaching of the gospel. He declared he would gladly walk twenty miles to hear Mr. Beecher or Dr. Wadsworth preach. He saw much that was genuine and inspiring in American religion, but he noted that much also was done for show. He did not enjoy the hot climate of Arkansas.

The doctor warned him that when summer came he would be sure to get congestive fever or chills, but he answered by saying that before this should happen, he would jump on a steamer and escape. Nevertheless on the 18th of June the stalking fever reached him. He had to go to bed, remaining there until the 24th of July, suffering reduction to the similitude of a skeleton. He sunk the little capital which he had accumulated in doctors' bills and nursing, yet he was very grateful for his recovery, for many young men around him had died of cholera.

This sickness was a turning point in Guido Verbeck's career. As he more than once told his relatives, he promised God that if restored to health, he should consecrate his life to service in the missionary field. How well he kept his vow, all know.

When able to walk again, he decided to return to Wisconsin, where his sister and brother-in-law were living. He was not able to leave Helena for Green Bay until August 1st. He came without any formulated plans for the future, but largely because his sister and brother-in-law were anxious to have him with them. After a long rest, which he greatly enjoyed, he accepted charge of Mr. Tank's foundry, spending the winter of 1854 and 1855 very happily. Then came the call, from no earthly master, to a different sort of service.

Let us now look at the other end of the earth and see what that service was.

The Crimean war, which in Europe was chiefly confined to the shores of the Black Sea, had its echoes in Japanese waters, even in Nagasaki harbor. The French and British fleets had entered the Black Sea January, 1854, and war was declared late in March. Early in September, 1854, Rear-Admiral Sir James Sterling came to Naga-

In the Land of Opportunity

saki with men-of-war. Intimating that hostilities might take place in the waters of Japan he requested also the privilege of obtaining supplies. Permission was given by the Bakufu, or Yedo Government, to make the ports of Hakodate in the north and Nagasaki in the south, ports of call and supply. Lord Sterling remained in the harbor somewhat over a month, during which time there was intense excitement among the Japanese, and the Bakufu was as anxious to prevent any of their people from getting out as to hinder foreigners from getting in.

To guard the coast and keep up both the policy of exclusion and inclusion, the daimio or baron of Hizen was given charge of the work of defence and surveillance. He appointed one of his karo, or ministers, named Murata, a brave and trusty officer whose title was Wakasa no Kami, that is, the honorary lord of Wakasa. In those days titles did not mean necessarily either rank, revenue, or office. Murata posted his troops at advantageous points, and set a cordon of boats around the harbor, so that no hungry scholar eager for knowledge, or student hoping to slip out from Japan to see the world, could break the blockade and get aboard the English ships. Japan was then like a dwarf pine-tree, laboriously prevented from growing, kept only as big as one's fist, with tap root cut and sunshine, air and moisture excluded or allowed only in doles. Neither light nor knowledge was then desired by the government. Nevertheless, though Deshima,

Verbeck of Japan

the little island in front of the city, on which a
dozen Dutchmen were allowed to live and trade,
was like a horn or dark lantern, it gave light.
Wakasa was powerfully impressed by a picture
of the siege of Sebastopol given him by a Dutchman. He asked many questions as to the secrets
of power possessed by Christian nations and
whence and how they had attained such vigor.

Wakasa frequently went out by night and day
in a boat to inspect personally the means of defence and of guard. On one of these excursions
he saw floating on the water a little book, which
in type, binding, and language, was different
from anything he had ever seen. Curiosity at
once seized him to know what it contained.
After much inquiry, conducted with wariness,
one of the interpreters, able to talk Dutch and
read words printed in European letters, told him
that it was about the Creator of the universe, and
Jesus, who taught His mind and truth, and that
there was much also between its pages about
morals and religion. All this only whetted the
governor's desire to know the whole contents.
He sent one of his men named Eguchi Baitei to
Nagasaki, professedly to study medicine, but in
reality to find out from the Dutch more of the
book, and they told him much. When he heard
there was a translation of this book into Chinese,
he sent a man over to China and secured a copy.
Murata's home was in Saga, the castle city and
capital of Hizen, and there with the Chinese translation he began the study of the New Testament.

In the Land of Opportunity

He waited patiently for the unknown teacher to come, who was then in America.

The life in Green Bay was very lonely to Guido Verbeck in a raw country far from the home land, and especially after his sister had left him. Sometimes the homesick young Hollander would bow his head on his desk and shed tears, as he remembered "the Koppel." Yet the exile sang songs of hope in the strange land. The sensitive young man found company with dogs and spiders, but not with bears. Of Mr. Tank's large dog called "Watch," he made a companion. The dog followed Guido about wherever he went. One afternoon as he was walking in the woods with Watch only, he met, when about fifteen minutes' distance from the house, a large bear. Mutually surprised, Bruin and Guido looked at each other for a moment, not knowing exactly what to do. Then the bear, seeing the dog, retreated. The man, believing discretion the better part of valor, retreated also. Both parties turning their backs on each other were not desirous of meeting again.

The laws of heredity were well illustrated in Guido Verbeck. His mother was peculiarly fond of the arachnidæ, and so was he. There was a pet spider in his room and the young exile from home would not allow any one to do it harm. Coming back from his work, he would play the violin, when the spider would be sure to come out of its hiding-place, to Guido's great amusement. The creature seemed to enjoy the concert given for its own benefit.

Verbeck of Japan

It is written by a sacred poet "The Lord looseth the prisoner. The Lord openeth the eyes of the blind." There is a reason why the caged bird born of migratory parents will beat its breast bloody in its attempt to obey the law of its being and fly northward or southward with the changing seasons. As matter of prose fact, Guido Verbeck was as the blind who had not yet won vision and as the prisoner who had not gained deliverance. In some such mood, as the caged eagle feels, he wrote from Green Bay, December 15th, 1855, "There is not much to communicate from these peculiar quarters. It is Saturday evening and the week's troubles are once more endured. We are fast striding toward the end of the year and I hope to enter into a better one than the last one was. It seems to me as if I were going backward in life —with its manifold relations—instead of forward, but perhaps I do not deserve a better fate. Oh, I wish I were an old man. Then I should be joyful and cheerful. I always loved the fall—the autumn best. I am sometimes led to think with Cowper—your poet friend—that 'if I were as fit for the other world as I am unfit for this, I would not change with a saint'; but God forbid that I should speak lightly about so serious a subject. I think I have lonely and dull moods as most feeling men have, and now I am in spite of all circumstances in my low mood. I feel as if I could do anything, at least in some directions. . . . I don't make any plans for the present or the future and act only from momentary impulse and as circumstances require, but these being in a rather critical state it is hard telling what may happen. You need not be alarmed about anything, as all will end pretty well whatever may happen."

The question will naturally arise as to how and why Guido Verbeck's mind was led from his career as civil engineer to that of the ministry of the gospel, and on this subject we have not all the light or information which we desire. Yet the missionary yearning and aspiration had been very strong in the young man from his childhood, and, as we shall see, it did not need much outside pressure or influence to turn the channels of Guido Verbeck's activity. Besides, were not Murata's prayers for light and a teacher, heard of God? It is to be noted too, that the year of Guido Verbeck's sickness was that in which the American Expedition under Commodore M. C. Perry's peaceful armada had been dispatched to Japan. The news of the treaty, made between the government of the United States and that of Japan, had already reached Green Bay. After the happy summer of 1855 Mr. and Mrs. Van Deurs left Green Bay for Auburn, N. Y., the former to prepare himself more thoroughly for the ministry in this Theological School.

The letter quoted above shows that Guido's mind was ready for an entire change of life. All that was necessary was to open the cage. Then the bird would fly. It required very little urging indeed from his brother-in-law to take the step that would open to him the glorious prospect of carrying the good news of God to lands far away. It required little urging from Mr. Van Deurs to Guido to come to Auburn to pursue the studies preparatory to entering the ministry. The late William E. Dodge was also one of the friends who encouraged and gladly promised aid. In due time the young Dutch American appeared before the Faculty, was examined and accepted as a student.

Guido Verbeck enjoyed his life as a student in Auburn. He had also the company of his two married sisters who then lived in this city. He lived in glowing anticipation of work for God and man in lands afar.

Having a deep rich tenor voice, he joined the Seminary quartette of singers. One who was a schoolgirl then and a busy mother now remembers the pleasure his singing gave, at her father's home on Thanksgiving day, 1858. Quiet in manner, reserved almost to shyness, he played his own accompaniment and forgot himself in giving pleasure to others. Not the least of the victories of Guido Verbeck throughout his life was the conquest of self. He overcame shyness when the good of others was in view.

One day he came from the Seminary and with beaming face and sweet rich voice sang the hymn, already, from 1841, old to Americans, though to him quite new, "I am a pilgrim and I'm a stranger." Both the singer and the song seemed never more in unity.

While absorbed in study at the school of divinity, the student found exercise of his powers in preaching in German to the people from the Fatherland, who met for worship in the Seminary Chapel. His heart went out to a maiden, Miss Maria Manion, to whom he was betrothed and in due time married. Meanwhile at Owasco Outlet, a beautiful spot near Auburn, his future colleague, Rev. Samuel R. Brown was pastor of the Reformed Dutch church. This genial pioneer of Christian education in China had been at Canton from 1838 to 1847 in the missionary service of the Morrison Education Society. Having returned home on account of his wife's illness, he had been settled at Owasco Outlet since 1851, hoping for an opportunity to return to missionary work in the Far East, or, shall not we Americans say, our New West beyond sea?

Let us look again beyond the Pacific, and see how prayer and works wrought together, even while Murata waited for his teacher. Japan needed true Christianity.

Nagasaki lies in the province of Hizen in the western part of the Kiushiu or the Island of the Nine Provinces. Its geographical situation makes it the most important port in southwestern Japan and the gateway from China and Korea. Not being easily accessible to the large open country beyond, it can never become a great centre of commerce, but must ever be an important coaling station. Near by are the coal mines and not many leagues away is one of the chief national navy yards.

Verbeck of Japan

Until 1568, Nagasaki was a mere fishing village. Then Hideyoshi wrested it from the local baron and made it a part of the imperial domain. It may be called the birthplace of Christian missions, both of the Roman and of the Reformed order. The Portuguese merchants and missionaries made this their centre of influence, while trade and conversions multiplied so that the city is one of great historical prominence in the story of Japanese Christianity. Early in the seventeenth century, the representatives of southern Europe were driven away and the Dutch were ordered to leave the island of Hirado and their factory there and come to Fore Island or Deshima in front of Nagasaki. Out in the bay, and in sight of the city, at the entrance of the long land locked harbor, is Pappenburg, from which, in 1643, after the uprising at Shimabara, the native Christians were, according to tradition, driven into the sea. As "geography is half of war," so also has it much to do with shaping of mission work in every land. Hence the rebirth of Christianity, this time not of the Roman but of the Germanic type, was at Nagasaki also. From the city on the Long Promontory, the call for missionaries was first sent to America, and at this city they first arrived. The origin of the missions is thus stated in The Life and Letters of S. Wells Williams, p. 284, by himself:

"I was much impressed with what Mr. Donker Curtius, the Dutch envoy, who had just signed a treaty, then said: that the Japanese

In the Land of Opportunity

officials had told him they were ready to allow foreigners all trading privileges if a way could be found to keep opium and Christianity out of the country. There were also then at Nagasaki (on the United States Steamship Minnesota), Rev. Mr. E. W. Syle and Chaplain Henry Wood, and we three agreed to write to the directors of the Episcopal, Reformed, and Presbyterian Mission Boards, urging them to appoint missionaries for Japan who could teach the people what true Christianity was. Within the coming year we all had the pleasure of meeting the agents of these three societies in Shanghai."

In a word, these three Christian men saw that it was simply ignorance, pure and simple, on the part of a Japanese governor to consider Christianity an evil on a par with opium. They resolved then and there to have the Christianity founded on an open Bible brought into the country. One agreed to write to the Episcopal, the other to the Presbyterian, and the other to the Reformed Church in America, urging them to send missionaries to Japan.

When the letter of Dr. S. Wells Williams reached New York, the Board of Foreign Missions of the Reformed Church in America, true daughter of the church in the Netherlands, began to consider their duty in the matter. The appeal from Japan was presented to the monthly concert of prayer for the spread of the gospel, held in February, 1859, in the now vanished South Reformed church edifice at the corner of Fifth avenue and

Twenty-first street. "As the Japanese had long been friendly to the Hollanders, and were now well disposed toward the Americans, the Reformed Church of America, representing both Hollanders and Americans, was above all others the church to carry the gospel to this nation of thirty millions of souls." Two elders of this South Reformed church agreed to give each eight hundred dollars annually for the support of a missionary in Japan, and the church as a church agreed to support a third. The board thankfully accepted the offer and began to look for brave and true men who must be willing to go into the caissons, as it were, to work quietly and almost unknown for years, and probably without any signs of success. One medical and two clerical missionaries, one of whom must be an "Americanized Dutchman" were needed. Even before the secretary had secured a dollar or begun to sweep the horizon for the right men as pioneers, Dr. S. R. Brown's offer to go came and even then he was inquiring for a companion.

Let "The Missionary Journal of Guido Verbeck" in his own handwriting tell how the "Americanized Dutchman" was sought, found and sent.

"About the middle of January, 1859, Rev. Mr. Charles Hawley, D. D., of the First Presbyterian church, Auburn, first told me that an Americanized Dutchman was looked for by the Reformed Dutch Church, to go as a missionary to Japan. About a week after Mr. Hawley had recommended me to Dr. Scudder, Rev. S. Brown

GUIDO AND MARIA VERBECK.

came to see me on the same subject, and on the 22d January told me I was invited to join him in a visit to New York before the Reformed Dutch Missionary Board. On the 20th I had sent a letter to Dr. Isaac Ferris, corresponding secretary, and on Friday, the 28th, went to New York with Mr. and Mrs. Brown.⌐ On Saturday I went on to Philadelphia and returned with George Van Deurs to New York on Monday, 31st January, when we had a meeting of the board at 3 P. M. On my return to New York, I stopped at Mr. William E. Dodge's, George with the son of Mr. Doremus. George returned on Tuesday, and I returned to Auburn on Thursday, 3d February.

" Under date of 16th February I received the appointment by Dr. Ferris with directions for ordination, etc.

"On the 22d of March I was licensed and ordained an evangelist by the Presbytery of Cayuga, at the Second Presbyterian church, at 1:30 and 7 o'clock P. M. Sermon by Dr. Condit, charge by Dr. Hall. Many of the Reformed Dutch clergy were present, and some took part in the exercises of the day.

"On the next day at eleven o'clock I was received as a member of the Reformed Dutch classis of Cayuga. From the 28th to the 31st of March I was at Albany to secure my American citizenship from the legislature,"[1] which he

[1] A letter from the deputy secretary of state, June 6, 1900, states that " this office has no records showing anything relative to the application of Rev. Guido F. Verbeck to secure Amer-

found could not be done. So he went forth, a citizen of no state.

Thus for one night, Guido Verbeck was a Presbyterian minister. The classis of Cayuga, named after the queen jewel in the tiara of lakes that adorns the Empire State, covered a region rich not only in Iroquois and Colonial lore, but famous for the number of Christian missionaries in that glorious number, already in the thousands, sent from New York, including J. L. Nevius and S. Wells Williams, born and reared within its borders. With his betrothed, communion was enjoyed at the Sand Beach church at Owasco Outlet. Bidding farewell to his German congregation, and to professors and friends, he left Auburn, April 15. A large party of students and friends wafted good-bye to the pioneers. In Philadelphia, on Monday, April 18, at 11 A. M., Guido Verbeck and Maria Manion were united in marriage by Rev. George Van Deurs. The bride of 1859 became for nearly forty years the devoted wife, and is yet living, the honored and beloved mother of the eight children born to bless the union. A bridal trip was made up the lovely Schuylkill Valley, then just putting on the first green tints of springtime, to Morristown, near the historic Valley Forge. The world remembers the camp and the sufferings of 1778, even though they know not the city.

ican citizenship. We have examined the State and assembly journals and documents of 1859 and also the session laws and find no reference to Mr. Verbeck."

In the Land of Opportunity

The missionary party, in which were Verbeck and his wife, sailed from New York in the ship Surprise, at noon of Saturday, May 7, 1859. They were bound for Shanghai, depending on the wind to waft them. Rev. S. R. Brown, D. D., who won an honored name as missionary, translator, and teacher, whose Japanese pupils have nobly adorned their country's history, and Duane B. Simmons, M. D., who made an imperishable mark in the annals of medical science in Japan and in the invaluable study of Japanese private law, continued by Professor Wigmore, with their wives, were also in the party.

"How well I remember the sailing of the good ship 'Surprise,' May, 1859, from New York harbor, with flags flying, and amid firing of cannon when the first missionaries to Japan, three men and their wives, set sail on an embassage of mercy to the far-famed Zipangu! How well I remember the youthful face and blonde hair of the tall, sedate, and thoughtful Guido F. Verbeck."

So spoke his co-laborer, Rev. James H. Ballagh, on March 12, 1898. As he said further: "Alas, that youthful form after exhausting labors, . . . is to-day to be borne by devout men to his peaceful resting-place in 'The Evergreen Mount,' Awoyama!"

Nagasaki is in our day distant, in time, from New York, about three weeks. Then the voyage required months. In thirty-one days they crossed the equatorial line, and on June 30 were at the cape of Good Hope. They celebrated the 4th of July and reaching Anjier in Java on the 28th, spent two days on land. Here they found a perfect paradise and enjoyed the luscious fresh fruit. It was not until the 25th of August, on account of baffling winds, that they stepped on shore at Hongkong, where they met the Rev. William Ashmore, now the veteran Baptist missionary, whose face and form at the Ecumenical Council of Missions in New York in May, 1900, those present remember so well.

On account of the storms and the ship's needing repairs they were detained a whole month, at Hongkong, during which time Guido Verbeck visited the Scotch, German, and the English missionaries and also the cathedral of the Church of England. Those whom he admired most of all were the German missionaries, Genaehr and Winnes, of whom he wrote:

"Oh! what a difference between their warmth, love and sympathy, and that of the English or American! I see anew that if a German is a Christian, he is one with his whole soul. The Germans here are also considered the hardest workers, the plainest livers, and they count some of the best Chinese scholars. The great difficulty is here, the hardness of the language. It takes a very long time of dry hard studying before one is able to preach in Chinese, sometimes many years. Yesterday I saw a German missionary with a sword cut across his face which he received of a Chinese who tried to strike off

MESSRS. F. VERBECK, S. R. BROWN,
AND D. B. SIMMONS.

his head last year, in order to secure the one hundred dollars premium which the governor of Canton had promised to pay for the head of every foreigner, but he was very providentially saved. Another one was attacked by an infuriated mob of about two hundred Chinese and had to bargain a whole day (with swords over his head and knives at his heart) for his life, but he beat them down from four thousand dollars to one hundred and forty dollars. He was rescued by an English steamer, but still he honestly paid the price. That was brother Winnes. But now peace and safety are established."

At Shanghai on the 17th of October, Guido Verbeck met Rev. C. E. Bridgman, Rev. E. W. Syle, S. Wells Williams and Chaplain Henry Wood of the United States Steamship Powhatan —all names of fragrant memory. After consultation it was thought most expedient that Dr. Brown and Dr. Simmons, leaving their families at Shanghai, should go on to Kanagawa at once. Finding a vessel sailing thither on October 21st, they set sail, arriving there October 21st, being met, welcomed, and taken in by Dr. J. C. Hepburn in his house, or rather his temple. Strangely enough the government authorities and the priests themselves opened the temples for Christian missionaries to lodge in. Drs. Brown and Simmons soon had houses prepared to receive their families. Leaving Shanghai on the 17th of December, the wives joined their husbands on the 29th of the same month, and so the right wing, as it were, of the Reformed Church mission took position in Japan.

In order that the missionaries should not all so crowd into one place as to alarm the Japanese at the invasion, Mr. Verbeck thought of staying first in Shanghai for a while through the winter to study the language, expecting to go to Nagasaki in the spring. However, on taking counsel of Dr. Williams and others, he decided to go at once.

On November 4th, leaving his wife behind and going ahead as a prospector and pioneer, he reached Nagasaki harbor on the night of November 7th. The next morning after a journey from New York of one hundred and eighty-seven days, he beheld the land of promise, Everlasting Great Japan, and touched its sacred soil with his feet.

A GLANCE AT OLD JAPAN

THUS far we have looked at the young missionary following the lead of the Divine Spirit
and making his home in that corner of the empire of Japan which had thus far been best known
to the world at large. Until the days of Marco
Polo, the existence of the Japanese Archipelago
was almost as unknown to European people as
was that of Australasia. Except to the geographers and map-makers, it had only a shadowy
existence, for the European peoples had not only
not come into full geographical consciousness of
their own continent, but were ignorant of the as
yet unveiled outlines of Africa and Asia. Hence
Zipangu, or Japan, was almost as mythical to the
average European, as were the Antilles or the
Seven Cities of Cibola, and to many even less
real.

As Marco Polo was dubbed " Signor Million "
because he used that term in arithmetic so often
and was ridiculed therefor, so Mendez Pinto,
who first from Europe, in 1539, landed in Japan
was punningly dubbed the "Mendacious" Pinto.
After Pinto, there followed about fourscore years
of mercantile and missionary contact between the
Iberian peninsula and Japan. During this period,

Christianity of a certain type had great vogue in the islands. The number of adherents including prominent men and local rulers was very great, possibly a million, and these "converts" were found not only in central, southern, and south-western Japan, but even up in the north as far as Sendai. The labors of the Jesuit Fathers, inaugurated by Xavier, seem prodigious. The history of these fourscore years (1540–1620) is very wonderful and the details of organization, and later of disaster and martyrdom, are sufficiently interesting. As to the material and tangible success, as of the mustard seed becoming a great tree with much lodging of a variety of fowls in the branches, with the noises of report and rejoicing, there seems to be no lack of evidence and the literature on the subject is large and full.

Yet on the other hand when we come to inquire into the dynamic influence of the Portuguese and Spanish missions in Japan in the sixteenth century, we naturally ask how far was the nation leavened. What transformations were made? Did Christianity, as then presented, influence the Japanese people in their literature, art, or ethics, or in those things which make the Japanese man what he is? Surely, the phenomenal in missions, though temporarily seeming of vast importance, is as nothing compared to the renovating and transforming power which true Christianity, though hid as leaven, exerts. Though the martyr roll of Japan is a shining one, and though there were here and there attempts made to resist unto blood, notably in the insurrection at Shimabara in 1637, yet it seems wonderful that after such triumphs of Christianity throughout the islands, so little should have remained to influence the national life, that the native extant records and monuments and relics should be so scanty, that the mark on the thought and intellect of the people should be so slight.

After critical research and even at the risk of being immediately considered bigoted and sectarian, one must come to the conclusion that the religion preached by Portuguese and Spaniards in Japan was more of the church and the corporation, than of the Heavenly Father and of His Christ.

Let us realize what the situation was, as known and unknown to the young missionary, Guido Verbeck, in the early sixties, when the Civil War was raging in the United States, and the war clouds were gathering in Japan. What was the religious and political situation?

Japan at this time had about thirty million souls within her borders. The population had stood stationary for over a century. The suppression of Christianity, the expulsion of foreigners from southern Europe, the confinement of the Dutch to Nagasaki and the limitation of all intercourse with outsiders to that port, the exclusion of all foreign ideas and influences and the inclusion of the people within an order of things expected to be permanent, was contemporaneous with the rise of the Tokugawa family, as founded by Iyeyasu, in 1604. The development and consolidation of feudalism went on with its centre in the Tycoon at Yedo. While the nominal fountain of authority was at Kioto, the sword and purse were at Yedo. The power of the Tycoon at Yedo weakened according to the distance from the capital. In the far off provinces, the barons or daimios had practically full control of their hereditary domains. In some, as in Satsuma, no agent of the Yedo government was allowed to enter. The great island of Yezo in the north was occupied only on the southern edge, the interior being practically unknown. The Kuriles were but rarely visited by government officers and occupied only by a few fishermen or soldiers. Saghalin, though nominally part of Japan, rarely saw a Japanese face. Further south, the Bonin and other outlying islands were unclaimed and uncared for, except as used for places of hopeless exile for political offenders. In the south the Luchu or Riu Kiu Islands received an annual visit of one junk from Satsuma, to receive the marks of nominal vassalage. Formosa was the far-off land, shadowy in mythology and known in fairy tales. There centuries before, Japanese buccaneers had won fame and glory. Indeed Japanese pirates, during the three centuries before Iyeyasu, had been making themselves lively and famous from Tartary to Siam. It is no wonder that as late as 1894, a Chinese emperor should, even in an official document speak of the Wo-jin, or "dwarf pirates" of Japan that had for centuries impressed themselves on the Chinese imagination, especially in the nursery, very much as the Normans in Europe had upon their minds of civilized people. On both continents the raids left their mark in many a blackened ruin and devastated and depopulated coast, as well as in litany, in nursery tale, and the frightening of rebel children by their maternal suzerains. Traditionally Korea belonged to Japan, for myth and legend, reinforced by invasions, notably the great one of 1592–1597, declared the peninsular kingdom to be but an appanage of Nippon. The country alleged to be of Japanese ownership was not only the land of tigers, of art, of wealth, and the fatherland of Buddhism, but also of the exploits of Kato and Konishi. Korea, in Japanese eyes, existed only by the suffrances and mercy of Japan.

Nevertheless at that one place of Nagasaki, the single window and gateway through which Japan looked upon the world, there was sufficiency of government, with constant scrutiny. The "walls had ears" and the velvet paw had claws within it. Here was the one place of foreign intercourse, trade, and traffic with Europe and China. The Dutch ships brought news, science, and apparatus, as well as material commodities from Europe, germs for the soil both earthly and spiritual. The Chinese junks made it possible for an occasional Japanese to slip away to China, or for Chinese to bring books. In the masonry of the Tycoonal system these messengers of the sea were as birds that dropped seed, which growing up with roots, threatened to dislocate the structure. Despite all the contempt and ridicule of the Deshima Dutchman, powerfully exaggerated through the jealousy and coveteousness of other and envious traders, these men taught the Japanese seekers after wisdom their language and science. Already in the empire, unknown to Mr. Verbeck or to other foreigners, there were hundreds of men of inquiring spirit, seeking knowledge through the Dutch language, practicing medicine according to the European principles and even seeking the light of Christianity through Dutch books, Chinese versions of the New Testament, the whole Bible, or such publications of Christian missionaries in China as were brought over from time to time by the Chinese sailors. There were also men, probably already thousands in number, politically opposed to the duarchy or division of power between Yedo and Kioto, who were bitterly hostile to the Tycoon. These were eagerly looking, awaiting the day when there should be revolution and change, through the overthrow of the Yedo government. They could not foresee just how this was to come, and in most cases the idea of each clansman was that his own clan should be paramount, even as that of the Tokugawa clan had become supreme and held power during two centuries or more. In many ways the desire for more light was showing itself and men were eager to know and possess the secrets of power held by the nations of the West.

A Glance at Old Japan

In alliance with the political usurpation in Yedo, for historically, we can call it nothing less, was the great Buddhist hierarchy and popular religion. Although divided up into sects and denominations, beside which even American Christianity has no need to blush, yet, priestcraft is one and the same thing the world over, for the priest stands by the fact, the thing done, the power invested and yielding revenue, and cares little for the truth, and especially for new forms and institutions. In Japan the Buddhist priests were united against any foreign religion that would curtail their power and they raged against a form of life like that of Christianity which, in its normal development, does away with priestcraft. To them was committed, by the government in Yedo, a business very much akin to that which within slavery's domain, in the old United States, was done by blood hounds and slave drivers. The system of inquisition in Japan, which ended in torture, imprisonment, crucifixion, and empalement of Christians on the bamboo cross, had been in vogue for centuries. By long experience in personal cunning, treachery, and power of espionage, many of the Buddhist priests had become experts in tracking out "believers." Furthermore, with the abundant material of fanaticism among men who to traditional erudition joined the frightful ignorance of insular hermits, there were always plenty of them ready to turn assassins, and to kill the foreigners, thinking thereby they were doing the gods service.

Verbeck of Japan

Soon the humble missionary scholar in his home, and the armed escort of the diplomatist, were to feel the presence both of the spy in the pay of united Japanese Caiaphas and Herod, and of the sword unsheathed by the order of Church and State. Thus together, like the ill assorted ox and ass drawing the plow, were to be found in Mr. Verbeck's classes, the sincere and admiring student eager for knowledge and the traitor-priest as destitute of principle as was his skull of hair. In the intellectual history of Japan, the priest first and then the samurai or gentlemen have been the leaders and usually the sole intellectual workers, furnishing the noblest and the vilest characters. With them is associated all mental initiative and monopoly of literary culture, the facts of the case being much the same in 1900 as A. D. 1600.

For a thousand years the Japanese have had writing and literature, intellectual culture, and mental discipline. From the time of the revival of learning in the last half of the seventeenth century, the samurai, or literally, servants of the emperor, have nearly monopolized intellectual culture. Bred alike to letters and to arms, the samurai was the gentleman and the soldier, in one person. Not as in China, separated in his interests, the military from the civil functions of life, he was equally at home with the sword and the pen, was trained to bodily exercises and accomplishments and to the powers and delights of scholarship. The samurai families comprised about one-tenth of the whole people. In a word, they formed an element large enough and powerful enough to swing the nation out of the ancient grooves of thought and policy into the new road and upon the new levels of the world's life in the nineteenth century. It was and it is the samurai, from whose ranks come the warmest friends and the bitterest enemies of Christianity.

Yet, while the impartial critic must award all due praise to the Japanese intellect and the record of its power and achievements, as manifested in a thousand years of its literature, yet the total output of the national thought is not of a kind or quality to be ranked either with the great nations of antiquity, or with the work of the leading European nations. It is very certain that the first intellectual attacks of Japanese writers against Christianity were not of a kind to command respect for the Japanese intellect. They seem even now more often like the work of children than of reasonable men.

Guido Verbeck was destined to be the target of one of the first shafts sped by an archer in the ambush of his own garden.

As soon as diplomatic relations had been established by the American envoy, Mr. Townsend Harris, and Kanagawa had nominally, and Yokohama really, become a place of foreign trade and residence, July 1, 1859, it seemed as though the signal was given for the long-waiting haters of the Tycoon and of foreigners to begin their work with torch, spear, and sword.

Verbeck of Japan

The breach between the emperor and the Shogun, between Yedo and Kioto, the court and the camp, widened daily. The emperor and Kioto court having refused to sign the treaties admitting foreigners, the regent, Ii, took the responsibility and signed the Harris treaty. Then, after the death of Iyesada, the Shogun, assuming high power at the Yedo court, Ii secured the election of his own nominee and punished severely the men who had favored the expulsion of foreigners.

Such severity developed the assassin and the incendiary, as heat and moisture make the weeds spring up. Since the old-style patriots—"the frogs in a well"—considered the emperor personally insulted and that such gods as the Japanese had, were angry, the cry was raised " Honor the Mikado and expel the barbarians." To a majority of the Japanese clansmen, who in the quantity of light enjoyed were little better than moles, a European or American was a "hairy-faced barbarian," fit only to die *inujini* (in a dog's place).

So long as these men, so eager to try their swords on foreigners, drew their rice and pay from the feudal masters, they were under control. Now, however, thousands of turbulent clansmen severed their connections of loyalty, ceased to be salaried gentlemen and became tramps, that is, ronin or wave men. While among these wandering and unsettled foreigner-haters there were the brave and true sons of honor, the majority of them were arrant cowards,

78

assassins, sneaks, and ruffians, morally no better than the roughs and toughs of Manhattan Island.

It is true that in the Old Japan, which Verbeck aided so powerfully to destroy, the people often glorified assassins and murderers, hailing them as martyrs, and piling flowers upon their graves. But this was nothing wonderful in a civilization founded on the morals of Confucius, which forbid one to live under the same heaven with the murderer of his father or lord, and where blood revenge and the vendetta were recognized as regular and popular forms of procedure. Nevertheless we note in all the days of the barbarian-expelling temper of Japan no mobs, as in China, but only individual instances of violence.

IT was on a charming moonlight night that the vessel bearing Guido Verbeck steamed up the beautiful bay of Nagasaki, so rich and so sombre in its memories of the past. Contenting himself with only a partial view of the city and surrounding hills from the deck, his heart was full of gratitude that having passed the many dangers of the deep he was on the eve of permission to set foot on the long longed-for land. He wrote:

"With the first dawning of the day I cannot describe the beauty that is before me. I have never seen anything like it before in Europe or America; suppose yourself to be on deck of a steamer within a port as smooth as a mirror, about sixteen neat vessels scattered about here and there, before you that far-famed Deshima, and around it and beyond, an extensive city with many neat white roofed and walled houses, and again all around this city lofty hills, covered with evergreen foliage of great variety, and in many places spotted by temples and houses. Let the morning sun shine on this scene, and the morning dews gradually withdraw like a curtain, and hide themselves in the more elevated ravines of the surrounding mountain, and you have a very faint picture of what I saw."

With the Japanese servant of the United States Consul, he quickly sought out the two young American Episcopal missionaries, of about his own age, who had been in China several years, but had been transferred to Japan the previous summer. They were both bachelors—the Rev. John Liggins, English by birth but educated in an American Seminary, and the Rev. M. C. Williams, afterward the beloved bishop of Japan. They offered the newcomer, for whom they had long been waiting, shelter and hospitalities. Registering under the United States Consul's protection, though as yet Mr. Verbeck was not a naturalized American citizen, he next sought for a house. Not finding one he desired in a foreign quarter, he tried to get one among the Japanese, who, though they did not absolutely refuse to furnish shelter, did all they could to weary out the stranger by vague promises and delays, so that he had to run about from place to place like a much-befooled apprentice among journeymen old in the craft of deception. He finally rented a very good house for six months at sixteen dollars a month.

There was no animosity felt against the new American because he was a missionary, for scarcely one of the natives knew that he was one. Furthermore the feeling of the lower classes toward Christianity was that of fear, rather than hatred. The fact is, at that time, the Japanese considered their civilization finished. Time was a drug in the market. In their eyes there was no hurry, nor any need of it. They were uncertain and suspicious of all foreigners. Above all, they were in no haste, while the Americanized Dutchman was in earnest. Investing about twenty-five dollars in repairs, including cash for fifty panes of window-glass to take the place of paper pasted over lattice work, and setting carpenters and wall-paperers at work, he soon had a place fit to live in. He was amused, as I have heard him tell, in recognizing on the lips of the Japanese, several Dutch words, such as *briki* for (blick, tin), *giyaman* (diamond), *karata* (chart or card), the names of medicines, *rauda* (laudanum) and various Spanish and Portuguese words, such as *andon* (lantern), *bidoro* (vidrio, glass), *castira* (sponge cake or Castile cake), *shabon* (sapon, soap), etc.

He ordered some foreign furniture made by native joiners. The product of their deft fingers, very cheap and exquisitely beautiful to the eye, went so quickly to pieces, through shrinkage and scamp work, that no doubt the young Dutchman often longed for one plain honestly made kitchen chair from home. Besides the tendency of pretty looking but flimsy things to divide and collapse, he found that Japanese servants are not in all respects delightful.

Soon a nice little study was fitted up, together with a good sleeping-room, and there was even a prospect that by summer there would be two

In Nagasaki: First Impressions

good second floor bedrooms. He wrote "Our kitchen is large and clean, with Japanese cooking apparatus. The whole house is beautifully matted with the celebrated Japanese mats, which spring as you walk on them." On the 5th of December he moved into his new quarters, at the foot of the hill, his two fellow-missionaries being at the top. He wrote "Both our houses are situated about a mile from the foreign settlements and at the opposite side of the city so that we live very undisturbedly, the only thing reminding us of Europe or America, being the shipping which we see from our quarters."

Having written to his wife, she arrived from Shanghai on the 29th day of December, on the same date that the other ladies reached Kanagawa, so that the mission of the Reformed Church in America was fairly established in Japan just before the close of 1859. They all spent a happy Christian New Year on their new field of labor.

The young missionary's birthday fell this year, 1860, on the Japanese New Year's Day, when the streets were bright with color and happy humanity showed that it was a time of rejoicing. The weather was very lovely, but while the new-comer enjoyed the new land and people, his memories went back to "the Koppel" and to his friends in America.

Housekeeping was begun with a Chinese servant man, who did all the cooking and housework at three dollars a month, boarding himself, with a Japanese boy, to help in the kitchen and go errands at a little less than half that amount. The new missionary housekeeper wrote : "We could keep two Japanese for one Chinaman, but the Chinamen are excellent cooks and workers and faithful, whereas Japanese are ignorant of our way of cooking and living, besides being slow, dishonest, and very independent. Yet next year, when I can speak with them, I intend to try them without Chinamen." This Mr. Verbeck did, employing Japanese servants all his life of thirty-nine years of active service in Japan, and finding many of them nobly faithful and honest.

A letter on the subject of domestics opens a window into the morality of the Japan of the early sixties. Let us hope that there has been improvement since.

"In your before-last letter you ask something in regard to the source from which missionaries were to get their servants, as mentioned by Mr. Alcock. I do not remember the place in Alcock, but it does not refer to us. We get our servants, usually young boys and girls, from among the people, without the least difficulty or hindrance. As a safeguard against pilfering, we usually get our teacher or other person of some standing to go security for the servants. Generally speaking, they make good servants, soon learn to cook foreign fashion, and are fond of children. At Kanagawa, I think, servants are obtained by application

In Nagasaki: First Impressions

at the Custom House, where a register is kept of them, and security given. It is possible that some of the missionaries wishing to get female servants were directed by the natives to public houses as the right source, but I never heard of such a thing.

"When Messrs. Liggins and Williams first came here, visitors would sometimes express their wonder that these brethren did not "keep girls" as others do. My being married precluded any native speculations of this kind. As a specimen of native notions on this subject:—the other day I walked alone along a country path, and fell in with a pretty respectable looking woman, who with another woman (a kind of servant) and two young girls was busily gathering tea-leaves from the bushes by the wayside. After talking a few words with them and picking a handful of the tender leaves for their basket, I asked the woman whether those young girls were her daughters. She answered in the affirmative, and immediately proposed that I might have the elder daughter, adding however that perhaps I would think her too young, as she was only just thirteen. And this she said quite seriously and in the presence of the whole company! And this is nothing uncommon in town or country! Oh, what degradedness, what moral gloom! Christian countries are not quite free from similar immoralities; but it is in darkness, a work of darkness and shame. Here vice stalks about at noonday; the people seem to be literally blinded and hardened, and all moral discernment lost! Of all the commandments, the fifth is the only one that is strictly inculcated and observed, and it is no doubt on this account, that their days have been thus long upon the land which the Lord their God gave them.

"But thanks be to God that the gospel will surely restore this people to holiness. Just as there was a proper 'fullness of time' for Israel when the Saviour and His gospel should be imparted to them, so I suppose every other people has had and still has its proper 'fullness of time.' For Japan, this comes late, but not too late, and no doubt it is to be now; the Lord will hasten it in His time. And yet, with all this present vice and this darkness, when once submitted to Christ, I am sure this people will be a 'peculiar people' indeed; I think one cannot fail to discover in them capabilities of the highest order, the germ of affections most amiable, which the new birth will bring forth."

One letter tells of daily diet.

"Of eatables we have an innumerable variety of fish, large and small, good goat mutton (we always call it mutton), liver, chickens, ducks, and rather tough beef, all of it tolerably cheap. Besides we can get eggs, many kinds of vegetables, especially nice sweet potatoes. Of fruit we have fine Japanese oranges, very cheap, persimmons, pummelos, etc., etc. We can get good sugar, good salt, but neither milk nor butter. The bakers bake excellent bread, sponge cake,

In Nagasaki: First Impressions

and many kinds of cookies. We take three meals a day, about the same hours as with you."

Mr. Verbeck thought that he had the advantage over the more northern port, "for Kanagawa is but a small place where one may be easily conspicuous, and become the subject of watching and spying, but in this large city (of Nagasaki) we seem to be unnoticed among the multitude, and are more unmolested in our operations, besides in course of time we shall have a much larger field of labor among so many thousand."

Neither Mr. Verbeck, nor others, not even Townsend Harris or Dr. J. C. Hepburn then foresaw that the splendid city of Yokohama would arise on Mississippi Bay to dwarf Kanagawa.

Nagasaki, or rather the island of Deshima in front of the city, had long been occupied by a company of Dutch merchants. Of these Mr. Verbeck wrote: "Of the Dutch residents at this place, I have only seen one or two, but am acquainted with none, nor am I very desirous of their or they of my acquaintance. I should indeed like to be of service for good to them, but much rather desire to be what I am called to be exclusively, a missionary of Christ to the Japanese; and missionary labor, and the preparations for it are so different from a pastor's labors, that it is difficult to be pastor and missionary at once. This is the general opinion of missionaries in the field, and I find it so."

Later he wrote of his once fellow-countrymen: "The influence of the Dutch residents is not so formidable as has been supposed abroad. Certainly they have exerted and are still exerting an influence most injurious to the Christian name and cause; but adventurers of other nations have done the same here and in other places of Japan; and as for the Dutch opposing an American Mission, I do not suppose they have the intention, influence, or power; at least I have been here now nearly three months, and as yet Nagasaki has been to me as though there were neither Deshima nor Dutch in it, and it may be so as well for the future. I should indeed rejoice to be of spiritual benefit to my former countrymen, but much more do I rejoice to be exclusively what I have been called to be: a messenger of the gospel of Christ to the Japanese."

It is only fair, however, to state, as Mr. Verbeck afterward found his grief, that it was not the Dutch only[1] who were either the Gallios or "hostiles." No bounds of nationality marked off the opposers, of either the commands of Jesus or of those who obeyed Him.

So in patient waiting, unable to preach the gospel, because dumb as to the Japanese language and bound by treaties and authorities restraining open propagation of a banned religion, the young missionary possessed his soul in hope. He wrote: "We look forward to years to come with warm hopes of success under God's blessing, knowing that the time must

---

[1] For the author's estimate of the Dutchman of Deshima see "The Religions of Japan," pp. 363-366.

surely come when His word shall have free course here, and the name of Jesus shall be magnified, and *then* humanly speaking, we shall have a good soil to sow in, for with all their present heathenish darkness and practices, the Japanese are a vigorous people, have a good appreciation of moral excellence and are willing to adopt what they can be made to understand to be better than what they have, and are."

It was an experience that seemed to open the windows of heaven into their home when, three days after its father's thirtieth birthday, the first Christian baby born in Japan since "the reopening" of the country saw the light of the day amid the camphor trees and bamboo groves and blossoming plum trees of Nagasaki. They called the little stranger "Emma Japonica." The story of her life is soon told. Let us read it in the language of the father's heart. "On the 26th of January, [1860], we were rejoiced by a dear little daughter, the first Christian infant born in Japan since its reopening to the world. After one week of apparent health, and another of ailing and drooping, the Lord in His wisdom took her little soul to Himself, on the 9th inst. On the Sabbath before her death, I baptized our daughter, 'Emma Japonica,' the first Christian baptism in Japan for centuries. Our sorrow at this sudden bereavment is deep indeed! How many hopes disappointed and prospective joys turned into mourning! The harder to bear in a heathen wilderness and solitude."

Verbeck of Japan

The Japanese New Year's Day, on that year, 1861, which was to see our civil war break out, fell on the 10th of February. According to native reckoning, the event was in the era of Man-en, and on its first and only year, the fifty-seventh of the sixty year cycle. Not till 1872, did the Japanese adopt the Gregorian or Occidental calendar, at which time, also, it was decided that there should be only one year period in each emperor's reign. "The Cycle of Cathay" is no longer in use in Japan, though a purely sentimental starting-point, based on mythology is that of the foundation of the Japanese empire, corresponding to B. C. 660.

His letters find him absorbed in the tedious and arduous work of mastering the language, which, he says "is as difficult as the Chinese, with some additional difficulties. Instead of going to preach the gospel, you are obliged to observe silence and almost keep it a secret what you are accustomed to proclaim as it were in the streets and from the house-tops, and then comes the plodding over a grammar and a dictionary instead. Nevertheless, I feel happy in my work, trusting that the fruit will come soon or late. Ours indeed is now to learn to labor and to wait." Their only visitors were good Christian friends among the officers on board the British war vessels on the China station. During midsummer and indeed for several months it was rare for one to go out of the house between 10 and 5 P. M., the hours being occupied in study.

In Nagasaki: First Impressions

In October he wrote: "A journal of my daily life would be as tedious, as brief to the reader and would run about thus: 'My teacher came this morning; went to study till a little after noon; took a short recess; continued studies till the time for exercise arrived, and so on day by day, perhaps now and then a Japanese visitor, or somebody to get a book from the Shanghai or Ningpo Missionary Press, and very seldom a pleasant change made by a visit of some or other missionary brother from the neighboring field of China.' "

Services of Christian worship begun by the Bishop of Victoria, were continued by Mr. Williams. At first the foreigners met in the Buddhist temple, the walls resounding in the solemn notes of our beloved Old Hundred. Then they were held in a large upper room above a warehouse on Deshima, "so that the first Christian service held on Deshima, since more than two centuries, are English services and held by an American." About this time Mr. Verbeck began to "load and prime" the vanguard of the innumerable army of writers who have each "perpetrated a book" upon Japan. Some of these knights of the notebook were merciless in their quizzing, as if Mr. Verbeck were an encyclopædia of knowledge concerning the Japanese and their country.

Times were peaceable in Nagasaki as compared with those at Kanagawa which, like Yedo, was becoming a political storm centre. Mr. Verbeck was glad that the missionary secretary and the Board of Missions of the Reformed Church in America had officially approved of his location at Nagasaki. It was also intimated that possibly a new missionary, Rev. James H. Ballagh, might be sent out in reinforcement. In February, 1861, he enjoyed a visit from that grand missionary, the apostle of Shantung, the Rev. John Nevius and his wife.

Along with this sunshiny experience, lay the dark shadow of the news of the assassination on January 15th, 1861, in the streets of Yedo of Mr. Heusken, Mr. Townsend Harris's secretary and the Dutch interpreter of the United States Legation. This tragic event was followed by the removal from Yedo of all the foreign ministers to Yokohama and of all the foreign consuls, except the American, from Kanagawa to the same place. Mr. Harris remained in Yedo keeping the stars and stripes afloat. For nearly ten years Japan felt the humiliation and all the world wondered at the strange spectacle of foreign legations in the country but not at the capital. Yet none of these events disturbed the quiet life at Nagasaki.

Though the clouds of civil war were gathering over Japan, things went on as usual in the sunny south. Mr. Verbeck wrote, "We pray that a general war may be averted and safety be restored at the North without bloodshed." Neither he nor any other foreigner then knew the real political history of Japan, nor was able to discern the signs of the times, which portended revolution and a new birth of national life. In a lecture delivered in Tokio, in 1898, a few months before his death, he said:

"Present Japan—this beautiful Japan came from beyond the sea. I, by saying this, have not a bit of mind to shame you, but am rather one of those who admire the wisdom of having implanted, within the short time of thirty years, all the western things, which have been the result of several hundred years' labor.

"Generally speaking, the people in those times seemed not to know anything of patriotism, so much spoken of at present. The word *chugi* was always on the mouth of the then warriors, by which they meant fealty to their lords, self-surrender to the cause of their masters. Those samurai knew of the existence of their clan, but nothing about Japan."

His first year's report as missionary was a faint cry, *de profundis*—just the kind which furnishes sport for all the Philistines, ancient and modern, who jeer over foundation work and sneer at the labor of bridge-builders, who invisibly toil in the caissons, as waste and ask with jibes "do missions pay?"

The civil war in the United States cast its cloud over the Americans in Japan. The Episcopal mission feared, as Dr. Verbeck did, that their medical missionary Dr. Schmid might, for lack of means, be called home from Nagasaki. This was because their supporters lived both above and below the slavery line. The Reformed

Verbeck of Japan

Dutch Church, more happily situated, never having any connection with the controversy which rent other churches, steadily maintained its mission without halt or break. Even after civil war had begun, the Reformed Church sent out, on the first of June, 1861, two missionaries to China and one, Rev. J. H. Ballagh, to Japan. The latter settled at Yokohama, seven years later in 1868, meeting Mr. Verbeck at Osaka.

Mr. Verbeck's experience of living at the foot of the hill in Nagasaki showed him that the situation was not as salubrious as that on the hill slope. During the rainy season in Japan, when all organic textures quickly gather mold, through combined heat and moisture, the house was unwholesomely damp. Finding a desirable location on the hill, whence a fine view over the city and harbor was obtained, they moved thither. Some of the pupils helped to move their goods. It was amusing—alas, sorrowful and exasperating, also—to see how the natives packed up things. Happy indeed is the foreigner who can think without woe and grief of these early days of packing, when if one did not watch, the bronzes would get on top of the porcelain and heavy things worth a penny would smash precious things worth many pounds. Mr. Verbeck soon found he was not living in the Garden of Eden, nor in the imaginary Japan of those rhapsodists who, at the end of this century, picture the Japanese as guileless or nearly immaculate. In short he was robbed, the burglars coming into his bedroom, noiselessly and very effectively. One of his pupils visiting a pawnbroker's shop and seeing the name "Guido F. Verbeck" on a telescope, recovered this article and also a clock, spoons, forks, and knives which the *pendulards* had stolen six months before.

These were the days of the unreformed prison| system in Japan when justice, such as it was, was administered, according to Chinese codes of| laws, when the torture of witnesses in court to obtain testimony was the rule. How different to-day when Japan has not only a prison system excelling that of some European states but has influenced Korea and China to like reforms. Hear Mr. Verbeck tell how, hearing cries for help, he chivalrously rallied forth and wisely interfered not.

"There were no lawyers but a kind of pettifogger, which went by the name of kujishi. They never defended clients at court but gave advice privately.

"How dirty the prisons were, words fail to describe. Gomon (examination of prisoners by torture) was always employed. It was at a certain night during my sojourn at Nagasaki, that I heard a plaintive cry, the remembrance of which is still a shock to me. Wondering what that was, I stole out of my house, and looked down, a musket in hand, far beneath, when I found that several warders were whipping the prisoners, who were the subjects of that cry. I, who was yet young was about to aim at the cruel officials with my musket, but was restrained from this by myself."

All over the land in city, town, and village, by ferry and in market, we must remember the anti-Christian edicts hung with the other ko-satsu, or little notice boards in plain view of all. We give the text of 1862:

"The Christian religion has been prohibited for many years. If any one is suspected, a report must be made at once.

"REWARDS.

"To the informer of a *bateren* (father), 500 pieces of silver.

"To the informer of an *iruman* (brother), 300 pieces of silver.

"To the informer of a Christian who once recanted, 300 pieces of silver.

"To the informer of a Christian or catechist, 300 pieces of silver.

"To the informer of a family who shelters any of the above, 300 pieces of silver.

"The above rewards will be given. If any one will inform concerning his own family, he will be rewarded with 500 pieces of silver, or according to the information he furnishes. If any one conceals an offender, and the fact is detected, then the head man of the village in which the concealer lives, and the 'five-men-company' to which he belongs, and his family and relatives, will all be punished together."

Seeing that he could not openly preach the gos-

In Nagasaki: First Impressions

pel, Mr. Verbeck was diligently disposing of Bibles in Chinese, which the educated samurai or wearers of two swords could read. Under his oversight, two young officers were already diligently perusing this version of the Bible and trying to understand it.

New cause for gratitude to God came into the missionary home, for a little baby (now Colonel William Verbeck, Head Master of St. John's [Military] School at Manlius, N. Y.) had made his advent upon earth. His father writes of him, "Willie is big and strong and affords us great pleasure and company. . . . Poor fellow, he does not know with which (language) to begin, English or Japanese, or even perhaps German, which I should like most of all." In the missionary home, the children not only had to be reared and protected against the contamination of paganism, but also against the diseases, such as smallpox and measles, then very prevalent and but slightly controlled, for the Japanese were then but slenderly equipped for the mastery of these contagious diseases. It was quite common for smallpox patients to roam around freely, the only notice to a stranger of infected children being the wearing of a pink cap. Dr. Kitasato was not yet. The procession of physicians trained by Dr. J. C. Hepburn, now a host, was just beginning to mark time.

By request from New York, Mr. Verbeck made researches and forwarded, with other matter, a note on epidemics in Japan.

Verbeck of Japan

"According to information received from a Japanese physician, the smallpox first appeared in this country A. D. 731. Ancient chronicles state that a renowned native scholar was on a visit to China for the purpose of studying Chinese sciences, when on his return home in the above year, he brought the smallpox with him. European vaccination was first introduced in 1846, and is more and more adopted. The measles, originating at Nagasaki, in 1471, are supposed likewise to have come from China. Of cholera, there occurred a few cases at Nagasaki about thirty years ago [1832]; and its introduction is also ascribed to the Chinese traders at this port. But it was not till 1858 that it began to ravage the country as a sweeping epidemic. Cholera, appearing soon after the opening of Japan to foreigners, is perhaps correctly supposed to be a source of antipathy to foreign intercourse. In nearly all the principalities, public or government hospitals for the free treatment of these and other diseases have been established. The European treatment of diseases finds great favor, and in spite of the opposition of a host of old-school (Chinese) doctors and a superstitious populace, its ultimate triumph over the Chinese method is clearly to be foreseen. And shall not in like manner the gospel of Christ prevail over Buddhism and heathen philosophies!"

Guido Verbeck was a true prophet. He cared not to predict, but he saw the truth clearly. He knew what was in man, read the Japanese heart through and through and could often foresee the fruits of a course of action, so that often men looked at him in reverence, supposing he had some magic power. Yet his was an open secret such as lies in two old proverbs, as pre-ancient as copy books. These are "Knowledge is power," and "Truth is mighty and must prevail."

Streams of influence were uniting. The Bible class at Saga in Hizen was still kept up by Wakasa, who needing more light and detailed instruction, sent his younger brother to Nagasaki. "Accidentally," shall we say? the seeker for truth found Mr. Verbeck and became his pupil.

VI

On January 24th, 1862, twenty-four days before the last day in the last year in the cycle of sixty years, the Japanese New Year, beginning February 18th, Mr. Verbeck wrote encouragingly, though his eyes were red with inflammation from poring over Chinese and Japanese characters. At the Episcopal church he led the singing and played the harmonium, but it was a good congregation when fifteen or twenty people were at church, for devoutness and love of worship are not the shining characteristics of the foreigner at the treaty port. Unusually the average Christian from home becomes a Demas when abroad. The extreme worldliness and secret or open immorality of people in the new treaty ports, who would be accounted highly respectable at home, is one obvious and sufficient reason why there is not usually much harmony or sympathy between the mercantile and missionary classes. As Mr. Williams was soon to move into the foreign settlement, the Verbecks and Dr. Siebold, " who was half a Japanese himself," were the only ones outside the foreign quarter, and the rents were one-fourth what he should otherwise have to pay.

In one of his letters concerning some curiosities

100

sent home to his brother, it is very evident that American appreciation of Japanese objects, either artistic or flamboyant, had not then reached the point of either a fad or a craze. The market was not overstocked and the unknown was the magnificent. Many things were appraised in New York at ten or twenty times their real value.

Another of his letters has some wholesome criticism of our country and people. He wrote : " My thoughts were much with you when in Zeist. Shall I ever re-visit that dear place ? Oh ! how I should enjoy once more to move among many of those dear people who knew nothing of that exterior show, with interior hollowness and coldness, so common in America. I love America, and I think God has great things in store for it, but if I were to choose a home for happiness in this life, an exchange of true affectionate feelings, I should not choose it in America. I do not wish to be misunderstood ; I consider America as a young giant, a country in a restless state of development. I love its institutions and should wish to see them established all over the world, but it is not in the bosom of such a fermenting country that I should look for what I consider real social happiness."

How that preparatory work went on, by which at Nagasaki he was fitted for his life in Tokio of nearly thirty years, as the nursing father of a new nation, is shown in his letters. Guido Verbeck began his great work as teacher in Japan, with a Bible class of two young men, of whom one was

Ayabe, a younger brother of Murata, Wakasa no Kami.

"I proceeded," he writes under date of June 5th, 1862, "in my studies about as usual, but have, at the same time, a beginning of opportunities for doing real missionary work. Again, I must say, the beginnings are small; yet, may we prove 'faithful in a few things,' and more will be entrusted to us. A short time ago one of my English pupils surprised me by saying, that he had bought an English Bible, but found it very difficult to understand. I told him I would come to his house the next day (Sunday), and would gladly help him read his Bible. When I went there, I found him and another of my pupils trying to decipher the contents of a small volume of the American Tract Society, entitled 'A Pastor's Counsel to the Young.' The book being of a merely religious character, made him think it was a Bible, perhaps thinking this to be a general term for religious books. Of course I corrected his error, promised, and afterward gave him a real Bible.

"It is remarkable how every kind of Christian knowledge has vanished with a people among whom Christianity had its thousands of followers, but a little over three hundred years ago, even though in a corrupted form—another proof of how thoroughly the work of eradicating every vestige of our blessed religion has been done. We are sometimes surprised to hear a man ask, whether Jesus was an Englishman, or another, whether

the places mentioned in the Scripture are at all
known to modern geographers, and whether we
now know of the persons of the Bible, if they
were born and lived in Holland, or England, or
Spain.   Such ignorance is common with the educated as well as the uneducated, since their
sources of information on such questions have
been cut off entirely for the last three hundred
years.

"For the two Bible students above mentioned,
I am now preparing a kind of 'helps to the
Scriptures' in English.   I give it to them from
week to week in single sheets, which they bring
to their regular lessons, when I have a further
opportunity to explain by means of English,
Dutch, and Japanese such points as seem still
difficult for them.   These men have their English
lessons with me at different times, that is sepa-
rately; but every Sabbath they meet together for
the re-reading of the explanatory sheets.   These
sheets are as yet only introductory to the reading
of the Bible itself, but by and by I hope to lead
these men on in reading it also.   This, my first
Japanese Bible class, is the more interesting to
me, as it originated at the suggestion of the pupils, one of whom, though otherwise an exceedingly nice man, I had not thought of having any
wishes in this direction.   God grant that these
two Bible students may be among the number of
the first fruits of Japan unto Christ.

"Now and then I give away a copy of the
Holy Scriptures in Chinese, but have not had as

many opportunities since the beginning of the present year as I had during the last three months of the past year. One reason may be that all my immediate acquaintances are now supplied. The proposed serial, [of which Mr. Verbeck had suggested the publication] if it be brought about, will also be the means of bringing many more people to my house than at present, even now people sometimes come to me for a number of the old Ningpo or Shanghai serial, though both of these have been discontinued for more than a year. And many people will want the Bible to learn more of the subjects, which the serial can only treat of in a fragmentary form. The serial is to form a kind of stepping stone to the reading of the Scriptures and religious books."

We must glance again at the political background, now so clear in the perspective of history, but then crowded with figures and events in such confusion, that no foreigner could see clearly or interpret intelligently.

In Yedo the regent had roused the ire of his political enemies and all reactionaries and fanatics by signing on his own responsibility the Harris American Treaty and opening the ports to foreign trade and residence. In Old Japan, government was "despotism tempered by assassination." A band of ronin desperadoes determined to "move a vote of censure" in the good old-fashioned way—by the sword.

On March 23d, 1860, a determined band of

seventeen of these ronin suddenly attacked the regent's escort while he was on his way to the castle and near the Cherry Field Gate. In the bloody battle which ensued, in the snowstorm, his followers being taken by surprise, had to draw so quickly that for the most part they fought at first with sheathed swords, until the splitting of the wooden scabbards freed their keen blades. Nevertheless, despite these drawbacks, no fewer than eight of the assailants were killed or died of their wounds. Of the escort, twenty-three were put *hors de combat*, of whom eight died. The Premier Ii was speared in his palanquin and then beheaded. For a generation his name was execrated and his reputation lay under a cloud of aspersion, until cleansed and made to shine with honor through the scholarly labors, in Japanese, of Mr. Shimada Saburo,[1] editor of the Yokohama daily newspaper, and of Mr. Henry Satoh,[2] who has condensed the story of vindication into flowing English periods. In fiction, the episode has been gracefully treated by Mr. Arthur Collins Maclay in "Mito Yashiki."

The danger to foreigners after the signing of the treaties was very great, especially in eastern Japan, and there were several murderers of Europeans and of their Japanese servants. The foreign diplomatists, missionaries, and merchants were warned against the two-sworded tramps, but early in 1861 the secretary of the American

[1] Kai-koku Shimatsu.   [2] Agitated Japan.

legation, Mr. Heusken[1] was cut to pieces in Yedo. All the foreign ministers, except Mr. Harris, then struck their flags and retired to Yokohama, leaving the American alone, with the stars and stripes, in the feudal capital.

The emperor's sister was married to the Shogun, and for a while Yedo was peaceful, gay and festal, but again the epidemic of assassination and incendiarism broke out, participated in by some of the men who afterward, at the end of the century, became high officers in the Imperial Government in Tokio. Their sincere purpose was to embroil the Tycoon with the Treaty Power in order that he could be overthrown and the Mikado restored to supreme power. Opposed to the Shogun's government, also, was the powerful prince of Mito in the northeast, besides the maritime daimios in the southwest. The latter soon began to arm and fortify, especially at Shimonoseki, against the Yedo ruler. When the Satsuma and Choshiu clans met together at Kioto, where they were joined by hundreds of ronin, things began to look very threatening, for a conspiracy was formed to take the castle of Osaka by assault, burn the castle of Hikone or Baron Ii, on Lake Biwa, and put to the sword the garrison of the castle of Nijo, or the Shogun's residence, in Kioto. The inflamed patriots hoped then that the emperor would come out of his retirement, and set forth in person to conquer

[1] See the author's " Townsend Harris, First American Envoy in Japan."

and drive out "the barbarians" from the sacred soil of Japan. Then the upright men who were in captivity, on account of their hostility to foreigners, should be released. The "Phœnix Car" would be carried over the Hakone Pass to Yedo, and the Tycoon and his minions be punished for their crimes.

The British Legation in Yedo was attacked, June 26th, 1862, and two marines killed, for which the Japanese government in Yedo were compelled to pay fifty thousand dollars indemnity. The Satsuma clansmen petitioned the Tycoon to drive out the foreigners, close up the treaty port, "appease the sacred wrath of the Mikado's divine ancestors" and restore tranquillity to the empire. The document embodying these absurd demands now reads very strangely, stuffed full, as it is, with ancient rhetoric and Chinese illustrations. It was presented by the court noble Ohara and the notorious Shimadzu Saburo. They were escorted by six hundred armed men, who marched to Yedo in all the bravery of flags, umbrellas, boxes, and other truck, now bric-a-brac, like old armor and spinning wheels. The result was that the eminent men made prisoners under the late regent's orders were restored to honor. Hitotsu Bashi, (literally Mr. One or First Bridge) or, in Chinese, Keiki, was appointed guardian of the young Shogun, and the prince of Echizen became supreme exerciser of the government authority. Meanwhile the Japanese envoys sent to London had secured from the British government a delay in opening further ports to foreign commerce.

The prince of Satsuma was for some reason in a very angry humor when returning from Yedo, on the 14th of September. In his train were about a hundred men, who preceded him in a single file on either side of the road. All wore swords, according to custom. Three English gentlemen and a lady were riding along the road and were attacked by the Satsuma clansmen, two of the Englishmen being severely wounded and the other cut to death. The wounds were dressed by Dr. J. C. Hepburn of the American Mission. Mr. Richardson was so badly wounded that he fell from his horse to the road. His body was afterward hacked and speared, for it was then the common custom for the two-sworded men to practice with their weapons upon dead bodies. Concerning this altercation, Mr. Verbeck wrote on September 29th:

" At first view it would seem rather strange that so many murders and attacks should be perpetrated at Yedo and Kanagawa, and not in a single instance at Nagasaki; yet I think this difference can be accounted for. The nearness of Kanagawa to Yedo, with its hosts of arrogant officials and petty nobles; its nearness to the Tokaido, the great highway of the empire, frequently thronged by travelling princes with their numerous retainers; the probable desire of the government to see all foreign trade carried on at the greatest possible distance from the two cap-

Political Upheaval

itals, perhaps at Nagasaki rather than at any other port in the empire; the foreigners' general want of appreciation of the higher classes and nobility among Asiatics, and the consequent seeming (to the natives) or real overbearing conduct of foreigners toward natives of high rank; the probably decided antipathy of a few princes at or near Yedo against all foreign intercourse whatsoever, all these, and perhaps a few minor circumstances more, sufficiently account for the frequent collisions between foreigners and natives."

In mid-July he wrote:

" My little Bible class of two goes on encouragingly; one of the scholars translates my notes on the Scriptures into Japanese. He told me some days ago, that he thought that the exclusiveness of his country and any past misunderstandings with foreigners, were owing to a want of knowledge of the nature and tendency of the Christian religion, and that the best preventive of future troubles would be to acquaint his countrymen with these, and that therefore he would write out my explanations in the common popular style of writing."

The Bakufu now began to go to pieces. The compulsory residence of the daimios in Yedo was abolished. The Shogun was summoned to Kioto, arriving at the end of January, 1863. In the swing of the political pendulum, the old party in favor of foreigners had fallen into disgrace and those wishing to expel foreigners and close the ports had risen on the arc. At vast expense, the edifices of the British legation were built by the Yedo government, on the hill of Goten, but the ronins burnt them to the ground. Kioto now became the gathering place of the clans. The Shogun entered with his train on April 21st, 1863, making handsome presents to the emperor and the nobles to an extent that greatly curtailed his exchequer. When the troubles thickened between the British and Satsuma, and the Bakufu and Choshiu, it looked as though the foreigners at Nagasaki and other ports were to be slaughtered. Ayabe came with a message from Murata warning Mr. Verbeck to fly for his life, as he and his household were certainly in danger. Leaving his city home on the hills, the missionary father moved with wife and children to Deshima the island in front of the city, writing as follows:

"NAGASAKI, JAPAN, 28 *April*, 1863.
"Deshima, Kaempfer's House.
" DEAR BROTHER:—
"From the above heading you see that we (the family) have been moving, and indeed to a historic place: the house of the historian of Japan, Dr. Kaempfer. This is not however the identical house and rooms occupied by honest old Kaempfer; yet from my window I see his name and that of the hardly less celebrated Thunberg engraved on a miniature rock in the garden, an indication that our present dwelling stands very nearly on the spot where his once stood. But why do we come to this place? is a more important question with a less doubtful reply."

Political Upheaval

The next letter is dated in Shanghai. It shows how he proposed to spend his precious moments even in exile from his post, in studying the Chinese characters, so necessary for the reading of ordinary Japanese books. It eventuated that Mr. Verbeck was of great benefit in getting under way facilities for printing Japanese script. In a sense, he was, with Mr. Gamble, the founder of the printing press of Japan.

At the first opportunity he returned to Japan, reaching Nagasaki, October 13th, making his home for awhile on Deshima.

The volcano of Japanese politics now developed a fresh crater of war.

While negotiations for indemnity between Yedo and London were going on, the three great clans, Satsuma, Choshiu, and Tosa, made that combination which lasted under the popular name of "Sat-Cho-To," until the dawn of Constitutional Japan and government by party, in the late nineties. The year 1863 had opened with an exodus of natives from Yokohama, terrorized by the ronins and the fear that the foreign squadron might bombard the place, but the British fleet went to Kagoshima. The American legation suffered from fire, probably from ronins on May 24th. Yedo and Kanagawa being rid of foreigners, steps were taken to confine them in Yokohama, but the Shogun reported to the emperor that the foreigners could not be expelled. The Choshiu clansmen, raising the flag inscribed "In obedience to the Imperial Order," erected, on the rocky and woody heights overlooking the narrow straits of Shimonoseki, batteries of heavy guns. They began indiscriminate firing on every foreign vessel that passed through, American, Dutch, and French, and even, by mistake, on a Satsuma vessel, in foreign style. After fruitless conferences, the British sent their squadron to Kagoshima and seized three steamers. Being fired upon, they bombarded and burnt part of the town. This took place between August 12th and 17th while Mr. Verbeck was in China.

Although the bombardment was condemned even in Parliament, it had the seasonable effect of bringing the Satsuma men to their senses. Indeed, this taste of foreign fire and iron was a turning point in the history of this most warlike of the clans. It opened the eyes of brave but narrow minded men, who had been educated under a ferocious system of morals. With that respect which a well thrashed bully looks upon the man that has administered chastisement, the Satsuma men thought better of the "hairy foreigners" and began to introduce foreign machinery and appliances. Soon they became, what they long were and continue to be, leaders in the material part of civilization, especially in matters of war, in the army and the navy. They paid their indemnity in cash. In modern Japanese statecraft, the men of Choshiu excel in civil, and those of Satsuma in military, affairs, thus making a superb combination.

The Choshiu men went to Kioto and attempted

to carry off the Mikado and were foiled, but Sanjo and six other Kuge or court nobles, who wore amazing large flowing garments and black caps that looked like bricks tilted endwise on their heads, went back to Choshiu with the clan. They were deprived of their honors and titles. The expulsion of foreigners was postponed, even though the Shogun visited Kioto a second time.

After the failure of the Choshiu men in Kioto, October, 1863, let us see how the situation appeared at Nagasaki, to which Mr. Verbeck had just returned from China. His letter is dated November 14, 1863.

"In my letter from Shanghai, I stated our departure from that place. After a long but pleasant trip of nine days, we safely reached our desired haven in Japan (13 October). I cannot describe our joy at again seeing and setting foot on this fair country. All things around looked very much as when we left, only there were a few new batteries, and more activity around and in them. Business had come to nearly a dead stop, and although there was no danger for the time being, yet the greatest uncertainty prevailed. On the whole, however, the prospects of peace seemed brighter; and at all events, the general opinion was and is, that the Japanese, though they are acknowledged to have fought well, have had a sufficient trial of foreign warfare to convince them that they are not able to cope equally with foreigners. They also have learned to respect the lives of foreigners, since they see that they

cannot endanger or take them with impugnity.
The delays on both sides in these troubles I
think, have been rather for good, as it has given
the native government time to think and arrange
its own internal confusions. The ronins, who
were the perpetrators of all the murders and attacks at Yedo, and who at various times caused
a good deal of apprehension here also, have
nearly all been seized, and many of them put to
death. The Prince of Choshiu, who so irregu-
larly fired on ships of all nations at Shimonoseki,
is to be, or is perhaps by this time, degraded and
punished. And the Prince of Satsuma is said to
be very sorry for his encounter with the British
forces at his capital. Yet with all this, we have
no certainty of anything. Nearly everything we
hear comes in such different forms, with such
contradictory variations and from so many (often
doubtful) sources, that it is hard to get at the
truth. Much is supposition, because hoped for.
Political news you must look for from Kanagawa,
though even that is often contradicted by later
reports."

VII

THE DOORS OPENING

" BEHOLD, I have set before thee an open door,"
seemed to be the Heavenly Father's message to
Guido Verbeck at the opening of the year 1864,
despite the turmoil of impending civil war.

In the ebb and flow of the fortunes of the
Bakufu, it looked as though the foreigners and
the Yedo government had triumphed, for the foreigner-haters and fanatics were in disgrace.
Choshiu became the rendezvous of ronins and
runaways from every clan in the empire. A body
of these regular and irregular clansmen marched
upon Kioto, with the idea of seizing the emperor's person. In Japanese politics, whoever
possesses his sacred body makes the government,
while those who resist are traitors. A terrible
battle took place in Kioto. After fighting and
cannonading, with much loss of life and awful
destruction of property in the war-fire, the
Choshiu men were defeated though still defiant.

The combined squadrons of four nations, Great
Britain, France, Holland, and the United States,
gathered at Shimonoseki in September to chastise
these audacious clansmen who attempted to fight,
on the one hand, the mighty Tycoon and all his
host, and the foreigners with their fleets on the

other. We shall see what happened, what good medicine of chastisement they took, and how they too, like Satsuma, repented and turned their faces in the direction of progress. Let us note how Nagasaki harbor revealed to Mr. Verbeck what was going on. To him Choshiu seemed like an old mediæval baron "with his brigand band." He wrote in August:

"The renewal of Choshiu troubles, and the expedition now fitting out for Shimonoseki, have brought eight native steamers and a large number of people from all parts of the empire to this port, and I get my share of inquisitive visitors. The troubles and expedition are entirely civil, not foreign. The Prince of Choshiu, after apparently submitting to the necessity of circumstances for a time, has again broken through the nets and seems determined to stand his own ground. An ultimatum has been sent to this obstreperous prince by the Taikun, and the general expectation is that its terms will be refused and war ensue. There is not supposed to be any danger threatening foreigners. Surely, war is a sad thing anywhere; but if ever good is to be hoped for from such a cause, it is in Japan, I think. These people, in many respects, live yet in middle-age darkness and institutions, from which it may be doubted whether they can emerge without at least one hard, it may be, sanguinary struggle. The mighty Lord overrule.

"There is an extensive inland and coast trade carried on from this port, which continually

The Doors Opening

brings strangers from all parts of Japan, but especially from this inland Kiushiu, to this port. Thus we come in contact daily with strangers as well as residents. The great majority of the people who come to see us in our house, in quest of books or for other information, are visitors whom trade or curiosity brings thither, so that our influence, especially when the country will be more open, but even now, is by no means limited to this place (of about 80,000 inhabitants). That our names and characters are thus carried much farther than we might superficially expect, was shown me the other day in rather an amusing manner. A steamer belonging to the Prince of Higo came into port, with a brother of the Prince on board, and stayed about a week. I did not know that either Higo steamer or Prince was here, when two days before their departure a Higo man, who got a Chinese New Testament and some books from me three years ago, came to see me and told that a high officer of his Prince wished to see me. When this officer came, he stated that he wished me to assist him in getting a steamer for his master. These people were strangers in this town, and when it was known that they came to purchase a steamer, they were so beset by a corrupt set of brokers and runners (natives) that they became as it were bewildered, not knowing whom to trust. In this extremity they applied to me. That they applied to me may also partly be owing to my sometimes having assisted native scholars or engineers in the solution of difficult, at least for them difficult, problems, especially in mechanics or engineering. In such cases the profession of my younger years, that of civil and mechanical engineering, proves useful even after years. In the present instance, however, I could give these gents but small comfort, as of course I told them that such business lay quite outside of my province, that I could do no business transactions of any kind, and that my business was to teach the doctrine. After some deliberation, I agreed so far with them that I would recommend them to the American Consul, Mr. Walsh, who no doubt would gladly undertake to get them new steamers from New York. They left with warm expressions of thanks, and I was glad to rid myself of customers of this kind. I did not expect perhaps to ever see them again, because they must have been disappointed that their last refuge proved so unavailable. But the next day a still higher officer called with this same request; yet, though he was one of the highest officers of his state, a karo or minister, I could but give him the same answers. They left much pleased with their visit on the whole, nor have I seen them since. The gratifying part is the manifestation of confidence in our character. Where one ran down the other, to whom should they go? To a missionary of the gospel! Oh, that they would come with weightier questions! But they will. The time will come, when we shall welcome them and say: You are the men

118

The Doors Opening

we have been waiting for these years; it is to
you we were sent. Come and welcome. Ask
the way and we will show it you! And then,
may they go away comforted instead of disappointed. May the Holy Spirit open their hearts
and Christ give them peace."

Before unchaining the dogs of war, the olive
branch was tendered. Two British ships, the
Barrosa and the Cormorant with two young
Japanese natives of the province were sent to
treat with the daimio of Choshiu. These were
two out of the five young men who in 1863 had
escaped the vigilance of the Tycoon's officers and
had been sent by the Prince of Choshiu to England to be educated. Having seen the power of
Europeans at home, these samurai wished to
warn their master of the folly of measuring resources with the foreigners. With them went
two young Englishmen, Messrs. Enslie and
Satow as interpreters. Yet although the two
young men were landed and had an interview
with their feudal lord, they returned to the ships
with no written answer and only an unsatis-
factory verbal reply from the daimio. This was
to the effect that he was acting upon orders received from both the Mikado and the Tycoon.
In total ignorance as to the value of time, for
the Japanese language then contained no word in
the ordinary vernacular, for either minute or
second, the daimio asked for three months' delay,
promising to go to Kioto and get the Mikado, if
possible, to change his mind.

Verbeck of Japan

At the present writing both of these young Japanese are still living, one being the Marquis Ito, who has been the Mikado's premier and repeatedly summoned in grave crises to form a cabinet, and who is probably the ablest all-round Japanese statesman, and at this writing in June, 1900, called for the fifth time to the premiership. The other is Count Inouye, who has been also for many years one of the purest statesmen and cabinet ministers. One of the young British interpreters is, and has been for many years, the Minister Plenipotentiary of Great Britain in Japan.

The Japanese sick man had now to take his medicine in the form of shot and shell. On the 5th of September, 1864, at 2 P. M., the combined squadrons of Great Britain, France, Holland, and the United States, numbering seventeen vessels, in three divisions, with two hundred and eight guns, and seven thousand five hundred and ninety men, began the bombardment. The battle was bravely contested on both sides but the superior force and skill of the foreigners silenced the batteries. These were captured and destroyed by landing parties and the guns removed. On her sea front Choshiu was now completely humbled.

It must be noted that in the previous year, 1863, American skill and valor were amply vindicated by an act which ranks among the most brilliant in the long and glorious history of the United States Navy. On the 16th of July, 1863, Captain

120

The Doors Opening

David McDougal, then in command of the United States Steamship Wyoming, a corvette of the same rate and force as the Kearsarge, that is, with two eleven-inch pivot guns and four thirty-two-pounders, being then in pursuit of the Confederate man-of-war Alabama, entered the straits of Shimonoseki. Instead of passing along through the channel, which was duly staked out along its edges for the benefit of the Japanese gunners, McDougal daringly ran his ship in toward the shore, and under the fire of six batteries, drove the Wyoming between two armed steamers flying the Choshiu flag. He engaged these and the six batteries, blowing up the steamer and sinking the brig formerly called the Lanrick. In the seventy minutes' fight, the captain fired fifty-five rounds and had five men killed and six wounded. The Wyoming was hulled eleven times, receiving thirty shots in mast, rigging, and smokestack. The ship grounded, but came off safely, having performed a most wonderful exploit.

In 1864, the only national ship we had on the Japan station was the old sailing vessel Jamestown. The American minister, Robert H. Pruyn, chartered the steamer Ta Kiang, and Captain Price detached Lieutenant Pearson, with a party of thirty marines and sailors, with one Parrott gun, which was served most handsomely by the squad. After the battle, Lieutenant Pearson, having the swiftest ship, conveyed the wounded quickly to Yokohama.

Verbeck of Japan

All testimony since the events at Shimonoseki in 1863 and 1864, and it has been sufficiently abundant, was to the effect that the chastisement was most wholesome. The Choshiu men then and there resolved not to oppose the foreigners, but rather to learn the full secrets of their power and make friends with them for the good of the nation.

It was very evident, also, that, apart from political reasons, the jealousy of the great daimios of the Tycoon's monopoly of foreign trade and their desire to share its fertilizing streams which have so enriched and transformed Japan, were potent causes of both the imminent and the actual hostilities. During the negotiations, it transpired that Choshiu desired to open Shimonoseki as a port of commerce. The foreign ministers would gladly have remitted indemnity if new ports had been opened, but the Yedo government preferred to borrow in London at ten per cent. and to pay down the money, rather than open new ports. So the indemnity of $3,000,000 was ultimately paid, in the main, by the Mikado's government in Tokio. The share of the United States amounting to $750,000 was, after some years' delay and discussion,[1] by order of Congress, returned to Japan, and there used for educational purposes.

During all this time, in a strange land, where

[1] See pp. 593–595 of the first edition of " The Mikado's Empire," 1876. For several years the author sent copies of these pages stating the facts, historical and financial, to every member of Congress, until the money was paid back to Japan.

122

STUDENTS IN THE GOVERNMENT SCHOOL AT NAGASAKI.

there were no newspapers or telegraph, the lone missionary at Nagasaki, like a sentinel on a distant picket line, could learn what was going on in the country only by fitful reports, through rumors and exaggerations often told one day and contradicted the next, the wish being usually the father of the thought. Like the trailing shadows of moving clouds, his letters reflect his own moods and the thoughts of himself and those around him. This year was rich in opportunities and in opening doors of usefulness, as we shall see by quotations from his correspondence. He was even invited to come to other provinces and teach. All Japan seemed to be in a ferment. A newborn hunger for knowledge had seized many.

The first teaching of young men outside of his own house, by Mr. Verbeck, was in a school which the governor of Nagasaki established for the training of interpreters. On coming back from China, Mr. Verbeck found that the two young men to whom in 1860 he had taught some English, had been twice promoted. The happy students to show their gratitude to their preceptor presented Mr. Verbeck with two black sucking pigs. Their idea was that foreigners were especially fond of pork. The governor of Nagasaki was so pleased with the attainments of the young men that, on going to Yedo, he proposed to the Shogun's government that a school of foreign languages and science be founded and that Mr. Verbeck be made the principal.

In due time the official application was made through the United States Consul, and Mr. Verbeck accepted, to be head of the school at Nagasaki, agreeing at first to teach two hours a day for five days in the week. The salary was $1,200 a year. Happily for the good of Japan and the furtherance of true Christianity, the Board of Missions in New York gave its hearty assent to this opportunity of influencing for good the promising young men of Japan. From this time forth, until 1878, Mr. Verbeck was a self-supporting missionary.

A schoolhouse was built and was soon filled to overflowing, with over one hundred pupils, Mr. Verbeck taking only the advanced classes. By June 10th, 1866, the two nephews of Yokoi Heishiro, "Ise" and "Numagawa," were started to America, the first of a host, and the beginning of a procession of five hundred or more, who, with Mr. Verbeck's introduction, were helped in various ways, when in America, by the Reformed Church and Mission Board.

The samurai not only from Hizen and the southwestern provinces, but from many parts of the empire, including two sons of the court noble Iwakura, who afterward became Prime Minister of the empire, flocked to Nagasaki to get under the care of a man whose name was already magnetic, potent, and to some apparently magical. Indeed the long sealed doors seemed now opening on every side.

The two great documents, expressed in English,

which Mr. Verbeck taught most and longest to the most promising of his pupils, including such future members of the emperor's cabinet as Soyeshima and Okuma, were the New Testament and the Constitution of the United States. Here at the feet of this modern Gamaliel sat by the score other young men also, who in the Meiji period (from 1868 until the present day) have directed the destinies of Japan. Mr. Verbeck's pupils have become the new sort of orientals, in a new kind of Asian state that has voluntarily placed itself under the leading of the two great Anglo-Saxon nations.

Yet even more joy was given to Mr. Verbeck by hearing that his as yet unseen friend and pupil, "Wakasa," had resigned his office and, now free from the cares of state, proposed to visit his teacher and in native phrase "hang on his eyelids."

When Mr. Verbeck returned from China he found that Ayabe had moved from Nagasaki to accept a government appointment. It seemed then, at first, as though all his prayers and labor had been in vain, but soon after Mr. Verbeck was made happy by the advent of Motono. He came as the messenger from Murata, to get explanations of difficult portions of Scripture which could not be understood without a teacher, and also to secure other Christian literature. For nearly three years Motono vibrated like a pendulum, making the two days' journey, between Nagasaki and Saga. Now, teacher and pupil were to meet.

Verbeck of Japan

On the 14th of May, 1866, to the joy and surprise of Mr. Verbeck, Murata appeared, with his brother Ayabe, Motono, his two sons and a train of followers. He was tall and dignified, a gentleman of frank, ingenious mien, and about fifty years old. After his greeting, which was in the impressive manner of ancient Japanese courtesy, he said to Mr. Verbeck:

"I have long known you in my mind, and desired to converse with you, and I am very happy that, in God's providence, I am at last permitted this privilege."

In the course of their conversation, this seeker after God said:

"Sir, I cannot tell you my feelings when for the first time I read the account of the character and work of Jesus Christ. I had never seen, or heard, or imagined such a person. I was filled with admiration, overwhelmed with emotion, and taken captive by the record of His nature and life."

Murata showed great familiarity with the Bible, quoting from it with ease and point. He was ready to believe all that Jesus taught and to do whatever He required. The conversation lengthened into hours. Then Murata asked baptism for himself and Ayabe. The missionary warned them that there was no magic in baptism. All superstitious notions they might have as to its efficacy must be laid aside. Those who received the rite assumed sacred obligations of service. Explaining the form of baptism as used in the

Reformed Church, they were asked to decide as in the presence of God. Without faltering they renewed their request, only asking that the act should not be made public. They knew too well that not only would their own lives be in danger, but that their families would have to die with them. Death by crucifixion on the bamboo cross for a commoner, *hara-kiri* for a samurai was the punishment.

In full confession of sin, with vital faith in Jesus as the Christ of God, loyally desiring One whom they had long before acknowledged as Master, they took the step. On the next Sunday, the evening of May 20th, the three men, Murata, Ayabe, and Motono, were baptized in Mr., Verbeck's parlor. Then, joyfully they obeyed the further command of Jesus, "this do in remembrance of Me." After the sacramental meal Murata told the story of the Moses of his deliverance,—the book "drawn out" of the water twelve years before. Then the three men went away happy.

Mr. Verbeck wrote out an account of this his first baptism of Christian converts, but no publication was made of the fact at home, and for a long time there were but few persons who knew it. At Saga, Murata reported the fact to his feudal lord, who knowing the character of the converts made no further inquisition. One of Japan's Christian samurai wrote in 1863:

"The Imperial Government on hearing of Wakasa's conversion commanded the prince to punish him. The only semblance of obedience to this order was, to burn some of the subject's books.

"Murata Wakasa no Kami's last years were spent calmly, he having retired to a villa in Kubota, where in rural quietude, surrounded by the most beautiful scenery, he lived in the sweet embrace of nature. It is said that in those days he was engaged in translating the Bible from Chinese into Japanese. At the end, he, praying for the future victory of Christianity in Japan, smilingly left this world in 1874, being sixty years old."

"His memory is deeply cherished by Christians still living, who in earlier days, felt the power of his earnest personality. In his own family tree there are good and fruitful branches that are green and flourishing in Jesus Christ."

Space does not allow of our telling the story of Mr. Verbeck's visit to Saga in 1868 and of his royal entertainment by the daimio, or of his own impressions and pleasures. Nevertheless, his wonder grew to inquire why, with all the charms of the Japanese character, the nobility of humanity seemed an idea unknown in Old Japan. In the public bath-houses, so carefully graded according to classes, one pool was for "beggars and horses," while the common numeral term for laborers was the same as that for animals. Etiquette seemed to be the sufficient substitute for both religion and virtue.

Along with some relics of Roman Christianity

The Doors Opening

recovered in Kiushiu and sent home as curiosities, Mr. Verbeck, having photography to help him, enclosed some "living" documents.

He wrote: "Herewith inclosed you will please find a picture of a crucifix, and one of Christ with the crown of thorns. They are exact copies of the two pieces that for about two hundred years have been used in the annual 'Ceremony of trampling on the Cross' in the vicinity of this place. It will be something to show in addresses on missions, etc. The ceremony is mentioned in nearly every book on Japan, as you know; but I think writers on Japan have much mistaken the object of the shameful wicked act. It was not so much, if at all, to abuse and disgrace the Saviour, as to find out who were Christians and who not. It was known that no good Christian would trample on the image of Christ; therefore, at the annual census of the people, these images were produced to discover secret Christians. This ceremony was discontinued a few years ago. If you paste the pictures on a card, they will last better. By this mail too I send you a larger photograph of the elder of the converts. He sits between his two sons, in front. Those standing around are some of his vassal servants that accompanied him to this place. His name is Kubota Wakasa.[1] Will you kindly forward the photos as directed on the back? When do you send me a colleague? There is room for more

[1] Murata, Wakasa no Kami, lived at this time at Kubota, in Hizen.

than one. An experienced young minister who has had charge of a congregation at home and knows active service would be desirable."

Unable as yet to preach Christ openly, the young missionary being in the spirit of willing service, was alert to do all and whatever work came to hand, in and out of season, and too often in time that ought to have been given to recreation. Young men came to him asking him to teach them Dutch or English and this he at once began to do, little thinking at the time perhaps that he should in later years, at the head of the Imperial University, direct the course of the streams that are still fertilizing the national intellect. He may not then have foreseen that he should lay the foundations and plan out in detail a national educational system for the empire.

In 1898, a Japanese scholar, Rev. G. Ogimi wrote what he knew to be the facts told him by many witnesses among his own countrymen:

"After the Doctor (Verbeck) came over to Japan, in a short time young men who were somewhat acquainted with foreign civilization came from various provinces, one by one to Nagasaki, and desired, in the use of English or Dutch, to investigate the sciences and arts. Since, with the exception of medicine, none of the sciences and arts could be learned from any one but the doctor, they received his instruction, bringing to him such books as they had, even books on astronomy, navigation, mathematics, surveying, physics, chemistry, and fortifications!

WAKASA, HIS TWO SONS AND RETAINERS, 1866.

FIRST SCIENCE CLASS, IMPERIAL UNIVERSITY, 1874.

The Doors Opening

Just to learn English, they bought such as these, and, using them as text-books, formed classes. Men like Mr. Kantaro Yanagiya, chief of the patent office, studied fortifications with the doctor, so he said himself."

On September 7th, 1867, Mr. Verbeck wrote:

"Last month the Prince of Kaga placed a fine steamer at my disposition to visit his country. He is the wealthiest of the Japanese princes, and wishes me to come to his state to establish a school similar to the one at this place. I have invitations more or less direct to the same effect from the puissant Prince of Satsuma, the Prince of Tosa of the island of Shikoku, and the Prince of Hizen of Kiushiu. These four are among the foremost princes of Japan, all wishing to go forward on foreign principles. Wish it were on Christian. During the last twenty-four months, I have had visits from relations of three powerful princes and of two Imperial governors. Without boasting, I can say that the name of your missionary stands high. I am sorry only that a lone missionary is almost under the necessity, in speaking of these and some other things, to offend against Prov. xxvii. 2, and hope and pray that our Master in time will grant us something better than mere name and fame."

A careful study of his environment had prepared Guido Verbeck to make the right choice as to the location and continuance of his educational labors. We can see also how all his previous training, of head, of heart, of mind, and

131

hand came to be valuable and useful. In the modern world, the engineer and the linguist make superb combination for largest usefulness.

After the official changes wrought by the Revolution of 1868, at which we shall glance in the next chapter, by which Nagasaki became an imperial city, the government school came under the auspices of the daimio of Hizen. Or, rather the two schools continued side by side, Mr. Verbeck teaching on alternate days in each one. A still more influential class of students now began to come under Mr. Verbeck's care. He had the immense advantage of having friends in both the old and the new government, so that the transfer of ownership and sovereignty was made without the loss of a day.

The photograph of the teacher and his classes, which he sent home, forms an illustrative document of the highest value to the historian of Japan. In this group of young men we can recognize many who afterward became powerfully influential in various government offices as heads of departments, as cabinet ministers, as diplomatists abroad, and even in the premiership of the empire. Among a few, whom the biographer, without assistance from book or person, can recall from memory or recognize in the picture, is Prince Iwakura and his brother; Count Okuma, whose potency in the new national life of Japan during forty years has been recognized as head of the treasury and the foreign department, and as founder of a college of literature, and whom, with Soyeshima, the Mikado's envoy to China in 1874 and minister of foreign affairs, Mr. Verbeck especially instructed in the constitution of the United States, besides making them familiar with the fundamental laws of most of the western nations; Kentaro Yanagiya, the chief of the Patent Office, besides many others who were members of the great embassy in 1874 to the nations of Christendom.

Most of the pupils of Mr. Verbeck, proved true and faithful to him, showing in the Japanese character a capacity for " friendship the master passion," but one vile exception was shown in the author of a virulent and lying anti-Christian pamphlet which was published in Yedo in 1867 and greatly disturbed the object of the slander. It was proved by Mr. Verbeck that the author had been one of his own pupils, to whom he had given many hours of unrewarded toil.

It happened in 1863, that Mrs. Verbeck, for her own health and that of the children, went to China for a short respite. During this time, it was uncertain whether or not all foreigners would have to leave Nagasaki, or the place be occupied by English and French troops. Her absence was made the ground of the most outrageous and scurrilous charges, and the idea of Christian doctrine held by the anonymous writer was one which only a very sensually-minded Buddhist priest could conjure up or entertain. The pamphlet was translated by Mr. E. M. Satow

now the British Minister in Tokio.   Mr. Verbeck
wrote July 16th, 1868:

" The internal evidence makes it pretty certain
that it is written by a priest.   And there is no
priest in Japan who knows the things, such as
names, numbers, etc., mentioned in the pamphlet, but the said priests, who possess volumes
of notes taken in my study.   I wonder he did not
put in the names of all my children, with the age
of each and further particulars, for the old fellow
evidently knows the rogues' principle that a few
undoubted truths, especially truths of detail,
will give the color of truth to a large number of
lies strung on them.   In reading it over for the
first time, I was struck at once with many things
that had been the subjects of conversation between the old man and myself.

" In my own mind there is not a doubt about it,
yet as two of the old man's pupils still continue
coming to me three times a week, I shall put
them to the test on the first opportunity, and I
expect that, although they are not likely to show
their true feathers, I shall be able to elicit sufficient proof to settle the matter definitely.   I shall
however do nothing rashly, and give them a fair
chance to defend themselves or prove themselves
innocent if they can.   They are certainly a
strange set of men, if my suspicions are founded ;
for they have bought whole boxes of Chinese
Bibles and Christian books and tracts, in fact,
hundreds of volumes, and all, as they said, for
the purpose of teaching their scholars.   These

books, perhaps got for bad purposes only, may yet turn out a blessing to many, and under the divine blessing, quite contrary to the wicked intention. For any one comparing the pamphlet with the original sources of all Christian knowledge must see what a bold and wicked perversion of the truth has been practiced.

"As to the contents of the pamphlet, many things about the Roman Catholics are sadly true enough, and the account of the Urakami persecution is correct in the main facts. But I am sure that what is said about 'conventicles' is nothing but a most wicked invention. They may have had night worship, but nothing licentious. That the native so-called Christians (they are so only in name) should have resisted by main force, is a great injury to the Christian cause in Japan generally, and quite inexcusable. That these people were finally released from prison was not for the reason stated in the pamphlet, but entirely at the pressing instance of the French Minister at Yedo. This the author took good care not to mention.

"As to my wife's going to China, as I wrote you at the time, the object was a change of air, a recruiting of physical health, not of missionary forces, and of weaning a baby that had been at the breast too long. Other ladies in the East, or most of them, have their babies attended and brought. up by wet nurses. My wife nurses them herself and none less than ten or twelve months. And this wicked fellow must try to give a most natural event the looks of a violation of what he

calls 'the social relations' or 'the five virtues.'
But what hurts me most is the blasphemous account he gives of the Saviour. I cannot imagine how he invents the foul stuff, unless it be at the instigation of the Father of lies himself. Shall I issue a crushing reply, or had I better keep silence? I shall let you know by next mail."

On reflection, Mr. Verbeck preferred golden silence to silver speech or iron ink. Disliking controversy, able to be silent in several languages and always anxious to present the positive side of truth, he kept on the even tenor of his way in teaching and satisfying inquirers. Indeed, Mr. Verbeck very rarely, if ever, entered upon argument with contumacious men of inferior mind or character.

Yet here again, comes out clearly the radical difference in the type of Northern, or Germanic, as compared with Roman, or Slavonic Christianity, both at home and in missionary aim and work. The prime object of the latter is to make churchmen. There is, too often, an oceanic difference between a churchman and a Christ-man. The former conforms to the corporation. The latter seeks his life out of himself in God. Reformed Christianity touches and re-creates art, literature, philosophy, and ideals individual, social, and national. It rebuilds anew in Christ Jesus. None knew and felt this more than Guido Verbeck. He wrote:

"What the author says about Protestants has reference to me only, for he never met any others; and that he considers me more dangerous or injurious to the country than a large number of Roman Catholic priests with a host of nominal converts, rather flatters me than otherwise. The fact is, the priests see that I begin to get a stand with the higher and ruling classes of society, with whom themselves have no show at all, and by whom they are looked down upon. It is an indirect concession on the part of an intelligent native to the fact that my way of proceeding is more likely to tell in the end than the rash course [*i. e.*, political opposition and interference] the Roman Catholics have chosen to follow.

"As an offset to the above, I have quite lately had another case of also a priest who had actually given up his priestly office, emoluments, and duties with the set purpose henceforth to serve the Lord. He has already felt the hand of persecution on this account and yesterday left me to go and live a while with a friend in a retired island."

In retrospect of the nine years' residence at Nagasaki, and especially during the turmoils of 1868, he wrote:

"We have not however escaped without serious and well grounded fears for our safety. We have been threatened with fires, attacks from the notorious "loonins" [ronins] or professional bravos, and even expulsion from the country. When I say *we*, I mean foreigners generally. As to ourselves, except in a general outbreak, I did not fear any personal violence, as I had numerous good friends on both sides of the question, and as our pacific character and calling are too well understood by all. But not a few of the foreigners, as I afterwards heard, had their valuables packed ready for shipment. All I did at the critical time was to reload an old revolver, so as to be ready for common thieves or robbers, who might avail themselves of the general confusion to try their wicked chance and who would probably be frightened off by the mere report of firearms; but especially did I commend ourselves to Him who is mightier than any that might be against us. By the mercy of God, we are now through the worst and there is not even the probability of personal danger. From a Tycoonal town we have become an imperial city. Our new governor is daily expected from Miyako, [Kioto] the imperial capital, and on account of my position of teacher at the Government School, which goes on as heretofore, I hope to meet him. On the whole we hope that all these great changes in the empire will lead to more liberal views on the part of the authorities, especially in regard to our religion. On the face of the thing, however, this is not at all self-evident; for these very emperors claim, or at least are from old held to be descendants of the gods and the supreme pontiffs of the empire. But I think we may reasonably hope that Japan is ready to give up such nonsense as antiquated, and show itself willing to receive a more reasonable, the most reasonable faith."

The Doors Opening

"During the years immediately preceding the restoration of the Imperial power," writes a veteran missionary, "Dr. Verbeck received numerous visits from the clansmen of Satsuma, Choshiu, Tosa and other provinces, who were then continually travelling back and forth via Nagasaki, engaged in discussing with each other what was eventually realized in 1868. Among these visitors, most of whom had never before met a foreigner, may be mentioned such men as Komatsú, the elder and younger Saigo, Soyeshima, and many others who distinguished themselves in those critical times."

At home the Reformed Protestant Dutch Church had by vote of the General Synod dropped the term "Dutch," and adopted as its name style and title, that of "The Reformed Church in America." Concerning this act, "the Americanized Dutchman" in Japan wrote:

"I suppose as missionaries, we are supposed to keep quite clear of anything approaching party politics; but where there is so much unanimity as in our late 'change of name,' I dare say we may express our opinion without compromising our character for impartiality. I, for one, hail the change as a good thing on mission ground. The name of a foreign nation in the very body of the name of a denomination cannot but do harm in a country to the church that bears it, and I only wonder that the foreign name has been so long retained by our Reformed Church."

Verbeck had the historic and true progressive conservative spirit. The ancient name of the church, since it had reformed its life, doctrine, morals, and government, by purging out the accretions from Rome, had been The Reformed Church in the Netherlands, and its name was but a "return," in spirit and fact, and not a departure from New Testament principles.

It has been well said that "the history of the Reformed Church Mission in Nagasaki for the first ten years is entirely that connected with the personal experiences of the founder" who, many years afterwards, wrote as follows:

"We found the natives not at all accessible touching religious matters. When such a subject was mooted in the presence of a native, his hand would almost involuntarily be applied edgewise to his throat, to indicate the extreme perilousness of such a discussion. If, on such an occasion, more than one native happened to be present, the natural shyness was, if possible, still more apparent, for there was little confidence between man and man, chiefly on account of the abominable secret spy system, which we found in full swing when we first arrived and for several years after. It was evident that before we could hope to accomplish anything in our appropriate work two things were essential; we had to gain the general confidence of the people and we had to master the native tongue.

"As to the first, by the most knowing and suspicious, we were regarded as people that had come to seduce the masses from their fealty to the 'god-country,' and to corrupt their morals generally. These gross misconceptions we had to endeavor to dispel by invariable kindness and generosity, by showing that we had come to do good to them only and on all occasions of our intercourse, whether we met in friendship, on business, on duty, or otherwise; a very simple Christian duty this!

"As to the other pre-requisite to successful work, we were in many respects not favorably situated, and our progress was correspondingly slow. We had none, or hardly any, of the helps for studying the language that have been so abundantly furnished to those who arrived at later dates. The discovery of a new part of speech, or of a new construction, seemed to us often like the discovery of a new land and often was the source of great joy.

"As to myself, I may say that, as an auxiliary in my endeavors to secure the above two requisites, I early commenced to give gratuitous instructions at my home in the English language, and various other useful branches. This course, under Providence, led to my being early identified with educational matters, and did much to give shape to my career in this country."

VIII

THE REVOLUTION OF 1868

THE intellectual movement of a century and a half in Japan was now nearing its culmination. What would issue? In the presence of aliens and of the forces of modern civilization, would there be collision and disaster or a union of forces?

It is easy now to see clearly what *did* happen. It was very far from being visible in 1868. Yet there were in Japan on the 27th of June, 1865, two men who were to influence mightily the issue. One was Sir Harry Parkes, the British envoy, a stalwart whose one idea in life was to "make England great." The other was Guido Verbeck, citizen of no country, whose consuming aim was to win disciples for the Master, whom each followed. Both were pupils of Gutzlaff of China and made so about the same time. In Zeist, this apostle had inspired Guido Verbeck. In Macao he trained Harry Parkes in the most difficult of languages.

Sir Harry Parkes reached Nagasaki from Shanghai, June 27th, 1865. With his coming, a new era in diplomacy opened, for Parkes, as he once told me at his own home, at the British legation in Yokohama, at once set about to find out who was master in Japan and where and what the government was. He "took precautions," as he told me, and then interviewed various high official figureheads and clan leaders. Aided powerfully by Satow and the other students of Japanese history at the British legation, he began to see the real facts. There was only one fountain of authority—the Mikado. Alone among all the foreign ministers, who wished to support the Shogun, Parkes held to the Mikado's side. He advised the loan of British money and otherwise encouraged the new government whose rise we shall describe. He served in the East forty-three years, with vigor in Japan from 1865 until 1883, and in China from 1883 until 1885, dying, of overwork in Peking. He was often made the target of abuse and even of slander. He was a stalwart for British interests, as Verbeck was for freedom of conscience and Christianity. Of both Verbeck and Parkes, the Japanese confessed that none was ever able to do what they so often did to other foreigners—twine them around their fingers.

In the military campaign on land, following the naval battle at Shimonoseki, the prestige of the Bakufu was ruined and that of Choshiu was increased. When the Shogun died, Hitotsubashi became head of the Tokugawa clan, and of the Yedo government. But by this time, the agitation for national unity, begun a generation or more ago and made perhaps a logical necessity from the study of native history and literature a century and a half previous, took phenomenal form in the combination in the southwestern clans. It was their desire to abolish the duarchy and have one source of authority, the Mikado, to be the sole ruler of Japan. Early in 1867, when the emperor Komei died, he was succeeded by his son Mutusuhito, now and since 1868, the sole ruler of the empire.

The new Tycoon, then a young man in his early thirties (now, in 1900, a hale and hearty gentleman living privately in Tokio) met the foreign ministers at Osaka. The interview was very satisfactory. Sites for the new settlement of Kobe and Osaka were determined upon and the west coast was inspected to see what harbors were best suited for foreign trade. Nevertheless, while relations between the Yedo government, which was the government *de facto*, and the foreigners were improving, yet opposition between the Tycoon and the vassal daimios was ripening into hostility. At this time the relations between the various landed feudal lords and the Tycoon was much like that of the various states of Europe, with such suzerainty as might be involved in a congress of powers, and it was held that the action of the emperor and Tycoon against Choshiu disturbed the balance of power. The clans of Satsuma, Tosa, Echizen, and Uwajima had therefore taken action in memorials to the rulers in Kioto and Yedo, the Throne and the Camp, looking to a change in the order of things.

The ex-prince of Tosa declared in a memorial

The Revolution of 1868

that the East and the West had risen in arms against each other, and that Japan had long been the stage of civil war, the effect being to draw on the Japanese the insults of foreign nations. The reason for this state of affairs was that the administration proceeded from two centres, and "the empire's ears and eyes were turned in two different directions." The march of events had brought about a revolution and the old system could not be obstinately persevered in. "We should restore the governing power into the hands of the sovereign, and so lay a foundation on which Japan may take its stand as the equal of all other countries." The clans hostile to the Tycoon, eager for foreign trade, and wishing a united country, now began to press matters so strenuously that the new Shogun, seeing the state of affairs, in a characteristic document resigned his office on the 9th of November, 1867. He did this with the understanding that a general council of daimios should be convened in Kioto to deliberate and settle the basis of a new constitution.

The 15th of December was the day fixed upon for the opening of the assembly, and the air at once became heavy with schemes of reform and programs to be discussed. Yet it was noticed, that on all roads to Kioto, instead of the councillor and the statesmen, armed men were moving, the troops from Yedo arriving by land and sea from the east, and various bodies of daimios' retainers, ronin and soldiers of Satsuma and

145

other clans, were entering from the southwest and the north. Soon the City of the Ninefold Circle of Flowers was full of the flower of Japan's warlike men. All wondered what was to happen. A few determined men believed that they knew. On the first of January, 1868, the flags of the United States and the European nations were hoisted at Osaka and Hiogo, city and port, salutes were fired and commerce began.

In Kioto, the soldiers of the combination, Satsuma, Tosa, Echizen, Owari took possession of the palace gates, surrounded the emperor with a new set of nobles and councillors favorable to their views, and on the 4th, the next day, obtained the emperor's decree, abolishing the Bakufu, establishing the new government, and admitting the Choshiu troops to the capital.

Meanwhile the troops of the Tokugawa family occupied the castle of Nijo, and each garrison kept watch upon the other. The Tokugawa men considered the action of the 3d of January as a *coup d'etat* and were annoyed at being excluded from the new government. Listening to the advice of his retainers, Hitotsubashi proceeded at the head of his troops to Osaka on the night of the 6th. This action was deemed so highly suspicious by the new government, that it prohibited the two clans most closely connected with the Tokugawa family, Kuwana and Aidzu, from reentering the capital.

The new form of government, or constitution, and the laws issued in the emperor's name were

The Revolution of 1868

published in the spring of 1868 in the official
gazette, a newspaper[1] established by two of the
young officers engaged in the revolution, or
restoration. In Yedo, the great *yashikis* of the
Satsuma clan, reputed to be the hiding-place of
ronins and robbers, were attacked and burned.
This increased the bitterness between the two
clans of Satsuma and Tokugawa. The new government finding itself without money resolved
on contributions from the Tokugawa and other
clans, and sent the ex-princes of Owari and
Echizen to Osaka to get the adherence of the late
Shogun and make him a gijo or supreme councillor,
one of the second highest officers in the government. He agreed, but, afterward, persuaded by
the daimios of Aidzu and Kuwana, he started for
Kioto with hostile intent with all his following,
probably ten thousand men, the clansmen of
Aidzu and Kuwana being in the van. This
action the court considered was in direct defiance
of its order and the troops of Satsuma and Choshiu
were sent to the two principal roads to block the
way of the Eastern army. A battle broke out on
the 27th, and continued four days. It was now a
fight between the "loyal army" and the "rebels,"
or, about two thousand young men, armed chiefly
with American rifles, lightly clad, and drilled in
the modern style of war, against men for the
most part cased in antique armor, with spears
and swords and old-fashioned guns. The

[1] The beginning of the journalism of Japan, in which there
are now nearly eight hundred serial publications.

147

Satsuma and Choshiu clansmen making excellent use of artillery, entrenchments, and flanking attacks, won the victory. On the 30th the whole eastern army broke, fled, and were pursued to Osaka, which was entered and the foreign legations were burned or sacked.

The Shogun, in disguise, with some of his followers, abandoned the castle, and on the 31st crossed the bar in a boat. He was received on board the United States steamer Iroquois, though it was not known at the time that so high a personage had fallen so low in fortune. Reaching his own steam corvette, the Kayomaru, he left for Yedo. The next day the magnificent castle of Osaka, famed for its ramparts and towers and gates, and the astonishing size of the stones in its walls, was set on fire, all the woodwork being turned to ashes and the wounded men inside of it perishing miserably. Now began the civil war, which lasted for two years, ending in the complete triumph of the Imperial army. Envoys from the emperor met the foreign representatives and signed the treaty in the name of the Mikado. In spite of the murderous swords of fanatics and assassins, the foreign ministers entered Kioto and had audience with the Mikado, who, on the 6th of April, proceeded in person to the castle of Nijo, now turned into an office for the Council of State, and took an oath in the presence of the court nobles and daimios to establish the foundation of the empire according to the five principles laid down, which were as follows:

The Revolution of 1868

1. Government based on public opinion.
2. Social and political economy to be made the study of all classes.
3. Mutual assistance among all for the general good.
4. Reason, not tradition to be the guide of action.
5. Wisdom and ability to be sought after in all quarters of the world.

It was this last provision making education the basis of progress, and the quest for talent and learning everywhere, to create a new order of ideas, that opened the way for the entrance into Japan of a great army of teachers, engineers, physicians, scholars, and experts in every department of human energy and achievement. They came from Christendom, excelling even that wonderful precedent of the Czar Peter the Great, in seeking from Holland the brain and skilled muscle for the making of a new civilization.

The new government found itself in a position of great difficulty. It had floated into power on the two ideas of the restoration of the Mikado and the expulsion of foreigners. Unable to accomplish the latter aim, they found themselves obliged gradually to come to some compromise between the foreigners, to whom they were constantly making protestations of friendship, and the fanatical and ignorant natives, to whom Christianity meant sorcery, witchcraft, and alliance with foxes and badgers, and who wished the defiling aliens driven into the sea and drowned.

The troubles of the Japanese ministers were very great.

Instead of the old edicts against Christians and the apparatus of inquisition by the Buddhist priests, the Council of State now issued a fresh defamation of Christianity and proclaimed a ban against believers in " the evil sect " of which the following is a translation. It was published in March and republished in October, 1868.

" The Evil Sect called Christian is strictly prohibited. Suspicious persons should be reported to the proper officers, and rewards will be given." Dai Jo Kuan (Supreme Council of the Government).

These edicts were published with India ink on notice boards which were hung up under roofs or sheds, set up upon a platform of masonry in every city, town and village, near ferries, markets, highways, and places of public assembly. The idea was not only to ban, but to stamp out the new doctrine.

The first outward activity was seen in the proclamation of June, 1868, which gave the anti-Christian and anti-foreign parties great glee. About four thousand Japanese Christians, living mostly in Urakami, a village near Nagasaki, were ordered to be distributed among the various provinces, many of them being actually sent out into lonely and remote places. They were to be employed as laborers or kept as prisoners, during the space of three years, by no fewer than thirty-four daimios. If during this time they repented, they were to be set free, if not, they were to be beheaded. The Christians were torn from their homes, tied together like so many bundles of fire wood, and arrayed in the red suits of criminals, were distributed throughout the empire. Kido, called "the pen of the Revolution," arrived in Nagasaki in June, 1868, to carry out this decree. He declared to the foreign ministers of state that the government was simply taking precautionary measures to preserve order between the Christian population and the lower classes of the Japanese. Kido, like most of his countrymen, brave and comparatively enlightened as he was, then shared the common superstition, of the more savagely ignorant of his people, that a missionary was a person sent to Japan to break the laws of the country.   Of this notion, Kido learned later to be heartily ashamed.   It was reserved in after years for Guido Verbeck to be the most potent personal force in Japan, using reason alone in paralyzing the arm of persecution.

Guido Verbeck, who was one of the noblest representatives of the land of William the Silent, and Hugo Grotius, was a champion of freedom of conscience and of the brotherhood of man. Ardent, doughty, wise, patient, far seeing, he delved in the mine or mounted the watch-tower of observation as occasion called.   In the new movement for nationalism, he saw his opportunity.   He would plunge into the crater of politics and war, if need be, to secure freedom of religion, the adoption of international law, the sending of more native young men abroad to study, and the introduction of more Christian gentlemen into Japan. As soon as news of the decisive battle of Fushimi reached him he wrote home for approval of a visit to Osaka, not forgetting things nearer home, for the canny and æsthetic Japanese have an eye for material advantage, as keen as a Yankee's, and wanted wealth by mining, as well as by commerce. He wrote:

"By the way, have you among your acquaintance perhaps a good scientific and practical miner? The Prince of Hizen wishes to explore and open his mines, especially coal, and I was desired to inquire for a suitable man to undertake this job. He would be sure of a good salary and it would be a fine thing to have a good Christian man occupy such a position; there are alas too few of these here. It is not as yet a sure thing, and I am not authorized to promise anything; yet it would well be worth to consider the inquiry. If we could succeed in placing one such a person satisfactorily, there would probably be a demand for more in time, and it would be well worth some trouble to supply the country with active Christian men in the various pursuits of life. You have no idea how the name of Christian is disgraced by most foreigners in Japan, and it would almost pay just to hire good Christian families and to make them live in various parts of the country to exemplify and adorn the doctrine. This too would put a stop to much of the open wickedness and immorality now prevalent among foreign residents of all nationalities and ranks.

"In compliance with your suggestion, I shall start to-morrow on a trip to Osaka, the heart and headquarters of the empire (*i. e.*, taking Miyako [Kioto] into account), and shall try my utmost to bring about the desired objects touching the young men,—imperial appointment to the Naval Academy and suitable support. As soon as I got your letters, I began my preparations, and have reason, I think, to expect a good welcome from my numerous acquaintances at the capital. It is no easy task I am about to undertake, and I should not think of entering on it so extensively unless at your express wish. My going North involves the suspension of my schools here (a vacation to about sixty or more studious youth), considerable expense (not chargeable in full to the mission), my leaving my home and my family alone among strangers. For five years I have not been outside of a circle of a radius of four miles and very seldom to the periphery of that. On the other hand, besides the advantages hoped for if I succeed, my trip gives me an opportunity to spy out the land in view of missionary enterprise and location.

"If a favorable opportunity offers, I shall not fail to impress upon leading men the reasonableness and importance of toleration of our faith in Japan.

"There is a good deal of preparatory work to be done, which, like the scaffolding used in rear-ing a new building, need not be publicly exposed, but which the master builders ought to know, and which the public will only appreciate after the building is ready for general inspection."

We have already seen that Mr. Verbeck had started a few students on their way to the United States, and that this was the beginning of a mighty movement. Most of those, to whom he gave letters of introduction to the missionary secretary Rev. John M. Ferris, D. D., were courteously assisted in one way or another, often at the expense of money, time and trouble—all most gladly given. In 1885, for the production of my pamphlet "The Rutgers Graduates in Japan," I wrote to Dr. Ferris for data and received with other information the following. It will be seen that the young Japanese financially stranded in America, by the revolution in Japan, were handsomely tided over all difficulties.

"When the movement was at its height, the revolution which deposed the Tycoon, began in Japan. Some of the students were soon out of money. They called on me and stated their case. I visited a few gentlemen and wrote to others. A company was quickly formed which engaged to furnish money as I might call for it, until the result of the attack on the Tycoon should be reached. The following persons were the contributors: Jonathan Sturges, James Schieffelin, James A. Williamson, D. Jackson Steward, General Robert H. Pruyn, and Mrs. Anna M. Ferris.

The Revolution of 1868

When the revolution of 1868 was decided, the advances, for which the students had given due bills, were repaid. When the last company of commissioners from Japan, led by Mr. Iwakura visited this country, they prepared a paper recognizing this generous kindness and saying that it had had more effect in confirming the friendly regard for the United States by the government of Japan than any event in their intercourse with this country. Some of the contributors advanced five to six hundred dollars.

"My impression is that three or four gentlemen besides those I have named, assisted in providing for the emergency, but I was at the time obtaining money for various objects and cannot speak of them positively. The chief contributors were those I have named. JOHN M. FERRIS.

"*New York, Dec. 30, 1885.*"

We also produce in English the august document sent by the imperial envoys, Iwakura, court noble and premier and Okubo of Satsuma, of whom we shall hear further in our narrative.

OFFICIAL ACKNOWLEDGMENT OF THE MIKADO'S AMBASSADORS, IWAKURA AND OKUBO.

"*Secretary's Office of the Japanese Embassy,*
                              "*Boston, August 5, 1872.*

"REV. J. M. FERRIS, D. D.,

        "DEAR SIR:—The Ambassadors, being on the eve of their departure from the United States, desire again to convey to you this expression of their thanks for the interest which you

Verbeck of Japan

have (for many years) invariably manifested in their people and country.

"The kind assistance and encouragement which were so generally extended by you to the Japanese students who studied in this country during a crisis of such importance in our national history, will long be remembered by us. These students are now far advanced in knowledge, and are very useful to our country, and the Ambassadors feel it is mainly due to your instrumentality.

"Until recently an impression has prevailed in Japan, that many foreign nations did not entertain kindly feelings toward our people.

"The generous conduct exhibited by yourself and other gentlemen in this instance, as well as in all matters of educational interest pertaining to the Japanese youth, will do much to correct this impression, and will do more to cement the friendly relations of the two countries than all other influences combined.

"Please extend to the gentlemen this renewed assurance of the Ambassadors' high appreciation of their kindness, and they will likewise, on returning to Japan, explain the matter satisfactorily to our government.

"We remain yours very truly,
"Iomomi Iwakura,
"Toshimiti Okubo."

IX

As we have seen, the great political upheaval of 1868 gave the alert missionary an opportunity, which seeing, he was not slow to seize. He had, months before, written home asking leave of absence from Nagasaki, to go where activities were more potent and promising. Happy in having a chief, who could discern the signs of the times, and who instantly wrote him from New York to go to Osaka, Mr. Verbeck with his body servant Koide, sailed at 2 A. M. on Saturday, October 18th, 1868. On Sunday, he passed the famous island of Hirado, where in the sixteenth century the Dutch had their first factory and settlement. At 7 P. M. he entered the historic straits of Shimonoseki, seeing the lights of the city but nothing more. Early on deck next morning, he enjoyed to the full the ravishing sight of the Inland Sea, with its enchanting coasts and islets, and its Island Without Death.

For nine years, with the slight exception of flight to China, and a visit to Saga in Hizen, Verbeck had been shut up to the hills and water view of Nagasaki. He now revelled in the wider expanse, as his eyes enjoyed the sight of what is probably the most beautiful water passage in the

Verbeck of Japan

world. At eleven o'clock at night, anchor was cast in front of Hiogo or rather Kobe, and he landed early next morning.

The harbor of Hiogo had been defended, or was supposed to be, by two miniature martello towers, made of wood, and already beginning to decay. Built by Katsu Rintaro, each was expected to mount twelve guns, but not being armed and already crumbling, they were not very formidable, and about as useful as the forts in Yedo bay. At the Hizen House, he breakfasted on rice, eggs, and soy, eating as one in the chairless room, from a table five inches high, must perforce do, while resting on one's " hams and heels." On trying to rise he found himself very stiff in the knees. Whereupon the hotel servant laughed, to the great amusement of his own servant Koide.

As in old Japanese style, the travelling barber came to the house with his brass-bound box of scraping tools, having many drawers and a hopper-shaped top, to shave Koide's head and face. In those days the Japanese had on their noddles from the forehead clear back to the occiput a great central avenue of space kept bald, over which, the long-grown hair of the cultivated area, duly stiffened with camellia pomatum, was gathered up. The resulting stick of hair, rigid enough to remain one of a Roman lictor's fasces, was first tied at the angle where bent, and then laid on the top of the head. As stiff as a ramrod, and in shape like a gun cock, the whole

158

suggested an old-fashioned musket on a small scale. The razors were in shape like Japanese sword ends. The chief emollient used, or the only one, was hot water. There were also curved and hooped tools of steel for excavating the ears and nose. When man or woman in Japan is shaved, the process extends all over the face, around the eyebrows and down the neck under the hair. The work is thoroughly, as well as neatly and comfortably, done. Already men were beginning to show their politics and preferences, radical and conservative, by the style of hair-dressing which they favored, while the street songs reflected the change of fashion.

The baggage and servants coming later, Mr. Verbeck and Koide set out on foot, the owner and the stuff meeting about ten miles from Osaka, at a place called Nishinomiya or the Western Shrine. One ri further, they came to Amako, where was a pretty, old-fashioned castle, with moat full of water, sloping stone walls, flanking towers, water gate, pine-trees planted inside, and the regulation white walls or ramparts built at the top of the masonry. Over one hundred of these feudal castles existed in the empire, and the aggregate amount of labor and engineering skill expended upon them had probably exceeded that spent upon the Great Chinese Wall.

Taking boat and poling, drifting with the current, or sculling, they moved along in the dusk through the slough, bayous, and swamps in a

wonderfully zigzag way, gradually approaching
Osaka. They heard the noise of drums and
trumpets on land and water, quite continuously,
for this was indeed war time. Landing at nine
o'clock, they looked in vain for a foreign hotel,
for the new settlement arranged for by treaty had
been just laid out and was but half finished.
The traveller was impressed on his river voyage
with the richness of the fields and vegetable
gardens, the general air of prosperity in the
houses, clothes, and looks, of the country and
townspeople, and the roads which were lively
with many travellers. He was not now in a
corner, but in the heart of Japan.

Osaka was the greatest commercial city of old
Japan. In it most of the clans had their yashikis
and trading-houses. After a long ride through
the canals and under the long bridges, of which
there were about eleven hundred in the city, Mr.
Verbeck was attracted to the Hizen inn. This
typical old native hostelry had its courtyards,
fish ponds, and a great matted parlor, with
bronze, keramic ware and kakemono wall-
pictures in the alcove. After a good supper our
traveller slept soundly and safely.

The next morning he rose and strolled all over
the foreign settlement, in the afternoon spending
the time among the book shops. He was pleased
with the politeness of the shopkeepers and
people, though he had one encounter with a rude
Japanese. He priced the great encyclopædia San
Sai Dzu Yo, (which in 1900 we see is under re-

vision and to be brought down to date), then costing only ten or twelve *rio*. Both he and Koide had forgotten their umbrellas, one of silk, the other of oiled paper, but the next morning walking along the boatman called them and returned these "portable roofs." This honesty mightily impressed Mr. Verbeck, who in Nagasaki had met with plenty of thieves, but not with the honor which the proverb doubtfully ascribes to them. He thought that the streets of Osaka were much quieter than those of Yedo—no jolting, singing of coolies, horseback riding, carts, etc. The reason of this lay in the rivers which like great arteries ramify the city, and the multitude of water courses on which most of the traffic and transport are done. On the same element also most of the pleasure was taken by parties large and small. At Nagasaki no attempt seemed to be made to save room, but at Osaka the wood was piled up for seasoning on the roofs and on the sheds, saving space and gaining sun and air. Like a genuine engineer, Verbeck notices, describes, and reproduces in drawing a teapot like a flue boiler, tobacco pipes that unscrewed in two parts, with two branches for two persons to smoke from the same pipe head, or, to be shut up and carried in the pocket. He noted a syphon for the pouring of soy, the condiment which forms the basis of various "shire" sauces of England, and a dish for holding this same Japanese product of salt and wheat. He found out how men raised up old piles out of the river by using boats and the "camel" principle, and he made diagrams of the "house-boats." His journal shows that he could not help noticing in Osaka what he and I together noticed later in Tokio, in ostentatious and prodigious quantity, the various forms and adaptations in art, use, and material, of the phallus. Until foreigners came in large numbers to Japan, the phallic cult had reached a frenzy that had ecclesiastical and commercial, as well as religious phases. Priest, shopkeeper, and deluded victim of superstition were alike interested in keeping up what, in civilization, is a caricature of religion.

The people of Osaka were polite and ready, but at Sakai less so. This latter port was the seat of the tragedy of March 8th, 1868, when eleven French sailors were shot to death by Tosa clansmen, and reparation made by eleven Japanese, out of the twenty doomed to vengeance, committing hara-kiri. The people of Sakai were said to call out, what they thought to be a European word "peke, peke," a Malay term which means "get out" or "go away."

In the foreign settlement most of the newcomers were from Nagasaki, very few coming from Yokohama. At the latter place the opening of Osaka was rather ignored, but the project could not be hindered. The location of the foreign settlement seemed well chosen, being on high land, accessible to native craft and capable of expansion. Yet while at Nagasaki, the native shops were full of "Ranguchi," foreign goods, or literally, "Dutch notions," and women dressed in foreign stuff, often after a certain approach to a European cut which made absurdities, here there were few shops or wearers, of such importations. The customhouse officers, interpreters, merchants, laborers, and other natives in the new settlement were Japanese from Nagasaki. With the aid of a kind and friendly Tosa officer, who gave him his card, he and his companion Mr. John Milne, who afterward became the authority on earthquakes in Japan, paid a visit to the castle, the woodwork of which had recently in the civil war been reduced to ashes. He admired its dimensions and shape, and the enormously large stones, which rival if they do not excel the wonders of the Egyptian pyramids and suggest like problems of engineering. The view from the castle, despite the haze and gloom, was fine. The splendid stone work had been greatly affected by the fire.

On his way back, he saw a large silk shop with a miniature bamboo grove growing at the entrance. At this time the governor of Osaka was Goto Shojiro. Other friends whom he met were young Mr. Pignatel and Mr. Ga Kinosuke, who brought bows and arrows for the children, silk for Mrs. Verbeck, and maps for himself. He told Mr. Verbeck that very soon in Tokio an English school would be required. Mr. Yoshida, formerly a pupil of Mr. Goble of Yokohama, and afterward in the United States as student, and later Minister from Japan at Washington, was in

Osaka, inquiring about teachers and schools for his native province of Satsuma. Visiting Mr. Lowder, Mr. Verbeck was impressed with the fine premises of the British Consulate. By inquiry he learned that much business was being done and "that Yokohama with its banks and big houses would not believe in Osaka, but they would change their minds too late and confess their error." Even Hartley, the bookseller, boasted of a good deal of business, for young Japan was ravenously hungry for the new knowledge of the West.

It is everywhere the custom in Japan for the natives to send their friends pleasant little remembrances, in the form of presents, oranges, eggs, etc. In Nagasaki Mr. Verbeck received from one admirer, a pig. In Osaka a basket of eggs was sent him. He gave them to the hotel servant who in a few minutes came back asking whether he should boil them all. The Japanese had an idea that the foreigners, whose drinking utensils were so enormously larger than the little cups of the Japanese, were very heavy guzzlers and devourers. In their late mythology and art are representations of red-headed Bacchuses and bibulous devotees who lounge by the seashore, ladling out by means of big dippers the inebriating fluid from large jars, which they drink from huge beakers. Perhaps the servant thought also that a foreigner could actually eat as he traditionally drank.

Next day Friday the 23d was spent among the

book shops. He was impressed with the fact that Osaka being a large city, particular streets could be devoted to particular products, such as crockery, tobacco pipes, books, etc. Three sets of the great encyclopædia with some other books were bought. One set in eighty-one volumes was for the Rev. James Summers in London, one for Rev. James H. Ballagh, and one for himself. The vast size of the temples, the splendid carving and imposing furniture impressed the visitor. On the pagoda he met some Satsuma soldiers. While Mr. Ballagh was talking with Captain Bonger and another gentleman, the laborers, not over polite, kept their head cloths on. Mr. Verbeck smilingly dropped a hint in praise of native politeness, when off went the scalp cloths. Whereupon, the old lady at the pagoda, became voluble in compliments at his being able to talk Japanese that could be understood both by Satsuma soldiers and the Central-country " coolies." In one temple he found the Five Hundred Rakan or primitive disciples of the Buddha, represented by as many idols distributed in three shrines, some of them two or three feet high.

There were many soldiers from the different clans roaming about the city, not a few of whom had foreign dress and arms. There was no real danger from these men of war, fresh from the battle of Fushimi, though the raw fellows were not nice to meet. On the road to Umeda he saw at a distance a number of people dressed peculiarly in white. These, he thought, were perhaps ronin, that had consecrated themselves to deeds of valor against any and all "foreign barbarians." In such case, what chance would he stand against so many men armed to the teeth. Yet even "supposing these strange looking objects were only sheep," wrote he, "I was not like Quixote bound for trouble. On the contrary I was bound to keep out of it as much as possible, but after all, my supposed ronin turned out to be quite as harmless as Quixote's sheep. . . As I was walking along remembering that I had a band of bravos at my back, all of a sudden turning a corner I came upon another body of the identical white dressed people, and what should they turn out to be but mourners in a funeral procession! At once I faced about again and followed at the rear of the mourners. My doing so drew others of the villagers along so that my following swelled the original procession to twice its number, making in all about sixty heads.

"I entered at once into conversation with the nearest, and it gave great satisfaction to the company that the foreigner went along. They told me the dead was to be burned, the teeth and some part of the bones alone being returned to the family as relics for worship. There are five or six such places for burning the dead and this Umeda burned daily eighteen or twenty. The body, exhibited a few minutes at the temple and prayer said, was then brought to the burning hall —a kind of vault with two doors. As we came in with our corpse, three fires were burning from previous bodies. Our coffin was placed in the central place and a light mat of straw hung over it. Then the friends came in, saying prayers in which 'Amida' (Boundlessly Merciful Buddha) and 'Gokuraku' (Paradise) were frequently audible. Then each took a whisk of straw and set fire to the mat covering. Then the outside case took fire. Just at this interesting stage of the performance, a bad, rough looking fellow bade all go out and close the door. By and by I sidled up to the side door and actually saw ghastly white knees and thighs jutting out from the debris of burning straw and wood. But again the operator told us to leave and he shut to the door. How he could stand it inside is hard to say, for where we first entered there was a disgusting smell of burnt human flesh. But soon the time came for the next comer and the doors were thrown open once more.

"I was anxious to see how far our corpse had by this time proceeded and horrid was the sight. The back was turned toward the front door and invisible on account of the fuel that covered it. But the fire contracting the arms and muscles, just as I looked, a white arm and hand holding a rosary came slowly moving out of the flame. Nobody seemed to care. Men and children (no women) stood around perfectly unconcerned and talked with me about my dress and other things. I told them about our mode of burying. I was the first foreigner ever seen at the temple, they said. Children played about and men laughed.

After we had had a long talk, finally I said 'come, let us go now,' to the great amusement of the crowd. Another coffin arrived before we left, and we met one more on our way through the village."

Arriving at his lodgings, Mr. Verbeck found Koide. He had returned from Kioto, saying that Soyeshima would call upon him next day. That night he enjoyed a walk in the moonlight with Mr. Ballagh.

The next day he learned from Ga that the son of Katsu would be appointed to the naval academy at Annapolis. Meeting Soyeshima, he was told that there would be no difficulty in appointing the six men (elect Japanese students) to the Naval Academy. The Vice Minister of Foreign Affairs, Komatsú, would settle the details of the matter.

"Soyeshima wanted me to accompany Komatsu to Yedo to see the United States Minister about the delivery of the 'Stonewall ironclad,' pleading that foreign neutrality was no longer applicable to the case of Japan, since there was no war between Yedo and Miyako, the former Tycoon himself being at peace and one with the Mikado's government. The last news from the seat of war was that Aidzu's forts had been taken, that his forces had fallen back to Sendai, and that those still resisting the government were a mere collection of outlaws now established in two places only.

By this time many United States naval officers

were in Osaka and a number of Japanese in the government service had called, asking for Mr. Verbeck. After the usual earthquake and heavy rains, he spent the evening writing out copies of permission for the Yokoi brothers to enter at Annapolis.

The next morning a guide being sent him, Mr. Verbeck went to call upon Mr. Komatsu who promised to give the appointment to the two Yokoi young men. Mr. Komatsu then stated the desire of the government to establish a school in Yedo for three hundred scholars, with three teachers besides Mr. Verbeck, one of the departments being for the study of Dutch. When Mr. Komatsu asked Mr. Verbeck about the Stonewall, the latter answered: "I told him he must convince the Minister of the fact that the opposing party are only a small faction, in no way able to affect foreign intercourse and commerce in the empire. An American naval officer had been engaged at a thousand dollars a month but dismissed after fifty days' service. He demanded twenty-five thousand dollars indemnification. They mean to offer ten thousand dollars and passage home."

From Komatsu's house, for passage to his own lodgings, Mr. Verbeck went on one of the famous Cha-bune, or house-boats, with three boatmen to pole him along, going swiftly with the current, which gave him a good chance to study the varieties and possibility of the native shipping. He noticed that all the dirt and garbage of the city was carried out in boats, nothing being thrown in the river. Everywhere at the landings along its banks were good broad flights of stone steps reaching down to the water. Riding to Sumiyoshi he noticed great stacks of straw looking at night like giants on guard. The cows were used for draught. Horses were larger and dogs rarer than at Nagasaki. Tea and cotton were very common in the fields.

Calling on Iwasaki, he was informed that the real mover in the affair of the school was Goto Shojiro, but he also learned that appointments had been made of Sugiura to military study, Matsumura and Nagai to the navy, Ohara to political science, Yoshida to criminal law, and Nagasawa to medicine. He also learned that the Mikado was to go up to Tokio on the 20th (Japanese) day of the month, but that it was doubtful whether he would be able on account of lack of funds. Already there was a tendency in the government to be conciliatory, even to their enemies, for peace and national consolidation were desired. The new paper money made in Echizen[1] was beginning to circulate, but counterfeits were already in vogue. Reports of its inflammability were very much exaggerated, as Mr. Verbeck found by experiment.

After seeing various matters of interest in Osaka, they took *kago* which seemed very amusing and ludicrous to Mr. Verbeck. One had either to tuck up feet and legs under him or

[1] Mikado's Empire, p. 425.

let his limbs dangle down, with feet near the ground.

This ended Mr. Verbeck's trip to the central port and province of Japan. After coming to their home in the south, Koide, on his way to Hizen from Nagasaki, fell off his horse and died soon after, from concussion of the spine, while Mr. Verbeck's life was spared for further and more glorious usefulness. He was now busy in moving forward the long procession of young men from Japan, whose faces were set toward Christian nations. Of one from Fukui, in Echizen, whom I knew at New Brunswick so well and who was soon, to " fall on sleep " in Willow cemetery there, Mr. Verbeck wrote May 4th, 1868:

" As to Kusakabe, I have put his affairs in train too, and I think we may hope for a good result. I was much pleased to see that his aptness for study attracted attention, and I must say that, although I know any number of what I would consider—humanly speaking—better men, I know but ten or a dozen that I would call smarter than Kusakabe,[1] among my Japanese acquaintance, I mean. It is encouraging to observe the general intelligence of these people, their avidity for foreign attainments, and their thirst for knowledge generally. Let the edicts against Christianity be removed, and I think we shall have one of the finest and most prosperous mission fields in the world."

[1] See Mikado's Empire, p. 430, 431.

Verbeck of Japan

Of the young men who were sent to America to study, the two Yokois, Kusakabe and scores of others, and much information about the students and men of 1868, one may read in the author's pamphlet: "The Rutgers Graduates in Japan," an address (with notes and appendices) delivered at Rutgers College, June 16, 1885.

Verbeck's Americanism has the true ring. He believed he had found his work, in becoming all things to all men that he might lead some, and as he certainly did lead many to Christ. He wrote:

"It is said that the American and Presbyterian Boards of Missions refuse to send out foreigners, even naturalized foreigners, under their auspices, because they think that such men are not fully imbued with the American spirit, and will not sufficiently uphold, stand up for, and propagate this spirit. As a general rule, these Boards may be right in using it; but in making no exceptions, as I found on inquiry they did, I humbly think they err. Some of the best linguists and missionaries of the American Episcopal Mission, are foreigners. There is, or rather was, Schwartz, and a large number of really illustrious German missionaries in the employ of the English Church Mission. In speaking of myself, I would do so in all humility, giving all the glory and praise, if any there are, to God the giver of all, and counting all things but loss and worse than worthless that do not directly or indirectly, in their results redound to the glory of our Lord and Master, and

172

A Japanese Graduate of Rutger's College.

to the advancement of His cause. Now I claim to have more of the true American spirit than any Americans in this part of the Japanese empire, and claim that as an American, I am more looked to and respected by the natives than any other of our countrymen here. In one sense, if you know how immorally all foreigners, Americans (alas!) not excepted, live here, you would not think this much of a boast; but I refer more to our general institutions. Further, as most of the Japanese are great admirers of our glorious Washington and of the institutions which he helped establish, I have many inquirers, especially at the present time, into these matters. Now, although I never lose sight of our Master's saying: 'My kingdom is not of this world,' and though I know that missionaries ought to avoid getting mixed up in political affairs, yet, when these people come and sincerely inquire after the most likely measures that would conduce to the welfare of their country, I do not feel at liberty to refuse them a hearing and advice, in a place where honest advisers are few, if at all extant. I am of course careful in such cases to state clearly that properly such matters are beyond my province. to avoid all party spirit and feeling, and to impress the idea that my private desire and hope are only for the welfare, not of a section, but of the whole country."

Which of our readers recalls the scene at Peking in 1873 when Soyeshima was received by the Chinese emperor as an envoy plenipotentiary

from Japan, the first of any nation that ever stood
in the presence of the " Son of Heaven " ? Who
can but remember the long and illustrious services
of Okuma? yet both of these makers of New
Japan were Mr. Verbeck's pupils. He wrote
early in 1868:

" More than a year ago I had two very promising pupils, Soyeshima and Okuma, who studied
through with me a large part of the New Testament and the whole of our national constitution.
The former of these is now a member of the new
parliament, lately formed at Miyako, to revise
the ancient constitution of the empire. The
latter is a member of the privy council of the
Governor-General of Kiushiu, and is to start in a
few days for the capital, Miyako, in connection
with the revision of the constitution. On Saturday last, I was invited to a special meeting of
some leading members of the said privy council
to be consulted on matters in regard to the revision of the national constitution, and to-morrow
a similar meeting is to take place. You may be
sure that my friends and pupils above named
will work hard, for not only the repeal of the
ancient edicts against Christianity, but if possible
for universal toleration in the empire. The meeting for consultation was very interesting and I
may be able to give you a sketch of it and to-
morrow's in a future letter. It was interesting to
see how their own reasoning, with a little guiding touch here and there, led these men to the
conclusion that at the bottom of the difference

in civilization and power between their own country and such countries like ours and England, lay a difference of national religion, or theology, as one of them, who speaks a little English, termed it."

What with his journey to Osaka and his trip to Saga, the Nagasaki teacher was beginning to be a traveller, as well as sedentary resident in the empire which he afterwards traversed so thoroughly as evangelist and proclaimer of the good news of God to his Japanese children. On January 22d, 1869, he wrote to a friend:

"You see that, although it is a long time since you had any lines from me, I am still at the old stand, by the great mercy of God. Yet of late I have done more in the way of locomotion than for several years past, and indeed I begin to stand quite loose in my shoes here. I mention this here at the outset, because my apology to you for my long silence rests on these very circumstances. After waiting long for letters from you, at last they came; but then also came my migratory turn and such a multiplicity of engagements that I barely managed to get ready the monthly letters to the Secretary, and those at long intervals to my own relations."

He refers jocosely to the philosophers and artists whom he had met on his trip to Saga. For amusement, he translates literally some of the Japanese names.

"As a specimen of Japanese table-talk during the last trip, [to Saga] allow me to mention only one of those little incidents that my notebooks are full of; this, however, was the best thing said. On Tuesday P. M., paid a visit to Mr. Marble, who for my entertainment had called Mr. Heavenprint, a painter of a good deal of celebrity in Hizen. Mr. Heavenprint soon squatted down and really performed astonishing things with his brush, by a few bold strokes, and lighter lines and shades, producing most powerful effects. Within half an hour he finished half a dozen paintings of natural objects on paper six feet long; besides one of a rat eating a hole into a big turnip, painted with his little finger and nail only. Toward the end of the artist's performances, just as he had finished a fine crane and was doing the ground under the bird's long legs, Admiral Leftyard, who was with us as usual, said with the greatest ease and off-handness: 'Mr. Heavenprint is quite a creator; there he makes storks, horses, trees and flowers while we stand looking on, and now again this beautiful crane;—but there is a difference: the Great Creator made the earth first, and then peopled it with living beings, whereas *this* creator makes his animals and birds and trees first, and then puts terra firma under them.' This was probably in its way the best thing said on the trip; but is it not fine and could it be excelled by any of us?"

Japanese art being a subject of deep and abiding interest, it may be well to quote Mr. Verbeck's opinion of some phases of this development of the national genius. The passages we quote are from his long and masterful review of Professor Basil Hall Chamberlain's volume on The Classical Poetry of the Japanese in " The Chrysanthemum " for 1881, Vol. I. 8, 9, 10:

" Art, in Japan, is exceedingly artificial. It is strange that it should be so with a people who apparently have an intense love of nature. Their birds, insects, and flowers, whether painted or carved or otherwise made, are generally true to nature; yet it is not uncommon to see even these disfigured by unnatural lines and touches. Their larger quadrupeds are almost without exception outrageously unnatural. Streaks of clouds run right through the foreground of many of the older pictures of scenery. All their singing is in an artificial voice. Once asking a connoisseur of native art (he had himself taken lessons in oil-painting at the Hague, nearly twenty years ago): 'How is it, Mr. Uchida, that your artists, who do so well in flowers and insects, fail so utterly in quadrupeds, and notably in horses? How unnatural, for instance, the horse on yonder screen.' 'Ah, you must not judge of them in this way,' replied my friend, 'they do not attempt to imitate nature in painting horses and some other animals. Years ago a celebrated artist painted a horse which was considered the perfection of equine beauty, and now all artists take that as their model; whoever succeeds most nearly in reproducing that ancient model is the best artist. It may be that the introduction of

photography will help to correct the error.'—
Something like this, I think, is applicable to the
poetry of Japan: it is exceedingly artificial. Mr.
Chamberlain has taken a number of such standard horses and transformed them into as many
fine English steeds.

" Japanese art has recently gained (or, as some
think, lost) much by an accession of foreign
elements. But in nearly all departments of
European art, too, more particularly in the
pictorial and decorative, may of late years be
noticed distinct traces of notions peculiar to
Japanese art. It would almost seem as if the
European artists' kaleidoscope, having refused,
after the exhaustive use of ages, to show new
combinations of form and color, had suddenly
been given a fresh turn, bringing to light wholly
unexpected and hitherto unthought of notions,
and patterns, and nuances. The result of the
mingling of elements so foreign to each other is
sometimes surprising, often agreeable, always
novel."

Referring again to his trip to Saga, he says:

"I wish I could freely write about some very
touching circumstances in connection with some
native believers for the interior of the country;
but you know my bump of cautiousness is
rather largely developed, and I really think that
publicity in such matters would injure our, the
Master's cause, and jeopardize—under the exist-
ing laws of the empire—the very lives and property of those who have entrusted their all to my

discretion. But I trust the time is not far off when we can ' publish in the papers ' full numbers and names for the encouragement of the churches. Till then excuse me, unless I should see you again face to face before that time."

Mr. Verbeck's reference in this letter is to his baptism of Wakasa's mother in her home at Saga. Years afterward, his daughter received the same rite at Nagasaki, and now four generations of Christians in this one household have illustrated the beauties of Christian holiness and have strengthened the prophecy of a Japan over which Christ shall rule.

CALLED TO THE CAPITAL

MR. VERBECK was now to have his field of labor changed from Nagasaki, "the quietest and safest place in Japan," in the extreme south-western part of the empire, to Tokio, the Eastern Capital, (Saikio, or Kioto, being then called the Western Capital), and the nation's centre. The restoration of 1868, with its accompanying revolution, was essentially a student's movement, but in its origin it must be referred to the early part of the eighteenth century. Many streams fed the flood which floated the Mikado to power and made a new nation. Native scholars began reexamining their ancient history, both on its religious and its political side. The revivalists of pure Shinto studied, wrote, and published, showing what Japan was before Chinese influence had been felt. The Mito scholars had compiled their great history, (Dai Nihon Shi). Rai Sanyo had published his volumes, (Nihon Guaishi) which were being studied by Japanese gentlemen in every province and shaping their political opinions. For a century the intellectual leaven from the Dutch at Deshima had been helping to transform the national mind. Foreign influences from without, and especially the work of Guido

Called to the Capital

Verbeck and his co-workers from within, were bringing to head and to union all the latent forces. The signs of upheaval and change were as manifest as in the hour before earthquakes or blossoms.

When in Kioto, in 1868, the coalition of the progressive clans, in which native and foreign learning had been most active, had been formed, the decisive battle of Fushimi had been fought, the new government organized, and the whole train of gathered forces were in momentum toward a new Japan, the situation may be thus roughly outlined:

Theoretically a union had been made between the Throne and the People, by abolishing the old and putting in new intermediaries who were first, the kuge, or court nobles, men of immemorial rank and high prestige; and, second, daimios, or landed noblemen of uncertain abilities; and third, a large number of young men full of eagerness, with their eyes set on the future, but without much experience and in matters of dealing with foreigners little better than children. In Kioto these young statesmen, most of whom had been students under Mr. Verbeck, or had learned a little in various ways from other foreigners, were fortunate in having the advantage of the wisdom and experience of Yokoi Heishiro. This man, who sent the first Japanese students to America, was, among his younger colleagues, very much as the aged Franklin was among our constitutional fathers in Philadelphia in 1787–9.

Verbeck of Japan

But on coming to Tokio, where should the young Japanese statesmen get advisers, in order to "reestablish the foundations of the empire," and to deal and cope successfully with aliens? Whom could they trust? Naturally they, that is, several of the leaders and scores of those rising in power, turned to their old teacher and called him to their aid. Mr. Verbeck, alert and ready, breaking up his home in Nagasaki, took steamer for Yokohama. We find him in Tokio writing under date of June 21st, 1870, and again under date of June 29th, 1870, where we see him under that terrible strain of work which continued for so many years, surprising those who, like myself, saw it going on in his own home. As we know well, the course of convalescence is not a straight one, nor is the path suddenly taken from mediævalism toward modern national life one of easy ascents. There was ebb, as well as flood, in the tides of political progress. Let us see how our hero's letters record them and his own feelings.

Let Mr. Verbeck's own letter tell how the invitation came to him from the Imperial Government to leave his " few sheep in the wilderness " and assume larger duties, even as it proved, to the shaping of the course of a nation:

"Herewith you will find two enclosures. One, a letter to Mr. Brown, which after perusal I request you to forward to him; the other, as you see, implying great changes in regard to myself. On the 13th inst., there came to me a high official of the Imperial government, now located at Yedo, who had been specially sent to this port to call me to the Eastern Capital, Yedo. As far as I know now, the chief object is to get me to establish a university, or something of the kind. I am not, however, given to understand much of the detail of the object of my call; only I am assured that some of my former pupils, now in the new government, are to meet me there and to arrange matters satisfactorily. As you see from the enclosure, the government wants me forthwith, next month, and I did not feel justified to refuse the invitation. You have no idea what emulation there is in this country, from the Ministers of all nationalities down to the commonest subjects, to get in with the men now in power in the Imperial government; besides, the Romanists exert themselves to the utmost for the same object, and under these circumstances it would never do to let such an opportunity as is now offered me pass by unnoticed or unprofited."

His answer was as follows:

"To Yamaguchi Hanzo, Esq.,
      "Dear Sir:
            "Having duly considered the proposition of the Imperial government in regard to my going to the Eastern Capital by the middle of next month, which you kindly transmitted to me, I have the pleasure to communicate to you that I shall be happy to accept the same."

And so, in the tenth year of his life in Japan,

Verbeck of Japan

Verbeck obeyed, seeing "the city that hath foundations." "He went out, not knowing whither he went." He had faith and saw Providence in the call. Like a tree that in autumn strips its branches in order to wrestle the better with winter's storms, he sent his family to California, not hearing from them for two months. How he left Nagasaki is told by his successor the Rev. Dr. Henry Stout:

"When I first met Dr. Verbeck, he was under appointment to go to Tokio to assist in establishing a school for the Western languages and sciences, and so we were together but ten days as associates of the Mission in South Japan. For him, those days were filled with engagements with officials and old friends, made up of dinners and visits of ceremony for the exchange of courtesies and leave-taking, from which little time could be found for preparation for his going to his new position and for his family's returning to America. But the morning of the day the steamer was to sail, was spent, from immediately after breakfast till a late lunch, closeted with a Buddhist priest. The explanation given at the lunch was that the priest was eager to have certain questions with regard to the Truth answered before his teacher should leave. Whatever else was neglected, this opportunity must not be lost. Lunch having been served, hasty final preparations were made for leaving. Bearers were called for the luggage and the start was about to be made. But some things yet unpacked must be taken. A blanket
184

was spread upon the floor of the sitting-room, and upon it went books, curios, a clock, cushions, shoes, a great medley of the last odds and ends of things, when the corners of the blanket were drawn together and tied, making a huge bundle, which was hoisted upon the back of the last man in the line of bearers hastening to the wharf. This was the scant consideration his personal affairs received. No wonder he found afterward that some of his most valuable belongings had been forgotten."

It was a band of students that overturned the old and set up the new government. They had so adjusted the whole political machinery that the throne, the pivot of national movement was now at Tokio in "the far East." Now seizing opportunity by the forelock, they were determined to make "education the basis of all progress." Hence they wanted Mr. Verbeck at once. They called him even when the city was still in political confusion. History was making itself so rapidly that years seemed compressed in days. He writes under date of March 31st, 1869:

"As regards my own special duties at Yedo, I do not myself as yet exactly know what they are. I can only say that I have full confidence in the parties highly connected with the Imperial government, who have been mainly instrumental in calling me hither; that the ostensible and no doubt ultimate object of calling me to come to the Eastern Capital (Yedo) is to get me to establish something like an imperial university; that

next month the Mikado is expected to come back
to Yedo from the Western Capital (Miyako); that
most of the powerful daimios are also expected
here for consultation on an improvement of the
constitution of the empire and on a revision of
the foreign treaties, as well as the probable sending of embassies to Europe and America; that
the government wanted me to be here previous
to these great events; and that finally I shall
stand in need of all the wisdom, grace, and humility that can be vouchsafed in answer to prayer.
Such seems to be the program for the summer
before me. I may be mistaken and overestimate
the probable events of the year, at least in so far
as I may be called upon to be concerned in them;
possibly I may underrate them. Whatever happens, I am convinced that I am not called here by
a mere chance, and that I have a work to do, in
the doing which, being quite aware of my in-
sufficiency, I look to the Master for counsel and
guidance. This confidence removes mountains
of difficulty."

"My change to Yedo took place at a most un-
propitious time. The plan which was laid before
me was that I was to be at Yedo in the spring;
in the summer all the daimios would meet in
parliament, and much in regard to reforming the
laws of the country would have to be discussed,
in which I could act as adviser. Then in the fall
or winter I should enter on establishing a kind of
Imperial High School. With such a program I
did not feel at liberty to refuse, especially as it

IMPERIAL UNIVERSITY OF JAPAN, 1871.

came unsought. I always make a wide distinction between whatever originates with myself and that which is brought about without my own design; upon the former I think and act cautiously, as there may be too much of self in it; in the latter I sometimes perhaps go ahead too confidingly, forgetting that there may be other 'selves' besides my own, that may stand in the way of success under the divine blessing. However, I came and found all things as had been represented and met a cordial reception from some of the high government officers. But it did not last long; when the northern daimios and others of the extreme conservative party (anti-foreign) made their appearance, there came a change in the whole engine of government.

"Now the anti-foreign party is so strong that even the most liberal men are obliged temporarily to keep quiet till the paroxysm is past. There is no ill feeling against me personally, but there is against all foreigners. It is a temporary spasm in the wrong direction, such as frequently occurs in any process of transition and reform, and often followed by a proportionate stride in advance; yet it is disagreeable to be near the centres of action at such times, and daily I wish myself back to Nagasaki, which for several years to come will be the quietest port in Japan, because far removed from the restless political centres. You may say or think, *why*, under the circumstances, do I not go back to my old post. Well, I should go at once, if I could do so without disappointing some parties. But I am actually at work with translators of Blackstone, Wheaton, and Political Economy; besides no less than thirty-six of my former pupils came after me to Yedo, and it would not be so easy for them to go back as for me. So I have made up my mind to go on to the end of the year, if I can hold out so long, and then if matters have not improved by that time, to go back to my old station to work there permanently."

Thus already, Mr. Verbeck had begun that work of putting into the language of Japan those great compends and introductions to the modern law of civilized nations and of the constitutions of western nations, which were educating the Japanese to take their place among the great nations of the world. We can hardly understand why the constitution, given by the Mikado to his people in 1889, was so liberal in its provisions, nor how it came to pass that Japan was so soon, that is in 1898, received as an equal in the sisterhood of nations, unless we know what Verbeck of Japan was doing twenty and thirty years previously.

Meanwhile, without regarding wind or cloud, the sower sowed. Before the summer of the year 1869 had ended (on June 11th), Mr. Verbeck had not only proposed (what took place in 1872) that a great embassy composed of the highest imperial officers should visit the United States and Europe, but had planned out its organization, itinerary, personnel, objects, and methods of investigation. Of this we shall read further.

Called to the Capital

On the 21st of February, 1870, he wrote in regard to the Bible in Japanese, in which work, also, he was a pioneer, even as he wrought at its completion:

"I have to thank you for your kind favor by last mail. The principal topic in it that requires a direct answer is the translation of the Scriptures. What I have, or rather got done in this is that I have the whole of the New and a few books of the Old Testament translated by a good native scholar out of the Chinese. This, being a translation of a translation by one in spiritual darkness, is naturally a very imperfect work, yet of some value, as I found on lending it out to inquirers who could not read either English or Chinese. In the same manner I got translated a number of catechisms and tracts, also lent out several times as above. Further, I must frankly say, owing to my engagements in the educational line, I have not been able to go; nor do I see any chance of being able to do so as long as I am thus engaged, for the simple reason that in my present circumstances fully one man's labor is making constant demands on my strength and time.

"Even if I had the capacity of two men, I should find good use for it all. It is not for ease that a man would undertake a post like mine. A simple missionary, being, it is true, bound in conscience by responsibility to the Master and His Society, but at the same time at liberty to lay out and use his time and talents according to the natural bent of his genius, leads comparatively an independent life. With the same double responsibility resting upon me, I in present circumstances bind myself with other parties for much the better part of what remains available for work in every day's twenty-four hours—no sinecure, indeed. Sometimes I feel this so much that I have a real longing for being, like most missionaries, once more master of my whole time and powers, to devote them to the noble work you referred to, which would and ought to engage all of a man's uninterrupted time and attention. But I do not say this by way of complaint, only of explanation. I have been so gradually, and I think providentially led into the path I have taken, that I feel sure I am not out of the path of duty in pursuing it. If I were an independent missionary, just come into the field, and an offer of a position like mine were made me off-hand, if such a thing is supposable, I am sure I should consider it as one of those openings that sometimes providentially present themselves to a man, not for him to be entered on, but to be passed by. But my case, as you know, is different.

"I have been so gradually led toward my present status, through a long course of years, and, I wish to say it with gratitude and in all humility, have gained such a name, and influence in it, that I should consider it unwise, according to present light on the subject, to throw it up except for the clearest and weightiest reasons. If I were not here, these hundreds of young people at the college would be under the influence of men openly leading immoral lives and enemies of God and His Word. Now the students have learned to like and respect missionaries, (I might say more) and the authorities of the school acknowledge that missionaries are their most reliable teachers.

"Only a few days ago I had a proof of this, being requested to secure the services of another "missionary" (named as such) for the college; and they were glad, and so was I, that I succeeded in getting the Rev. Mr. Cornes (of the Presbyterian mission) for one year, to enter on his duties next week. Besides, my position brings me in contact with people, high, low, who otherwise would be quite beyond any reach. But I do not like writing so much about self, and it is only necessity that induces me to it for your information. But I may take it then for granted, I suppose, that with the respected Board of Directors' permission, I am for the present to continue as I am, at the same time not neglecting to exert according to ability a direct influence for the gospel of love, and always considering the great aim and end, the regeneration of this people.

"In view of this state of things I have a request and proposition to make. Could not the board send out a man for the express purpose of becoming, under Providence, a translator of the Scriptures into Japanese, selected and appointed with a special view to this purpose? I take the liberty to enlarge a little on this, speaking as one in the field. A man for this purpose, besides of course being a devoted man with a warm heart for the Master's work and a good constitution for hard labor, had best be a young man of studious habits, just out of seminary, who would be content to remain single for the first three or four years; besides a thorough knowledge of Hebrew and Greek, he ought to have a taste and talent for linguistic studies, though preaching, when he comes to that, would prove a good auxiliary, he ought studiously to abstain from everything else that would be calculated to draw him aside from his great life-work, and always look to that chiefly.

'' You may think that in asking for such a man for Japan, I ask for the cream of the land. True, that is just what is wanted, and is there not missionary spirit enough in the land to send us talents as well as piety, or gifts as well as graces ? It would be painful to think so. There is room in this and other fields for any number of willing workers without any special talents and acquisitions, and they are all heartily wished for and welcome; but there is an actual want of a few picked men, especially for the work of translation. If anywhere there is a place to offer ample scope to the noblest enterprise and sanctified genius, it is right here and now. Are any kept home by a noble ambition for a wide influence for good, here is their place, here they find a great and most promising field for their holiest aspirations. This is no exaggeration. It is the simple truth, which, I think if well understood by our promising young men ought to go far to lead some chosen man among them to throw up all other plans and prospects, to devote himself without reservation to the Lord's cause in this particular land.

" But, dear brother, I leave this matter now with you. I have been writing nearly all through the night and it is going toward the morning. I never have time to write long letters during the day. I would only add privately that, if such a suitable man could be found and sent out, I would—while I keep my present post—give him rooms and board free, and gladly bind myself to pay about a quarter of his annual expenses. At the beginning of his career I think I might be of much assistance to him in his studies and by general advice, though I believe in a man's working most profitably according to his own conscientious convictions.

"I have no later news about the converted priest of whom I wrote you that he was arrested early in January. We pray that the God whom he loves may save and strengthen him in his sore trials. While at one end of the country there is temporary persecution, at our end there is quite a demand for the Scriptures, and I have been able to dispose of quite a number in Chinese, English, and French.

"Dear brother, please remember us and ours at the throne of grace, and believe me, yours faithfully   G. F. VERBECK."

Verbeck of Japan

We must now take up the thread of political narrative and show the framework of events amid which this toiler on the foundations of New Japan kept perseveringly on. It was like working with sword and trowel as we shall see.

After the formation of the confederacy of the northern clans, a battle between their adherents and those in Yedo was fought July 4, 1868, during which the great temple at Uyeno was burned to the ground. This was the day and hour, when the great Fukuzawa "intellectual father of one-half" of young Japan, decided not to take up sword and gun and go to the battle, but to sit down with a few companions to the study of Wayland's Moral Science.

The theatre of war shifted to the north at Wakamatsu, where the castle of Aidzu after a thirty days' siege, was besieged and taken, November 6th. On the 7th of November, 1869, the Mikado's birthday was celebrated throughout the empire and the chronological era was changed to that of Meiji, or enlightened civilization. It was made a rule for all time, thus putting an end to much confusion, that for each reign there should be one chronological period. In response to a memorial of Okubo, the imperial palanquin or "Phœnix Car" at last moved overland and was carried over the Hakone mountain pass to Yedo, not to expel, but to cultivate friendship with foreigners. The name of the City of the Bay Door, Yedo, was changed to Tokio, or Eastern Capital, and on the 26th of November the Son of Heaven

194

slept in the castle of the usurpers, whose power had vanished. Then all men saw that he had resumed his rightful place. The last Tycoon had returned to his ancestral seats in Shidzuoka and the old notions of a "spiritual" and a "temporal" emperor must now vanish like the morning mist. On the 1st of January, 1869, the foreign quarter of Tokio as well as the city of Niigata on the western coast, were opened to trade.

The emperor returned to Kioto to marry Haruko, a daughter of the princely family of the house of Ichijo, on the 9th of February, on which day the neutrality proclamations were withdrawn. This last action enabled the American minister, Van Valkenburg, to hand over to the new government the ironclad steam ram Stonewall, which, reinforcing the fleet of the loyal navy, quickly made an end of the wooden war vessels and of the very short-lived republic inaugurated by Enomoto, a brilliant Japanese who had been educated in Holland, but who has, for thirty years past, as a statesman of marked abilities, been a most loyal servant of the emperor.

During the same month the court noble Iwakura, Minister of Foreign Affairs and Junior Premier, resigned the office of prime minister on the plea of ill health, but while giving up the former he held the latter office. Though not in form, he was in reality the chief officer of that government which had been established on the theory of a closer union of the Throne with the people, the intermediary being a kuge or court noble of bluest blood and of immemorial lineage. To those who knew the political methods in vogue, Iwakura simply followed the usual fashion, which was to lose the form, in order to gain the substance. Nearly all offices in old Japan were like our antiquated frigates and ships-of-the-line, which had painted and gilded figure-head at the prow, near to, corresponding with, or representing the name of the ship, while the real commander and executor stood on deck or was invisible in the cabin.

Indeed, in America, it was more than once noted that when the young hermits of Japan stepped out of their clogs and sandals into the tight boots of civilization, their favorite amusement in hotels was first to climb the stairway and then to descend on an elevator. They enjoyed the paradox and the sensation connected with it. So Iwakura and many men like him, who preferred real power, usually descended on what was really an elevator. It is highly probable that Mr. Verbeck took hints from what he saw and gladly put himself in harmony with his environment—remained in shadow, in order to increase light.

By the end of June, 1869, the war came entirely to an end. One of the purposes for which Iwakura had taken a lower office or rank, in order to carry out a great scheme, was now manifest to those able to read the meaning of the signs of the times.

Called to the Capital

In reality the great restoration of 1868 was in-augurated and carried through mainly by a com-mittee of four men, Iwakura, Kido, Okubo, and Okuma, who, seeing the need both of money, unity, and power, and the necessity of a strong front before foreigners and the world, resolved to abolish feudalism and have real national union. The daimios of Satsuma, Tosa, Choshiu, and Hizen, leading in this patriotic purpose, yielded up their quasi-sovereign rights, and handed over the lists of their possessions and retainers to the emperor, that he should do with them what he would. As usual, the figureheads knew little of what was going on, but the able men of inferior rank carried through the project. The memorial penned by Kido was published in the ófficial gazette on the 5th of March, 1869. The com-position is rich in that peculiar oriental rhetoric which is dominated by the Chinese classics and is overweighted with those peculiar expressions of Japanese orthodoxy, which it is even yet dangerous in Japan to challenge. The history of the empire is also given in brief epitome. Here are some of the sentences:

"Now that men are seeking for an entirely new government the Great Body (the Imperial Government) and the Great Strength (the Em-peror) must neither be lent nor borrowed."

" The place where we live is the emperor's land and the food which we eat is grown by the emperor's men. How can we make it our own ? We now reverently offer up the list of our possessions and men, with the prayer that the emperor will take good measures for rewarding those to whom reward is due and for taking from those to whom punishment is due. Let the Imperial orders be issued for offering and remodeling the territories of the various clans. Let the civil and penal code, the military laws, down to the rules for uniform and the construction of engines of war, all proceed from the emperor; that all the affairs of the empire great and small be referred to him. After this, when the internal relations of the country shall be upon a true footing, the empire will be able to take its place side by side with the other countries of the world. This is now the most urgent duty of the emperor, as it is that of his servants and children. Hence it is that we, in spite of our own folly, daring to offer up our humble expressions of loyalty, upon which we pray that the brilliance of the heavenly sun may shine, with fear and reverence bow the head and do homage, ready to lay down our lives in proof of our faith."

The answer from the Throne was that when the emperor returned to Tokio that this matter of reorganizing the empire would be publicly debated in council.

As matter of fact, Mr. Verbeck, when asked by Iwakura concerning national policy advised that everything possible, even to army, navy, and administrative systems of post, lighthouses, education, etc., like those in the West be immediately formed.

Called to the Capital

That Kido was the author of this document, there can be little doubt, but that Iwakura backed by Okubo was the chief force in its promulgation, can hardly be doubted. In Mr. Verbeck's parlor in Tokio, I was present at an interview between himself and Mr. Verbeck and heard Iwakura say, concerning the measure and the expectation, that coercion of some of the daimios would be necessary, "We were prepared to shed blood and expected to do it."

Yet the bloodshed was not necessary. Example being so much more than precept, the action of the great clans was quickly imitated by the smaller ones. In less than six weeks, by the 16th of April, 118 out of 276 daimios of Japan had published memorials requesting permission to restore their lands and registers to the emperor, and before many months the number reached 241. The daimios were returned to their own territories.

It was a great and inspiring example to the other court nobles and to the imperial families, when Mr. Iwakura (well named Rock Throne) having long known and trusted Mr. Verbeck and consulted him on the gravest affairs of state, now, under his direction, sent his two sons, Asahi and Tatsu, to America for education. In his letter, Mr. Verbeck turns the Japanese kaleidoscope for us, showing the amazing changes during the decade.

Verbeck of Japan

Yedo, April 21, 1870.

"Rev. J. M. Ferris, D. D., *New York,*

"Dear Brother:—Last mail came so unawares upon me that I lost all chance of writing you, if the few lines are excepted that I sent you in behalf of the five young men, Asahi, Tatsu, and their companions, who started for New York by that mail. The fact is in the daytime every available moment is so taken up by all sorts of engagements, principally teaching, as is also a good part every evening, that only the quiet of the night is left me for writing anything like a proper letter. The young men above mentioned, I trust, reached their destination in safety, and are probably now deep in their exercises and studies. They are an exceedingly interesting party, and will prove to be eminently useful to their country, when once they return with the advantages of a good education. In the meantime I am sure they will be liked by all who know them on account of their real amiableness, docility, and gentle manners. May the Lord bless them and lead them to a purer faith and higher love.

"As I have nothing of special note to communicate this time, I shall endeavor to give you a brief sketch of some features of progress made by this wonderful people in the space of about the past ten years. The Japanese, ten years ago, were in nearly all respects in the same primitive condition so quaintly described in the musty pages of old Kaempfer, purely native, in ideas as well as in appearance. The few articles and little information brought by the annual Dutch ship of the hundred years preceding the reopening of the country found their way almost exclusively into the palaces of the emperors and princes, the people at large realizing little more than the highly prized (and priced) Dutch vermifuge. In the midst of this state of things came Commodore Perry with his bundle of huge keys to unlock and open these secluded, ocean-bound ports, and well did he perform his work. Then followed the fleets of the other great maritime powers, and after that the merchantmen of the chief trading nations bringing merchandise from all the markets of the world.

"Yet the country cannot be said to have been fairly opened for trade and foreign residence until about ten years ago, in the very year that your missionaries were first sent hither. Even then, at first, we were far from enjoying free intercourse with the people, for it was yet the time of official interference, espionage, and suspicion which, indeed, being the old custom and inveterate habit of the nation, could hardly be expected to be shaken off at once.

"Now the people had a chance, if not a fair one, to see and learn to know the foreigner, and his merchandise, and forthwith they took kindly to them both. The sight produced the desire of possession, and so things went on till now the open ports and their vicinity teem with shops retailing foreign merchandise; and foreign cloths, blankets (worn as shawls), flannels, calicos, hats, boots

and shoes, watches, umbrellas, and fancy articles
are worn and used, in some form or other, by all
classes, from the daimio to the poor "betto" or
groom. Besides the stores kept by foreigners,
there are at Yokohama and Yedo alone many hundreds of native shops selling foreign goods. A
large portion of the middle and upper classes—at
least the male portion—dress entirely in our style.
Even old men, too old to sport the new costume,
look with delight upon their little grandsons
dressed in hats, boots, and what belongs between, and take pride to show off in the streets
their "young Japan" thus apparelled. The Army
and Navy are remodelled on European and American systems in organization, arms, and uniforms,
down to the common trumpet, drum, and fife.
We have several lines of stages, hackney-
coaches, and two steamers running between
Yedo and Yokohama, natives and foreigners
competing with each other on both elements.
On the same route there is a telegraph in operation, and a contract is said to have been made for
the construction of a railroad from here to Osaa.
There are two extensive foundries with foreign
machinery in the country, and several docks. As
to matters of diet, beef, the abomination of
Buddhism, begins largely to be consumed, and
bread is much liked. You would be a good deal
surprised, if, in the very heart of the capital, you
passed by some of our "noiseless" sewing ma-
chines rattling away with a will! But so far all
is material.

Called to the Capital

"The desire for possession is by no means limited to the mere material part of our civilization. It is true, there are many, a great many, who fancy that a pair of high-heeled boots and a suit of clothes go a good way to raise them in the scale of beings. But there are also a good many who, without change of costumes, look deeper and desire something more potent than appearance. There is a wide spread demand, an actual thirst in many, for western learning and science. Here is our college with its hundreds of English, French, and German scholars; besides this there are several private schools, carried on by natives, for the study of chiefly English; and there are numbers of students who study independent of any school whatever, by books and their own efforts only. Then there are hundreds more at the other open ports.

"There are three large hospitals and medical colleges, in which eight foreign physicians are engaged. Western medical science has nearly quite superseded the old Chinese system of quacks and immense doses of drugs.

"Newspapers are published in several places, with their columns of 'Foreign' and 'Telegrams,' clipped and translated from our standard home papers. Book stores selling English and French books are seen in many places, and the quantity of books imported is prodigious.

"All these and many more things are but the earnest expression of this thirst for western knowledge. And many brave young men have left their pleasant homes to satisfy abroad, in our own and English schools and colleges, that thirst more thoroughly than it is possible for them to do at home, and nobly to serve their country, on their return, with the acquirements thus bravely won. On the first opening of the country, of course, mere language was the chief object of study. Gradually the object has become the means for further researches, so that now law, political economy, and even intellectual and moral science are embraced. Nor have the efforts so far made been without fruit. Several good books have already been translated and published by native scholars, and many more are to follow, so that even those whose age and circumstances preclude their learning foreign languages are thus enabled to get an idea of our useful literature. At present there is being translated and published by our college, from the French, the 'Code Napoleon,' from the English, 'Perry's Political Economy,' and from the Dutch, 'Humboldt's Cosmos.' Of the former two, some parts have been already published. It is a real pleasure to hear a man say: 'I just read the first volume of "Buckle's History of Civilization," and am going on to the second;' or to have a man come and request you to help him solve some hard passage in 'Wayland's Moral Science.'

"And of all this there was next to nothing only ten years ago! What! is this not progress? Even those inveterate philosophers of the old school who, in the midst of an age of chemical analysis, have stuck like leeches to four elements till there is not a drop of life-blood left in their philosophy, and who reduce all things material or immaterial—quite irrespective of their true nature—into just as many elements as will agree with the number of the fingers of a hand or of two,—even those bigots begin to feel the general impulse and come forth to the light of day to get some true life, some real knowledge. Some celebrated ones of this class came to me the other day, saying that Japan was created in perfect harmony with the heavenly bodies, for as there were sixteen planets, so Japan had originally been created in sixteen distinct parts. When I told them that there never were exactly sixteen planets and gave them a correct list, their faces grew rather longer than before, and I actually believe they doubted themselves the harmony they had gloried in so much, as no doubt many had done before them, but fewer will do hereafter.

"Of course, such things are transacted in a spirit of gentleness and kindness; but in reconsidering that men capable of better things should spend their precious powers and time (to say the least) in trying to harmonize the distinct parts of their country (which never had sixteen such distinct parts) with the sixteen planets of our solar system (which never had just sixteen planets), one cannot help being provoked at the waste and stupidity. And yet much of the old philosophy of the country is of a similar nature. But let them come out of their darkness to the light, let the spell be broken, and forthwith they are fine, clever men.

"But there has been progress on a large scale in departments yet unmentioned. The time would fail me to enlarge on government reforms, the suppression of rebellion, the pacification of internal dissensions, the development of an extensive commerce properly so-called, etc. But there have been, no doubt, some drawbacks, some disadvantages to balance the advantages. So there have been, perhaps, many. Yet the general movement during the past ten years has been one of unmistakable, remarkable progress, in spite of all drawbacks. And those who ask for more, ought to remember that whatever of progress there has thus far been made, has been made as it were during ploughing time; after that comes the blessed seed time and finally the full harvest home. God hasten the time!

"But dear old brother, I come to a close and only hope that in the above there may be something of interest. Last mail I did not have news of you, so I am sure of some this time. Remember us and our work in prayer, and believe me.   Yours faithfully,

"G. F. VERBECK."

Mr. Verbeck found that earthquakes were more frequent in the north than in the south. On May 21, 1870, he wrote:

Called to the Capital

" The ground under us is very shaky this season and the northern parts of the country are going through some severe couvulsions, physically. A few nights ago we were waked up (at three o'clock) by a tremendous shock, which kept our house rocking and creaking for about a minute in an appalling manner; yet by our good Lord's mercy, no harm was done. The earth's crust is evidently not so firm in this part of its surface as might be desirable for comfort. The waters in some of the thermal springs are said to have risen above their usual level, and there is even a rumor of a new volcano having been opened in the northwest of the country.

" The country is quiet at present, innovations and reforms are being carried on in a silent unassuming way, and the general prospect is promising. As might be expected, there is yet a numerous and powerful party holding to what they consider as 'the good old times' and opposing reform and progress, so that those who otherwise would be willing and able to push forward have their hands tied. The bulk of the people sit as yet in the thickest darkness and know nothing that is good. Yet with all this there is a general awakening and a desire for larger knowledge, and as the younger generation grows into power we may look for great changes. Among these the Lord of the harvest will see that His gospel of love, holiness, and salvation shall come in for its share, and among much that is merely on the surface there shall be some deeper work. In the meantime our plain duty seems to be perseveringly to labor and pray, while we practically wait and hope."

On June 21, 1870, he wrote:

"What with six hours daily teaching at college, several scholars at home, and many other calls on my time, I hardly ever get time in the daytime to sit down to write without interruption. This fall some more young men are coming to join the New Brunswick band. I hope they are all doing well and being educated to become eminently useful to their country.

"All is quiet in this country. Foreign dress, foreign wares, and foreign science are daily gaining favor among the people, and a few years more will make great changes. Our religion, alas, is still proscribed, but cannot possibly remain so long. Our trust in the Lord is that all these changes are not and that we labor not in vain.

"At last, [July 21, 1870] I have got an order for young men from home to come out as teacher, a thing I had long wished for and that may go on if once introduced. But in the carrying out I have again to rely entirely on your kindness. What is required at present is a young man to teach principally chemistry and natural philosophy and a doctor-surgeon.

"The place is far in the interior [city of Fukui, province of Echizen] and he would never see a foreigner outside of his colleagues, except once a year, when in the summer vacation (of a month) he could go for a fortnight to one of the open ports; this is in the contract. His colleagues are to be two; one of whom [Mr. Alfred Lucy] I have sent thither early this month.

"He will stay a few days or a fortnight with me before proceeding to the interior. As I take whomever you think fit to send, he may consider himself engaged whenever you make the agreement to come sure between you and himself.

"It is safer by far in the interior than at Yedo where we live, as you are among the subjects of one prince who maintains strict order in his own country, only for a lady it would hardly do yet. The young man ought to be smart (to use a common word), kind-hearted, well up in his special branches and generally, especially in chemistry, of spirit enough to rely on himself, and particularly a man of firm and practical piety. The temptations in this country are fearful, and many a one has fallen who would have been safe as iron at home. In fact very few indeed, outside of ministers and missionaries, that have not fallen. Yet I would rather this young man were not a 'Reverend,' though if he be it is also right. We will hope and pray that the right man will be brought forward by the Guide of all, and all will go well.

"As to the doctor, his terms are the same, except his salary which is to be $3,600. But there is one condition in the contract that makes me fear that you, with best will, may not be able to find in New York, though I wish you could and it may be you can. He is to be a Dutchman, a Hollander; or if not, be able to read Dutch as a real Hollander. In case no Dutchman is to be found, a German who knows the Dutch language pretty well, would do. Can such a one be found with you? If not, I must send to Holland for one. The doctor's prospects in Japan are always good.

"If you can find the proper men, please let them come on with as little delay as possible. We are waiting for them. I shall make it so that no eventuality to myself shall effect the certainty of their engagements. All they have to do is to report themselves to me at Yedo, or I shall meet them at Yokohama."

It was about this time that Mr. Verbeck was called on to decide what language and system were to be Japan's medium of medical culture. The Rev. G. Ogimi wrote in 1898, how in 1870, the native doctors were asking,

" 'In the future what shall be the language of our science of medicine?' There was such a difference of opinion that no one could decide. Then the doctor (Verbeck) memorialized the government to the effect that so far as medicine is concerned there is undoubtedly no better way than to employ German. The Council of State in accordance with this advice adopted the German science of medicine; and the result is the prosperity of the science as it is to-day. So our medical fraternity owes a great deal to the doctor, says Surgeon-General Ishiguro."

This eminent officer who was in charge of the

Called to the Capital

Japanese army and the military operations in China and Korea, during the war of 1894-95 also wrote in the *Tenchijin*, a Tokio newspaper, after attending Dr. Verbeck's funeral:

"Although I was not in any way an intimate friend, yet I felt much regret when a paper informed me of Dr. Verbeck's death. I was not invited to attend the funeral, but I went to the church and attended anyhow. Toward the year 1870 or so, many agreed to the opinion that Japanese education should be English and American, and that English and American teachers should be employed. In those times, Drs. Iwasa, Sagara, Hasegawa, and I held the view that the science of medicine should be German. How we were ridiculed and criticised by the public! Dr. Verbeck was already in those times respected and believed in by the people. One day, Dr. Sagara got an interview with him, and talked about the necessity of enforcing our opinion about the science of medicine. With our view this American teacher expressed his sympathy. It was through his advice to the government that German professors of this science came to be employed. The present prosperity of the science owes a great deal to the deceased doctor. This is the reason why I attended his funeral."

On application being made to the German Emperor, two of the most eminent representatives of the science and art preservative of human life, Messrs. Muller and Hoffman came to Japan, serving long and honorably. I remember being with them when we were together given audience of the Mikado. Dr. Muller laughingly remarked to me that he had attended emperors of three colors, white, black, and brown, in Prussia, Africa, and Japan. How honorably German science is regarded in Japan may be seen in the rewards and dignities conferred upon Dr. Baelz in May, 1900, during the marriage of the crown prince, the doctor receiving the decoration of the first class of the sacred treasure.

New openings for teachers presented themselves. Concerning Higo, Mr. Verbeck wrote August 20, 1870:

"Numagawa is to write to his brother about it, too, and by next mail will write to you. I feel backward about troubling you with this new request and fear I shall exhaust your patience; but I really have no one else to whom I could or would entrust such matters of importance, and yet not within the direct line of your office. I consider, however, that this placing of good Christian men in various parts of the empire will operate as a very useful auxiliary to our main object, the Christianization of this nation, and as such only, would I at all dare to enlist your kind offices in behalf of the movement. If we could supply a few places with competent and good men, I expect there will be numerous applications of the same kind. At the same time this measure offers a fine opportunity for those of our young men of learning who may desire to make a career abroad without becoming missionaries.

Called to the Capital

"The government of Higo would like to get an ex-lieutenant of the army, and would prefer a married man with his wife."

The rage for foreign travel had now seized upon the upper classes and we find the relatives of the emperor setting their faces eastward to the United States and Europe. Most of these parties I had the pleasure of meeting and often of entertaining, during 1868, 1869, and the early part of 1870 before I left home for Japan, which I did in the month of November, 1870.

Mr. Verbeck wrote to Dr. Ferris from Tokio, Sept. 21, 1870:

"The bearers, his Highness Kacho-no-Miya, and Messrs. Yagimoto, Shirane, and Takato have requested me to furnish them with letters of introduction to you. The officers of the high government, too, who feel a deep interest in the welfare of these young men, and who know your good name and the interest you so obligingly take in their countrymen who came to the states for an education, have joined in the same request, being assured that they have the best guarantee for the future good of their students while under your prudent patronage.

"Knowing your invariably kind disposition toward and care for all students from Japan, I do not hesitate to commend this interesting party to your favor and good advice, all of which are always gratefully acknowledged.

"The Kacho-no-Miya, whom in his introduction I style 'His Highness,' is a relation to the

213

Mikado—the reigning emperor. He comes, however, incog. and only intends to resume his rank the last year or so. He is to stay some years. Your name is already well known to the officers of the high government, and this man's meeting you will do the rest to get your kindness to all Japanese properly noticed and acknowledged by them."

Soon there was not only a stream of students moving from Japan to New Brunswick (for scarcely any other centre of education in the United States had yet been discovered), but the calls now began to come for teachers from the daimios to organize schools and begin work inside Japan.

Naturally one of the first of the feudal lords, to apply and to receive permission for foreigners to enter this country, was Matsudaira, Lord of Echizen, for here the soil had been already prepared for the good seed. The ground had been well ploughed and harrowed by Yokoi Heishiro and a band of scholars from and visitors to Nagasaki. In Fukui, the castle-city, a medical and a literary school had already been established. Echizen being a relative of the Tokugawas and yet a friend to progress, very acceptable to the new government and holding a position under it, applied for a staff of five trained professional teachers, one of English, one of the physical sciences who was to be superintendent of education, a mining engineer, a military instructor, and a physician.

Called to the Capital

Under date of July 21, 1870, "the second day of our summer vacation of a month," when Mr. Verbeck had assumed the principalship of the college, which greatly increased his duties, we find him writing as follows; for toleration of Christianity had not yet come.

"What you wrote in your last I have deeply felt and taken to heart. The time does seem long and I too sometimes feel like crying out, how long shall the heathen rage and the people imagine a vain thing? It is such a difficult thing to locate with precision the division line between human prudence and unquestioning obedience. Sometimes the goal seems almost within reach and then again recedes by several removes. Religious intolerance to us appears so entirely unreasonable and wicked that we should think it cannot last many days longer. Yet again, considering in what a maze of difficulties, political, diplomatic, and financial, this new government is as yet involved, it is not strange that they stave off as long as possible what many of those in authority consider as another (foreign) cloud fraught with danger and confusion. As to myself, however, I see well that a time must come when patience and forbearance (if I may adapt the word so) shall have had their full share, and when it will be proper to take a bold stand and openly to say, we have long enough shown you that we are honest men, desirous to labor for nothing but your happiness; we have waited long enough for you to allow us to do the Lord's work freely and in His appointed way; now we must even disregard altogether what man can do against us and commit the issue to our God.

"Such a crisis must come of course sooner or later. In the meantime we use every opportunity to gain an influence and a good reputation, which will be a powerful means in the day of direct attack; while with many we must vindicate our very character and prove to them satisfactorily that we are not such dreadful beings as tradition and superstition had once taught them we were. But perhaps I ought not to have entered on such a momentous subject in a hasty note like this. It is no easy matter to keep seven or eight foreign teachers, picked up at this port and of four different nationalities, in order and peace. I have my hands full, yet do not like to complain on that score. I feel dreadfully lonely, and if it had not been necessary for our dear children, should never have consented to this new family separation. Pray for us and our work, is the request of Yours in Christ."

XI

THE BIOGRAPHER IN TOKIO

IT eventuated that of the four or five men desired for Echizen, Mr. Alfred Lucy, from Birmingham, England, became the teacher of English. He spent some months in Fukui, Echizen, four of which were while the present writer was in that city. The faculty of Rutgers College, to whom the matter of the teacher of science and organizer of popular education was referred, unanimously voted that the present writer, the biographer, was the man to fill the post. Nevertheless, as the idea, when first propounded, of going to the turbulent Japan of that day, beyond treaty limits at least, seemed like venturing into Central Africa or into the regions of eternal ice, the offer when first made was promptly declined. It was reconsidered, and accepted after it had been reinforced by the urgent wishes of the secretary of the Board of Missions, and then only after very peculiar and searching personal experiences.

I found that the insurance companies would not, except at a heavy premium, insure the life of one going inside Japan. To this day, as if it were yesterday, I remember the incredulity and surprise expressed by business men, that "an intelligent young man should trust a people like the Japanese to keep a financial engagement."

After purchasing Hoffman's Japanese Grammar in October, and learning a number of Japanese phrases from my friends and pupils, chiefly from Satsuma and Echizen, noticing even then a difference in their dialect, I left home in Philadelphia early in November and crossed the country on the Central Pacific Railway. There were no stations, though plenty of drinking places, between Omaha and Ogden, so I laid in four or five days' cooked provision before leaving Nebraska. At the stopping places I saw plenty of wild Indians with scalp locks, one or two scalped white men, others that wanted to "rub out" all the red men, and squaws that not knowing what a nickel coin was, but not ashamed to beg, would throw away as a joke and fraud, the money fresh from the mint at Philadelphia. Herds of antelopes, millions of prairie dogs and occasionally a bear were visible from the car windows. I was impressed with the talk of the average western man, whose own comment on projected schemes was uniform enough to make a continuous chorus, "Well sir, it's a fact, and *you'll* see it."

Leaving San Francisco December 1st, in the roomy and comfortable old paddle-wheel wooden steamer, Great Republic, I landed on the soil of Japan, after a beatific vision at daybreak of snow-crowned Fuji-Yama, on the morning of December 29, 1870. Among the first to greet me were the Rev. James H. and Mrs. Ballagh and

The Biographer in Tokio

Dr. and Mrs. J. C. Hepburn. I was at the New Year's reception given by the United States Minister Hon. Charles E. and Mrs. DeLong. At that time, strange as it may now seem, not only were the French and British soldiers camped on the bluffs at Yokohama, but all the foreign legations, including the American, were not where they ought to have been, in Tokio, the capital of the country, but at the commercial seaport.

My first impressions, in the new wonder world of Japan, seemed more like those of fairy land, than reality. Here was a region of amazing contrasts in things both lovely and horrible. Notes of my journey over the Tokaido to Tokio may be read in "The Mikado's Empire," but let me here give my impressions, on first reaching Mr. Verbeck's house, which was to be my home for seven weeks during my stay in Tokio, before going in the interior. I felt convinced before I left him, that this quiet, forceful man, was then, as I now know, from 1859 until 1898, not the least among the living leaders and the actual makers of new Japan. Yet I imagine that "official" Japanese history will take no note of the "Yatoi."

From his letters, the lights and shadows of his life trail over the paper as clouds over the landscape. In one lies a great burden of grief. The Japanese so quick to learn, gained their experience often at a great cost, while handling the machinery of a government with new motors, whether of a nation or of a ferryboat. The little steamer, City of Yedo, had plied for several months, between Yokohama and Tokio, and on this the Rev. Mr. E. Cornes, his wife, two children and Japanese servant took passage. This promising American missionary who, at Mr. Verbeck's request, was acting as a teacher in the new school of Foreign Languages in Tokio, had served as a soldier in a cavalry regiment in the Union Army during the civil war. He was about twenty-eight years old and his wife was four years younger than himself. Both were strong and full of hope for the future. The boiler of the steamer burst shortly after it had left the dock. In the terrible dismemberment, his heart was wrapped around his neck. The only survivor of the four was the little baby boy, born in the May previous. With his Japanese nurse he escaped with some scalds. An English girl of fifteen was also killed. The Rev. David Thompson, since so rich in good works, took Mr. Cornes' place temporarily in the school. Of course the disappointed, the incompetents, and others who do not approve of missionaries, had their sneer about people who, coming to convert the heathen, turned aside to capture their shekels. As simple matter of fact the unsophisticated "heathen" soon discovered and discriminated between the counterfeit and reality in the men from "Christian" nations.

Mr. Verbeck wrote again concerning the low moral grade of such waifs as he was able to pick up, asking also for men of pronounced Christian character:

The Biographer in Tokio

"They are an inferior set compared with what I might get at home (private), and this I wish to show the authorities. They already know that if they want men to trust and believe, they must have missionaries, and I should like to prove to them that our country produces honest and honorable men outside of our order who yet will stand by us.

"Great progress is made by the people in becoming enlightened, but it takes time to move a nation of perhaps twenty-five or thirty millions and to affect public opinion so as to make the people give up their prejudices and traditions. There are many enlightened men among government officials and the private classes; but there are more who prefer the old state of things to the new. Besides all, the government, just newly established, has so many vexed questions to settle in diplomacy, finance, internal policy, and innovations of various kinds, that it is not to be wondered at that it staves off religious toleration as long as it may. But that turn will come too, and we hope and pray for a favorable issue at last. I am lonesome and dreary alone in this heathen capital, yet it was necessary for my wife to make a trip home. I only hope she can make suitable arrangements for the children and feel strong enough to come out again soon, to stay with me till 1876, when, if the Lord will, I promise myself the pleasure of a trip to civilization and Christian surroundings. Hoping to hear from you in two or three days, and requesting an answer to the inquiries above, I remain,

" I am anxious to inaugurate this new movement to their full satisfaction, because I consider it a fine opening for our able and enterprising young men, and as a means of indirectly aiding our missionary work by placing Christian young men in situations which otherwise would, nay certainly will, be fitted by our warmest enemies. If we can give satisfaction this time, there will be a demand for more, and later for young ladies in similar positions, of which I have seen some indications already."

The fruition of hope for the education of Japanese women, was not until 1873 when the first school for education of the daughters of the gentry was established by the Department of Education, of which Mrs. Veeder and Miss M. C. Griffis were the first instructors. Out of this grew the Peeresses' School in which taught Miss Alice Bacon, the author of that delightful classic " Japanese Girls and Women."

The Echizen men were especially eager about one point concerning the physician and surgeon. Dutch was then the language of science and medicine in Japan. Mr. Verbeck wrote, " The parties who engage him have come to me two or three times since to say that the doctor must by all means be one who knows the Dutch language well, all the native doctors' knowledge and nomenclature of the medical science having been got by reading and studying medical works imported from Holland, long before the opening of the country and since. There are some thoroughly learned men among these native doctors."

The openings for men of ability from Christendom were multiplying. To his house flocked as doves to their windows, officers for teachers from many provinces. In the same letter he wrote : " Through Numagawa's exertions, I have a similar application for a young man to go to the Prince of Higo's country." By September 22, 1870, Mr. Verbeck had already filled five similar places " with people I have found at Yokohama, but prefer getting them from home." By November 23, 1870, he had engaged twelve foreigners for the college of which he was principal. In his letter expressing the hope that he might be able to visit America during the Centennial year, he declared with emphasis his desire to get regularly trained men of character and ability from home.

The time is now come when the biographer must tell the story of how and when he first reached Tokio and saw Mr. Verbeck. It was on January 2, 1871, at half past ten in the morning. At this time Tokio had become definitely the capital of the empire, all the departments of the government being in full activity there. Twice the emperor, " the son of Heaven," a youth sixteen years old had shown his " dragon countenance " in broad daylight and in public to myriads of his subjects, who had never looked upon the face of a Mikado before. Two princes of the blood, and scores of young men had crossed the ocean to lands afar, and seen how big the world outside of Japan was. The leaders of the nation were in the van of a movement toward foreign civilization which, despite reactionary conservatives could not be checked. Two years before, such events as were now, in 1871, of daily occurrence, could not have been possible. They would have been too shocking. The ancient diet of rice, vegetables, and fish, and sake was giving way to beef, bread, and beer, and the old voluminous costumes to the tight dress of civilization. Yet many a time, in walking through the quarter devoted to the nobles and gentry, did I see kuges from Kioto, riding on horseback, who seemed to me as if figures from a pack of playing cards had been suddenly turned by some magic wand into life. They were swathed in what appeared to my gaze to be damask quilts or comfortables, each with a black brick strapped to the top of his head and bound around the chin with white tape. Numerous attendants were around each rider, all looking like figures on a chess board, suddenly become animated. It took me a long time to get over the association of broadly figured dress patterns with bedclothes, and of white tape, or broad bands, around the chin, with cerements. I could not help thinking that these solemn looking grandees were as actually in physical, as they certainly were in political life, " laid out."

The Biographer in Tokio

Henceforth in the new Japan, personal abilities far more than rank or birth were to count.

At this time the members of the Privy Council of the cabinet consisted of the Kioto nobles, Sanjo, Iwakura, and Tokudaiji, who formed a sort of triple premiership, beneath whom were the ex-Prince of Hizen, Okuma of Hizen, Soyeshima of Hizen—all of them Mr. Verbeck's personal friends—with Okubo of Satsuma, Hirozawa of Choshiu, Kido of Choshiu, and Sasaki of Tosa. Of this little company of ten, probably the lives of all were attempted by the assassins, while of four who saw their assailants and the weapons forged for their slaughter, Okubo and Hirozawa were killed at once and by night. Iwakura escaped from a hedge of spears and swords that at night, in a lonely roadway inside the castle, cut his carriage to pieces, by tumbling down the grassy side of a moat, thus eluding his pursuers. Okuma, some years afterward, lost a leg by a dynamite bomb made of a gas pipe carried in an umbrella by a native, clad in the full evening dress of civilization, who afterward killed himself. Arinori Mori, whom I met in 1871 and often afterward in Tokio, when a cabinet minister, in his official dress and in broad daylight and on the glorious day of the promulgation of the constitution in 1889, was stabbed by a young ruffian, a disappointed student, whose grave, though he had been executed as a murderer, resembled for some months, a Decoration Day. Katsu Awa, another cabinet minister, was often menaced with the butcher's sword.

Early in January, 1871, the Satsuma men were in very bad humor. They considered themselves the chief agents in the success of the Revolution, and did not like it that certain men, court nobles who had been shut up all their lives in Kioto, were trying to carry on the national business, and that Hizen had three members of the cabinet, while they had but one. Hence it was that one clansman named Yokoyama, in approved feudal fashion, first offered a protest of indignation against this state of affairs—in which the spoils were withheld from the victors—and then, going outside of the chief yashiki of the clan in Tokio, he duly opened his body according to the most correct method of hara-kiri. The Satsuma men withdrew their forces from Tokio and returned by steamer to Kagoshima.

It was now necessary to placate both the spirits of the dead and the minds of the living men in Satsuma. It was the fashion then, as it had been for ages in Japan, to manufacture gods out of men, by erecting innumerable shrines and giving high-flown pompous names to a mob of dead men, who were duly worshipped. One could watch the effigies of scores of such "gods" in the popular processions on festival days. Surmounting lofty structures on wheels, around which, in their phrensy of hilarious and often obscene delights, the crowds of devotees played, the scholar could recognize figures of men or

The Biographer in Tokio

women having each three names and titles, the first historical and human, the second posthumous and Shintoistic, and the third Buddhist and popular. One of these gods was Shokoku Daimiojin, or the Great-Named Man, Shokoku, who had been a daimio or head of the Satsuma clan and province. It seemed necessary for the government to send an envoy to "take an oath to the god to exalt the destinies of the State," and at his shrine to present a sword.

So Iwakura, in company with Okubo, proceeded with a commission from the emperor to Shimadzu Saburo, then head of the Satsuma clan, together with a letter written in the proper style and full of complimentary phrases culled from Chinese documents and precedents. The answer of the great Shimadzu Saburo, who listened "prostrate to the imperial decree," though "his bowels are rent with the effort," and he tried to "forget himself for the sake of his country," is characteristic. Read in a cold English translation it seems diplomatically vague to the last degree, yet it was wholly acceptable. Did not Shimadzu depend upon his "Majesty's wise and sagacious supernatural virtue"? Did he not "pray that the heavenly heart may be pure and transparent"? Did he not "adore his Majesty from afar, and with genuine fear, bowings of the head, and contempt for death"? And was not all this according to Japanese orthodoxy? Surely yes.

Okubo, Kido, and Iwakura formed the triumvirate or committee, which really made the new government, which heretofore had rested almost entirely on the reverence inspired by the Mikado's sacred name. They were successful in getting the three great clans Satsuma, Choshiu, and Tosa to furnish the central government with troops, which in Tokio formed the nucleus of an imperial or national army. The three great men arrived in Tokio on the 2d of April, 1871. Early in 1872, Shimadzu Saburo and some hundreds of his loyal clansmen arrived in Tokio. I shall never forget either them or my feelings when, in a narrow street, I met a large detachment of the red-sworded men. Fierce and wild indeed seemed these swarthy fellows, with hair shaved off their front temples as well as from their midscalps, their tremendously long swords in scarlet scabbards, their wide sleeves thrown back over their shoulders, exposing bare and muscular arms, and their faces set to a scowl, they seemed the very embodiment of pride and jealousy—exactly the kind of pride and jealousy which only ignorant hermits, believing themselves to be the favored children of the gods, could cherish. They had rescued their own land and wished to keep it safe from foreign defilement.

I had during our own civil war looked on Arkansas and Louisiana "tigers," had read of ancient fanatics in Jerusalem, had seen Pawnees on the war trail, and even in Japan beheld in paint, at least, the face of Yemma, the Lord of the Buddhist hells. These had all done excellently in scowls, yet I am not certain but that I thought the Satsuma swashbuckler of 1870 excelled them all.

My first arrival in Tokio took place while Iwakura was absent. I bore a letter of introduction to him from his own sons whom I had known in New Brunswick. Tokio was then garrisoned by the soldiers of other clans. Passing through Tsukiji, or the foreign quarter, seeing that already the new settlement was doomed to failure, chiefly on account of the shallow harbor, I passed at the limits a barrier and guardhouse painted black and looking grim enough to keep out, as was intended, all ronin from entering the settlement. To get into the main city, one had to pass by "the flowery meadow" or Yoshiwara, where sat hundreds of young girls and women, practically slaves, but fair by nature and prettily dressed or made attractive and all ready to ply their trade for the benefit of their owners. This and a customhouse were the two institutions supposed to be indispensable to a foreign port.

With a little Japanese map in my hand, I found my way through the various streets, until I reached the great Tori, or main highway, which was thronged with moving humanity, including soldiers in every style of hybrid costume. Near the Nippon Bashi or Bridge of Japan, which was the centre of the empire, from which all distances were measured, I stopped to note, having already recognized. the anti-Christian edicts which hung

with the other laws under roof.   At noon, having
passed through, or rather along the district occupied by the castle and great Yashikis, some of them
occupying many acres, I reached a street opposite
the castle gateway and bridge named after the
last of the Tycoons, Hitotsubashi, where, in the
vast space, of old called Gojingahara, were built
the sheds and bungalows, comprising the Kai
Sei Jo or Place for the Promotion of Civilization,
then called the Dai Gaku Nan Ko, or Southern
Branch of the Imperial University.   Within were
about a thousand barefooted or sandaled, top-
knotted and two-sworded pupils, who wore
what seemed to me bedroom wrappers and petti-
coats, often with slates and ink-bottles slung to
their girdles.   In the "compound" lived the
foreign teachers.   The inclosing fences were of
the regulation official black, high, tarry, and
gloomy.   Entering through the gateway, duly
received, and my business made known to the
mom-ban or gatekeeper, I was escorted to the
door of the superintendent's house.   There I
met the house "boy," a young samurai with re-
fined face and exquisitely dainty hands and taper
fingers, who invited me to wait in the parlor,
until lunch was ready, which was in a few moments.   Soon my host with a face stamped in
every line with seriousness, honesty, penetration,
and the enthusiasm of humanity entered and
warmly greeted me in welcome.   Then began
my six weeks' stay under the hospitable roof and
a lifelong friendship.

The Biographer in Tokio

Let me first of all describe that parlor or reception room, in which, early in 1871, I spent many days in study, rest, conversation with the host, and pleasant social intercourse with both Japanese and foreigners.

Again, early in 1872, on my return from Fukui, I was in that same room for weeks. Often I remained, by request, when Mr. Verbeck was giving audience to high ministers of the cabinet and heads of departments who came to consult him on grave affairs of state.

To sit in a cozy armed chair, which afterward became temporarily the imperial throne, to study Japanese maps and books, to read the literature from Europe that loaded the superintendent's table, were privileges I counted then as delights and now enjoy as memory pictures.

Often I had good opportunity to learn the etiquette of the gate and the door, and to notice how careful this grave, serious, and spectacled man was to do the right thing to the right person, at the right time and at the right place. Yet, whether statesmen, to talk of imperial matters, or teachers and students to ask of education in theory or practice, or Samurai from any and every part of the empire to propound questions on every subject under the heavens, I think I can honestly say, all were politely and patiently heard.

Yet these are not the only visions now in memory's hall. There were also, in 1872, after Mrs. Verbeck had returned from California, children in the house, for this was a home, also, and many a merry romp do I remember with the children, especially with little Guido, the pretty boy, who seemed as the incarnation of Japan's sunshine—a fair bud of promise, whose petals of life closed at sixteen. The fact that there was a little maid in the house attracted other little maids also. More than once, it seemed like the bursting of a cherry-tree into flower, or as if some old man in the fairy-tale had thrown magic ashes on a winter tree, to see the door open and the pretty virgins of Nippon trip in, arrayed in all the glorious color and the dazzling dyes of silk for which the Sunrise Land is famous. On Japanese New Year's morning, such a vision unexpectedly greeted me, as the young daughter of the minister Sasaki, not knowing that any one was in the room, was ushered in to make her congratulatory call. For color and brilliancy, for gorgeousness of hair, ornament and dress, and perfection of girlish loveliness, I thought I had never seen anything to equal it, though I had been in the capitals of Europe, as well as dwelt in America, yes even in Philadelphia, Queen City of fair women. Knowing some Japanese, I was able to put the little lady at her ease, until her girl friend descended from above stairs.

That part of the room which fascinated me and was most typical both of my host's toil and of Japan's new era, was that just within and to the left of the door. There on a space, if I remember right, of about ten feet by four, were piled dictionaries, text-books, and literature in several languages, with files of the best periodicals of the West, from countries on either side of the Atlantic, also catalogues of publishers and instrument makers, and other material necessary for the head of a nascent university in which six languages, English, French, German, Dutch, Japanese, and Chinese were taught, and in which courses of instruction had already been formulated.

It must not be forgotten that education and intellectual reform had been inaugurated by the Bakufu, or old government, and long been opposed by the Bakufu's opponents, and that this institution was the development of an older one. To be exact, let me quote from the Historical Summary, in the Imperial University Calendar, for the year 2556–57 of the Empire, or A. D. 1896–97, translating within brackets the Japanese words.

"Inasmuch as the Teikoku Daigaku (Heavenly Dynasty Country Great Learning), or Imperial University owes its existence to the union of the late Tokio Daigaku (Great Learning), Kobu (Department of Public Works), Daigakko, and Tokyo Noringakko (School of Forestry and Agriculture), it seems fitting that, in tracing its history, reference should be made to the origin of these three institutions.

"The four departments of law, science, medicine, and literature, which composed the Tokio Daigaku, sprang, with the one exception of the department of medicine, from an institution of some antiquity founded by the Tokugawa government, and known first as the Yogakujo (Place of Western Learning), and afterward as the Kaiseijo. This institution was, after the restoration of 1868, revived by the imperial government, and in the following year, the college received the name of Daigaku Nanko, and was attached to the Daigaku, which was then established at Yushima."

In the year 1871, the Daigaku Nanko came directly under the control of the department of education then first established, and was called simply the Nanko, and in the following year, when the country was mapped out into educational districts, it received the name of the "First Middle School of the First Grand Educational District." It impressed me mightily to see what a factotum Mr. Verbeck was, a servant of servants indeed, for I could not help thinking how he imitated his Master. I saw a prime minister of the empire, heads of departments, and officers of various ranks, whose personal and official importance I sometimes did, and sometimes did not, realize, coming to find out from Mr. Verbeck matters of knowledge or to discuss with him points and courses of action. To-day it might be a plan of national education; to-morrow, the engagement of foreigners to important positions; or the dispatch of an envoy to Europe; the choice of the language best suitable for medical science; or, how to act in matters of neutrality between France and Germany, whose war vessels were in Japanese waters; or, to learn the truth about what some foreign diplomatist had asserted; or, concerning the persecutions of Christians; or, some serious measure of home policy.

Week after week I saw Principal Verbeck at work and knew his routine of life. He rose early and wrought much before breakfast. Immediately after this meal, he would go to school, supervising details during three morning and three afternoon hours. Then, often, from four to six, he would join me in my expeditions in various parts of the wonderful city of Tokio, or its suburbs. Usually we went on horseback, when going some distance. We could not make use of the jin-riki-sha, for early in 1871 this vehicle was hardly known outside of Yokohama. Besides travel on foot or horseback, the usual means was by the kago or bamboo basket hung on a pole set on the shoulders of two men, or by the norimono, hung from a beam and borne by four men. The ba-sha, or horse carriage, was still a great curiosity. The locomotive and railway were still only in the dreams of hope, or as the breath of a clam—a fairy-tale clam, of course. When we walked out in the city or went to Uyeno, the scene of the battle of July 4, 1868, or to Asakusa or Shiba, we were accompanied by armed guards, who were responsible for our lives. Hear what Mr. Verbeck says in his lecture given early in 1898, to some Japanese young men, and thus translated:

Verbeck of Japan

"There were yet no *soshi* in those times, but a worse kind of persons who went by the name of ronin. I now remember some thirty or so of the people, whose lives were cruelly destroyed by these vagabonds. In the year 1869, I was invited to the Kaisei Gakko in Tokio, and lived within the compound of the school. Being now employed by the government, I was always guarded by bette (a kind of policemen). Whenever I went out for exercise or for business, I was escorted by them; if I rode, they also rode, and if I walked, they also walked. How troublesome this must have been for them!

"It was on a certain day that a chief of the bette came to me and asked me not to go out for some time, because many ronin had entered Tokio. Thus, I was obliged not to go out even for a short walk, and to spend about two weeks in weariness, when, feeling it to be unbearable, I called one of the bette and prevailed on him to let me freely enjoy fresh air. Escorted by four bette, though two bette were usual, I was as happy as a bird let out of its cage, about to leave my house, when two samurai of the Hizen clan called on me and offered themselves to follow me also as escorts. I, being thus assured of my safety by twelve swords (for each of these samurai and the bette wore a pair of swords about his waist), started for Oji. When we almost came to Dokan Yama, I was frightened by a ronin, who, seeing me, changed his color and touched the hilt of his sword, but, being

The Biographer in Tokio

prevented from any mischievous effort by my six escorts, passed us, so chagrined that he grasped the hilt as if he was going to crush it. I was so much terrified by this incident that I at once returned home, only too glad to become again imprisoned within my dwelling."

I noticed that Mr. Verbeck always looked carefully to his revolver to see that it was in good order. He carried it in the right-hand pocket of his loose sack coat, for he told me that this was the best place to have it instantly ready. The murderous ronins, to say nothing of drunken loafers, ruffians, and wild characters of every sort, were numerous in the capital city and Verbeck of Japan did not propose to throw his life away. "The two British military officers assassinated at Kamakura," he said, "were killed because they had their revolvers in their belts around at their back, whereas the ronins when they attack, rush at you as quick as lightning and may cut you down before you can draw your pistol." Mine was a Smith and Wesson's revolver, bought, just before I left New Brunswick, by the advice of my Japanese friends. It was snugly kept in a special pocket made inside the left lapel of my walking coat, whence it could be drawn quickly, as it seemed indeed more than once necessary. I am not certain but that the mere gesture of putting my hand into my bosom was more than once a means of impressing upon some scowling patriot that he had better not draw.

237

Verbeck of Japan

"The moral uses of dark things" were finely illustrated in a way outside of Dr. Horace Bushnell's lines of thought. Soon the mean cowards that disgraced the name of samurai and misrepresented the untarnished reputation for valor belonging to Japan, found that the foreigner had teeth that would bite. The public decapitation of a few of these misguided men on the common execution ground along with thieves and incendiaries, after they had committed assassination, cooled their zeal and made the assassination of aliens unpopular. The determined attitude in private defence completed a needed reform and stopped the epidemic of murder. It soon come to be known by this gang of cowardly ruffians that a little lead, packed ready for delivery at a moment's notice, was inside the alien's coat, and his species gradually made way for a better sort of "gentleman" and to the encouragement of a new model of patriotism.

It is not for a biographer to revel in a flow of words over the glories of the imperial city of Tokio, its pageantry and splendors, its gala days, its museums, theatres, temples, and gardens, river delights, its scenery, the fascinations of glorious Fuji ever in sight, its floral attractions in winter and summer, its literary and social charms, and in time the beauties of holiness and joys of worship. These can only be hinted at, to suggest an environment, which, during thirty years, the child of God, though ever "as one that served," gratefully enjoyed as from the hand of his Father. Mr. Verbeck was not able to give any time, but that absolutely needed for recreation, to what was around him, though keenly sensitive to the charms of nature and society.

How the lights and shadows played over the landscape of his life in Tokio during the early part of 1870 is seen in his letters.

CHAPTER XII

AMONG ALL SORTS AND CONDITIONS OF MEN

A WONDERFUL variety of human nature was oftentimes gathered under Mr. Verbeck's hospitable roof. The host had to employ steadily every one of the five languages which he knew so well how to use, even though most of his guests spoke the tongue which is yet to be that of the world. The fact that the Japanese, just born into the world of new thoughts and ideas, as constantly hungry for new food as young robins, kept as busy as a father bird the one man of all others then in the empire best able to fill the hungry maws. The fact that positions were opening for teachers with good salaries attached to them, brought a constant string of applicants from among the men who had sailed, drifted, or were dumped into Yokohama. The necessity thrown upon Mr. Verbeck to supply suddenly the teachers needed, was a pressing one. Yet while the great harvest was ripening, the laborers able to handle skillfully the sickle were few indeed.

In the ports of the East there are now, as there were then, many typical specimens of the highest manhood and womanhood, but there was also much floating wreckage of society. There were men once with superb and shining abilities, that had buried both their talents and their napkin, and were no longer rich in power or clean in character. Others had been graduated out of the army and navy, the bar and the office, and the counting room because of too long dalliance at the cup, or for causes that spotted their moral as well as physical nature. Yet if they spoke and read the English language and were immediately on hand, they might serve when the Japanese were so eager for teachers and no others were to be obtained.

It could not be surprising then, that teachers who would smoke their pipes in the class-room, swear at the students, absent themselves from their post because alcohol had fuddled their brains, or who would be found in disreputable rows and places, were more than common.

Let me picture as best I can the remembrances of one week's experiences. At dinner time, noon, the table is spread for eight. At the head sits mine host, busily attentive to the wants of the hungry men, while trying to make each one of the varied company happy. An oval-faced, taper-fingered, bright-eyed young man, reared as a gentleman, but serving as a waiter in order to learn English and foreign ways, waits on the table. He has the assistance of a "pudding face,"—another servant of heavier build but much less intellectual face and evidently of ancestors who, unlike the samurai, have not for a thousand years or more enjoyed intellectual culture. The first course is soup, the second is steak and fried potatoes, the third is shrimp curry and rice, the fourth, dessert. The host must not only supervise, provide, and teach, but must be hospitable out of his own charges. Yet there were those who wondered how the missionary could roll in wealth and they abused him roundly for it.

Opposite to mine host sits a Japanese young gentleman, whose younger brother is in America. I knew the latter as a timid, frightened looking boy, yet with an unquenchable thirst for knowledge. Fearfully handicapped in the race for life, by that hereditary disease which used to desolate humanity in Japan, science and surgery in Philadelphia had already renovated him. Now, writing after thirty years, we see in that youth, after the healing and helping of the education, abroad and at home, one of the leaders in industrial education and an honored envoy, able to martial and represent Japan's best products at the World's various expositions.

I sat in 1871, beside his brother, who had never handled knife or fork or occidental tools. With that restless Japanese eye—sure sign of Tartar or North Asian, not Chinese ancestry— that watches each detail and takes in all, this polished gentleman gets through the ordeal, from napkin opening to finger bowl, without one slip or fault.

Let the American teacher stand in the shadow, for he is enjoying the novelty and the fun. Have we not opposite to us a vast and pompous personage who, from the lofty height of that "R. N." on his visiting card, looks down upon us ordinary mortals who have never been in the royal navy? He diffuses around and beneath him a general air, both of mild omniscience and of extreme condescension, and we all of us are expected to think him a wonderful man. Of his subsequent history, I know only this, that, being temporarily engaged as a teacher of English, like the next rather modest and quiet gentleman, also an Englishman, who sits next to him, both are told that in addition to their salary, their expenses of carriage, or transportation, from their lodgings at the hotel at Tsukiji to the college will be paid. The distance was about three miles. Now to show the variety of interpretation, as well as contrast in characters, the next morning the simple gentleman reached the scene of his duty promptly in a jin-riki-sha for which the charge was half a bu, or about twelve cents, whereas the mighty man in the fraternity of Drake and Nelson appeared in a barouche drawn by four horses, with a native driver, for which in due time the treasury of H. I. J. M. had to pay. The feat was almost equal to the sale in Yokohama to a native of a shilling Shakespeare for fifteen dollars.

Then there were two other gentlemen, once representatives of our gallant army and navy, and both possessing the fine physique which West Point and Annapolis secure. Each of our country's defenders were able no doubt, to take a city or storm a fortress, but, alas, as events past and future proved, were unable to rule either their own spirits or those of the bottle. A mighty man in mathematics, and a hero on the plains, was he who had so long made king alcohol and John Barleycorn his companions, that between brandy and whiskey he had become a social exile, even as in Tokio he proved a failure. The man of the deck, with a history somewhat similar, was now hoping to recoup broken fortunes and character at two hundred dollars a month. Various indeed were the characters met with in that conglomerate of humanity which came under my eye during my first seven weeks in Tokio. Some were coarsely vulgar and unconcealedly ignorant. Because of alcohol, ostentatious sensualism, or manifest illiteracy, they ran through their probation and career, in periods varying from one to six days. It was as pathetic as it was disappointing, to discover stranded on the shore that in more senses than one is scoured by the Black Tide, the wrecks of so many brilliant men.

One must not forget that Tokio was then much like the witch's caldron in Macbeth's tale, seething with manifold strange and uncanny elements. The old order of society had been broken up by a great tidal wave, caused by political upheaval *de profundis*. Much of what was good in old Yedo had gone out and the new wave coming in had not only brought new and strange things afloat, but had scoured up and forced to the surface may evils long repressed. Furthermore it is doubtful whether vice in the chief city of Japan was ever more rampant than in the third quarter of the nineteenth century. Besides the lust and villainy, life was held to be cheaper than dirt by the swash-bucklers, ronins, and other strange characters and outlaws then infesting Tokio. With the rough soldiery of the various clans and thousands of young men and boys from many provinces then living in the city as real or nominal students, but ever ready for adventure and all armed with two swords, there was a sufficiency of the elements of danger. Only a few days before my arrival, within a few yards of Mr. Verbeck's door, a man had been cut down by some sword-bearing ruffian. It was a good many hours before the bloody carcase was removed. How it was done let Mr. Verbeck tell again as he did early in 1898 :

"There was still another thing, so cheaply estimated, that is, the life of the hemin-class (common people). It was not so serious a matter for a samurai to despatch a merchant, a farmer, or an artisan with his sword. Of course, this was not done without reason, and yet this took place very often. Suppose a young samurai procured a new costly sword, and you will see him taking a walk with his friends, when a poor beggar comes to him and asks for alms, and all at once the new blade glitters upon the beggar's head ! When I lived at Hitotsubashi, Tokyo, I walked out of my house early in the morning, and found a dead body on the ground, upon which doubtless a new sword was tried. After a little while, a certain official came to examine the corpse, and let two coolies bind the limbs and carry it with the pole running through the rope. They seemed as if they were going to bury a dead dog !"

We were soon to have a taste of contemporaneous Japanese manners and customs and the results of interference by foreigners. About ten days after my arrival in Tokio, Mr. Verbeck and I had planned to ride to Oji to see the flowers and the beautiful landscape. About 4 A. M., Mr. Verbeck called me, telling that great changes had occurred during the night and that two of the European teachers had been cut with swords and perhaps were dead. Dressing quickly, accompanied by a servant carrying a lantern, we went through the dark streets passing the watchmen, [1] who as they walked by the houses jingling their poles with iron rings at the top on a metal tip, called out "look out for fire," and seeing here and there beggars sleeping under matting.

[1] In 1898, in his lecture in Tokio, Mr. Verbeck said: "There were no policemen or constables but okabiki and torite (one of the young men in the audience did not know what these were. What a rapid change was made!) Since these okabiki or torité did not wear uniform, they could hardly be distinguished from common people. It often happened that the people regarded ordinary folks as detectives. To the school at Nagasaki, in which I was employed, this kind of officials frequently came, but soon they disappeared."

Among all Sorts and Conditions of Men

In Rice Pot street, we reached a house where were lying two men with fair faces. Both had been cut down from behind. On the one the sword tip had cut partly into the head and down through the shoulder. On the other was a terrible cut, crosswise, like a great canal, from the right shoulder down across the region of the spine and loins, one of the ribs being severed. He had also received a heavy cut downward, on the other shoulder, both gashes deep and long and then bound together with the admirably thick and absorbent Japanese paper.

I remember my strange sensations in being for the first time in a native Japanese house. On the walls hung the mask of the laughing goddess Uzume, and various other emblems and tokens of Japanese religion, enjoyment, and superstition were visible. The Japanese fairy-tales, which my college classmate, son of our American minister in Japan had told me, appeared to me in new lights. Out in the kitchen I could see the preparations for food, the cooking, and the household economy which was simple enough. Many hours during several days did I spend in meditation while sitting up at night with these wounded men and during the day assisting them, especially the worst wounded one of the two.

The outward story of this affair has been told in Adam's History of Japan, (Vol. II., pp. 235-239) and in " The Mikado's Empire " (pp. 374-377) but the true inwardness is better expressed in Mr. Verbeck's letters, which show that it was anything but one-sided. It is to the credit of the government that they acted so energetically, searching every house in Tokio that might hold the assassins and examining every sword in the city to see whether it had the stain of blood upon it—a stain which only grinding will remove. I remember distinctly the sense of importance as well as the fun enjoyed by many of the school-boys who had delegations of grave inspectors visiting them to see their swords, which had never had any practice beside the common experience which dogs and cats might furnish. The perpetrators of the outrage, arrested some months after the attack, were carefully examined. Two of them afterward were put to death by strangulation and the third was sentenced to ten years of hard labor. One interesting fact was brought out that the government had made a new compilation of the criminal code then in force, which was already printed and accessible.

Mr. Verbeck's account by letter is as follows:

"You will probably see in the papers that two of the teachers of our college were attacked and badly cut in the streets of this city. This is something that might unexpectedly happen to any of us here and our merciful Father defend us against our enemies, the haters of foreigners and progress. But I can privately assure you that in the present instance it was the fault of the sufferers, and almost a punishment. Whenever any of us go out we are allowed two armed guards to follow us. We have twenty such guards belonging to the college, exclusively for the protection of the foreign teachers. Of late several of the teachers had been going about without guards, and only a week before the attack I had given all the teachers official notice that they were desired by the authorities not to do so. On the night of the attack two of them went out with guards, but dismissed them at seven o'clock, an hour and a half after dark, and were attacked from behind at eight and one-fourth o'clock as they walked on in the dark street, in the company of a native girl. It is evident that they were on an errand that they wished the guards not to know of. If they lived a moral life, they would have been safe enough that night. And now they wish to throw the blame on me because I forbid them having such girls in their houses in the school lot! With all this, we are all of us glad that they escaped with wounds and are fast recovering. The attack was barbarous, and cowardly, made in the dark and from behind. The government put the whole city and vicinity in a regular state of siege for several days for the purpose of discovering the culprits, but so far have not got beyond suspicions. It is to be hoped they will be found."

I spent seven weeks of life under Mr. Verbeck's roof, in the new imperial capital, rambling in the nooks and corners of old Yedo as well as along the highways full of the new sights and scenes of the shops and crowded thoroughfares of Tokio, riding out to visit the suburbs and lovely rural places and the famous temples and gardens. I studied the Japanese language, history, and geography in the morning and spent the afternoon outdoors, usually with mine host, in the evening reading or paying visits to Americans or Japanese friends in Tokio, but always securing an hour or so of conversation with Mr. Verbeck. His evenings were usually spent in multifarious labors, but before bedtime, he refreshed his soul with music and his spirit with prayer. To this hour, I can remember some of his favorite strains on the harmonium, and recall that when he played in public worship he liked to be behind a screen.

The time came for my departure to Fukui. The contract and papers with the Fukui officers, the dinners and feastings in the Echizen Yashiki, the meetings with daimios and the famous men of new Japan were over. Before I left, I had also taught a number of Japanese in various ways, made many acquaintances, had seen lordly Fuji Yama in varied splendors of sunrise and sunset time, now a pyramid of silver against velvety blue, now a diadem of fire, anon a table-land whose crest and potencies were hidden under defiant clouds, and again a landmark that seemed to wear a hood of white vapors that foretold storm, yet ever glorious and inspiring, though sometimes seeming to pour upon us mortals its disdain of our weakness. Coming out into the glorious air and under the cloudless blue sky, after some terrible earthquake that silenced all animal nature and made the human heart sink, Fuji seemed to look down with cold contempt at human weakness rather than with tender pity. Fortunately before leaving Tokio I enjoyed with the Japanese their New Year's congratulations, thus revelling in the delight of two celebrations, one Occidental, the other Oriental.

Mr. Verbeck wrote on the 22d of March, 1871:

"Our college is as prosperous as under the circumstances can be expected. At the opening of our new term a month ago, we had one thousand students minus four, more than two hundred having been refused admittance for want of accommodation. We have twelve foreign teachers besides myself, that is, for the three departments, English, French, and German. By this mail I again send a few students home, who will probably call on you and whom I again take the liberty to commend to your kind offices.

"I consider myself highly favored by our heavenly Father in having been permitted to receive my wife and all the children back again. I cannot tell you how wretched I was without them. We shall get a teacher for the children here and make a home school for them in our house. We feel it is too much for all of us to send children under twelve away from home, with the Pacific rolling between. We shall not soon repeat the experiment."

I bade my host good-bye on February 16th. After four or five days in Yokohama and delightful visits to Kamakura, enjoying the seashore and the storied scenery, I, with my baggage left on the steamer Oregonian, spending Ash Wednesday and Washington's birthday on the water, studying also Japan's rocky and mountainous shore, arriving at Kobe on the 23d, to meet the first missionary of the A. B. C. F. M., now the veteran Dr. D. C. Greene. Thence by way of Osaka, Otsu, and Tsuruga, by horse, boat, palanquin, and on foot, reached Fukui to spend in this feudal city, under the shadow of its castled towers and in this stronghold of Buddhism nearly a year of most varied and in the main delightful experiences, described in part in "The Mikado's Empire." On the breaking up of the feudal system, I was called by the Department of Education to organize a polytechnic school in Tokio, which is referred to in Mr. Verbeck's letters. I made the journey overland in February, 1872, to Tokio, reaching again the hospitable home to rest, after toil, and to begin a three years' residence in the great city, there to witness amazing changes.[1]

Among those whom I called on in Tokio with Mr. Verbeck were Fukuzawa, the reformer, and Mr. Arinori Mori, afterward minister in Washington, of whom Mr. Verbeck speaks:

"This time, again (January 21, 1871) some of my acquaintances come seeking our centres of civilization, and as they are such intelligent and English-speaking men (I refer to Mr. Arinori Mori and his party), I must beg of you to excuse

[1] See "The Mikado's Empire."

the shortness of this letter.   Mr. Mori, the newly
appointed Consul-General to the United States,
and his assistant secretary, Mr. Yatabe, can tell
you a good deal about me and my work.

"Mr. Griffis I think will prove to be the right
man in the right place.   In a few days it is to be
decided whether he will go to Echizen or stay
here."

Yatabe came to Cornell University and returning to Japan made his mark in literature, science,
especially in botany, and lost his life by drown-
ing in 1899.

"I am in the midst of reforming and reorganizing the school.   It is likely that after all I shall
call Mr. Griffis here to this school."

The last reference is to the Polytechnic School,
a proposal to found which I had made, while in
Fukui, to the Minister of Education.

In Tokio, I found Mrs. Verbeck, with the children back in Japan and at home.   A glimpse of
the father is caught from one of Colonel William
Verbeck's letters to a friend, in 1899:

"Those were happy days to me.   My dear
father made my childhood and boyhood days
more happy and beautiful to remember than it is
the lot of many people to have.   He was father,
big brother, and chum to us all.   Shut off from
the amusements and companionships of children,
in this country, our father was more to us than
can be imagined.   He was an ideal playmate.
Athletic as he was, he could outrun and out-
jump any of us.   He entered with great zest into

all outdoor sports. He was a beautiful story teller, and he was charged with Dutch fairy-tales and German Black Forest robber stories. As you undoubtedly remember, he had a beautiful baritone voice. He had such a sympathetic voice that we could not easily forget his songs. I even remember the lullabies he sung to me in Nagasaki. He played chess and checkers with us, and did everything to amuse and interest us, and in his play we always learned something. He had a great passion for scientific toys and always kept us loaded down with them. With him as our playmate, our playtime was school, and our schooling under his tutelage was a liberal education. Knowing these things as you do, you can appreciate what we have lost in losing such a father."

XIII

PROBABLY the most remarkable event of the year 1871 was the dispatch of the great embassy to Christendom, that is, to America and Europe, of which it may be said, without any exaggeration whatever, that Guido F. Verbeck was the originator and organizer, as we shall see.

From Tokio, November 21, 1871, Mr. Verbeck wrote:

"Yesterday morning I rose as the clock struck four, was engaged all day, finishing off with an interview with the United States Minister and the Prime Minister of Japan, which lasted from five to eleven o'clock P. M. On Friday last, the 17th inst., I had the honor of an audience with the emperor.

"The government is going to send a very superior embassy to America and Europe. I shall give some of the members letters (special) to you. The ambassadors expect to sail on the 22d December for San Francisco. The chief of the embassy is the father of Tatsu and Asahi (of New Brunswick), the Prime Minister and most influential man in the empire. It is my hope and prayer that the sending of this mission may do very much to bring about, or at least

255

bring nearer, the long longed-for toleration of Christianity."

This last was one of the first direct results of the embassy (which Mr. Verbeck had planned two years before), as we shall see. One month later the diligent and happy missionary who had already, "stood before kings," wrote to Dr. Ferris:

"I also enclose a letter of introduction to Mr. Iwakura, who knows me very well. He is Tatsu and Asahi's father, the second man after the emperor. I have had more to do with the getting up of this mission than I could now say, nor would I have such a thing even distantly hinted at in public, unless the Japanese should choose to do so from their side. I like to work silently.

"By this mail, too, I must beg of you to be satisfied with these scanty, shabby lines. I am very busy for my friends going abroad by this mail. In the *Tribune* you will see the best account of the embassy. Eight or nine of the names are of former scholars of mine. We pray that the results may be good, and further, under the Divine blessing, the boon of religious toleration. I have worked it in that direction all I could.

"Would you kindly send the enclosures to Mrs. Doremus and Mr. Dodge with my compliments? I told Mr. Iwakura that I gave these letters. If Mrs. Doremus would take several ladies with her to plead the cause of female education, I am sure it would please and have a good effect."

The Great Embassy to Christendom

We need only add that "female education" in Japan received a powerful influence because of the interest of Mr. Iwakura in the advancement of women.

One prominent object of the embassy was to secure the removal of the extra territoriality clause in the treaties, that Japan might receive full recognition as a sovereign state. For this, however, the envoys were not, as our American Minister, Hon. Chas. H. DeLong, told me before they started, armed with full powers from the emperor. So after reaching the United States, Okubo returned to Japan to secure the necessary authorization. This did but give Mr. Verbeck a further opportunity of helping his friends. He wrote under date of June 22d, 1872:

" My dear Brother Ferris,

"Enclosed I again take the liberty to send you a first of exchange to go by halves to Mayeda and Takahasi. I am so crowded for time again, that I can just only fill this one page. For words I send you some more of my work. With their Excellencies Ito [now 1900, for the fifth time premier of Japan], Okubo and Terashima, [afterward minister at Washington,] come some more of my pupils, especially Dr. Okada, whom I hope you may meet. The Lord is leading this people wonderfully."

Let us now glance at the inside history of that great visitation of Japan's leading statesmen to the western countries which resulted in definitely and permanently committing her people to vital union with the nations of Christendom.   On August 1, 1872, Mr. Verbeck wrote to Dr. Ferris:

"I am very much obliged to you for your last kind letter.   From it I infer that this will not perhaps find you at your office, though it may come after your vacation.   I am in vacation too; but to show you that vacation sometimes may mean extra work, I send you under other cover two copies of specimens of this extra work.

"You ask me for something for publication; but I am sorry to say that—even if otherwise they were of a general interest—I can by no means offer either of these papers to the public. My usefulness in this country would be at an end, if I made a show of what I do.   It is just because these people know that I do not, like many, tell all about what I do and know about them, that they have implicit confidence in me. One of the papers, on the 'press,'[1] is a common thing enough.   The other is of more importance. It, in fact, as Iwakura, the Prime Minister and Chief Ambassador, told me more than once, 'helped to help' the government out of a great difficulty, and started off the embassy such as it passed through the States.   I wish I could see you and tell you all, just as it happened.   But I can give you the merest outline at present.

"When I came to Yedo in 1869, a strong anti-

[1] An elaborate plea for the freedom of the press, which belongs to the history of journalism in Japan.

foreign feeling pervaded the nation, happily but for a short time. But influential friends spoke to me of an embassy abroad as among the probabilities of that fall or winter. This suggested to me the composition of the paper, which on or about the 11th June, 1869, I privately sent to my friend Okuma, one of the leading men at the time and now. Satisfied with its having reached his hands, I left the matter there, never spoke or inquired further about it, and not hearing about it from the parties addressed, I gave it up as so much matter thrown away. In the meantime, time rolled on, until the government was very much perplexed at the near approach of the time appointed for the revision of all the foreign treaties: the 5th July, 1872.

"On the 26th October, 1871, Iwakura requested me to call on him. After the common demands of etiquette were satisfied:

"'Did you not write a paper and hand it to one of your chief officers?' was his first question.

"'I do not recollect; please be plainer.'

"'Something, a good while ago, that you sent to Okuma.'

"I, reflecting: 'Ah! two years ago, or more? About an embassy to Europe and America?' A significant nod of his Excellency's head.

"I answered, 'At that time it would have been the thing. I hardly remember all the particulars now. The times have changed; it might not be expedient now.'

Verbeck of Japan

‘ ‘It is just the very thing now. I have not seen the paper yet, only heard of it three days ago. I am to have the translation to-morrow. But please tell me all you remember of it now.’

“And so we went on and finally appointed an interview three days later, the 29th October, to go over the whole ground once more, paper in hand. And so we did, clause by clause. At the end he told me it was the *very* and the *only* thing for them to do, and that my programme should be carried out to the letter. A number of interviews followed, some of them till late in the night.

“The embassy is organized according to my paper (that I had sown in faith more than two years before). It sailed in two months from the date of my paper becoming known to Iwakura and the emperor. How could they get over the perplexity of the near revision of the treaties? If Iwakura was not on the spot, no revision could take place at all. How could they qualify themselves for the great task? By carrying out my program. I had the appointment of two of the members of the embassy, though not chief members. I laid out the route for them to follow. But all this is nothing, compared to that which lies nearest our hearts. I count all parts but loss for those that touch on *our cause* and toleration. If the Master on this and other occasions has given me an opportunity to show this people what toleration really is, and what is expected of them in regard to it, this is what makes me say:

'Bless the Lord, Oh my soul!' And that the men on whom it most depends, had mistaken it, and understand it now, I have had many proofs of since.

"You may ask, why did Okuma keep this paper so long to himself? I asked so too, I was told that Okuma (a former pupil of mine) at the time I gave it, a time of intense anti-foreign feeling, (1869), was afraid to show it to any one, because it might have endangered his high position, as he was already suspected by many conservatives to be a convert. But after a while he showed it to his friends and colleagues and thus it did its work quietly, till it reached headquarters, just at the most opportune moment.

"I assure you I felt ashamed of my impatience. I learned once more in a striking manner that God's time is not man's time. But I fear you will not appreciate and understand (excuse me) all this, because you cannot know all the circumstances involved. But it will show you at least that, if I do not have much to say or write for publication, I am not wasting my time and opportunities altogether, and that while I am ostensibly engaged in educational pursuits, I have the greatest cause of all at heart and in hand, as God gives opportunities.

"Now all this I only write to *you* and *not* to the *public;* for, as I said before, publishing such things would be directly contrary to my invariable principles of operation, would ruin my reputation, and make me lose the confidence of the people, which it has taken me twelve years to gain in a small degree. Besides, there is a tacit understanding between Iwakura and myself, that I shall leave the outward honor of initiating this embassy to themselves. And who cares for the mere name and honor, if we are sure to reap the benefits, toleration and its immense consequences, partly now, but surely after the return of this embassy?

"Moreover, there is quite a band of foreign ministers and consuls, who look with envy on me and my doings, and it would not be right or expedient wantonly to stir up their ire. I prefer to work on quietly and at peace with all. Each man has his sphere of action; I like to keep within mine without intruding myself on others. The name is nothing, the real results are all. Except to an old friend and a brother, like you, I would not have ventured to write the above, for fear of being misunderstood. Please receive it in charity and confidence. Dr. Williams (of Peking) is staying here a day or two. Ise is coming out this mail. Yagimoto cannot come at present.

"Please excuse this hasty conclusion, and believe me, with fraternal regards,

"Faithfully yours,

"G. F. VERBECK.

"REV. J. M. FERRIS, D. D."

The original document proposing and outlining the purpose of the great embassy, which so augustly introduced Japan to the world, is in Mr. Verbeck's own handwriting and covers twelve foolscap pages. In it he recommends that all parties, political and religious, should be represented and full details of organization and route are given. It is subscribed "Sent to Okuma, 11th June, 1869. Came up the 26th and 29th October, 1871."

Probably the best book descriptive of the embassy is Mr. Charles Lanman's "The Japanese in America," New York, 1872.

More mighty in work than in word, Dr. Verbeck's letter of February 22, 1873, which apologized for his long silence, showed also that he was longing for change and rest.

"My silence is by no means owing to forgetfulness or common neglect but to an absolute want of time. With the supervision of a school having near 500 students, eighteen teachers of four different nationalities, with many applications for advice or instruction at my house, with constantly one or other of the great topics of reform in hand, for research or essay writing, and with a large family,—with all these to be daily and hourly attended to, it happens, not unfrequently that I have to stint myself in my hours of sleep. The effect of all this is that I am become very nervous and inelastic. I feel the want of a change, if not of positive recreation, to recover my nerves and elasticity of body and mind. With this view I have applied for a seven months' leave of absence, to be taken between this and the close of the year. If I can get it and can leave my post so long, I shall, the Lord being willing, leave in a month or two by the India route, spend a couple of months there, and return by the states hither."

One of the first results of the embassy was the opening of the eyes of these men so long "hermits in the world's market-place," or rather, "frogs in a well" as their own proverbs describe them, and as they laughingly called themselves, to the fact that Christianity was the force of forces in true civilization. With reflection came action. To make a long story short, the imperial ministers abroad telegraphed back to the government of Japan their impressions. The result was that the anti-Christian edicts hung up on the notice boards disappeared like magic. I remember very well how the particular edict board so long hanging with the others at Nippon Bashi did on a certain morning "glare by its absence."

Although I tried hard to get one of these as a curiosity, I could not succeed. Others were more successful. At the museum held in connection with the Ecumenical Council of Missions in May, 1900, in New York, there were three specimens, one containing the text of 1683. There are others in the museums in Japan. The time for which Verbeck of Japan had long prayed and hoped for was coming.

Ever alert to his opportunities, Mr. Verbeck had also foreseen the time when Christianity would be recognized as a tolerated form of faith and not as sorcery, or a thing to be outlawed. Religion in Japan had for ages been a political engine, a matter of priests and corporations, for revenue and control of conscience. The free, spontaneous action of intelligent men who formed religious societies in order to educate and govern themselves and who regulated their own property was a thing unknown in Japan. The idea of lay trustees free from the dictate of priests, parsons, or other religious men of the official class, was something wholly new to the Japanese and as I have reason to know, Mr. Verbeck's suggestions were gratefully welcomed. As we now see, Japanese public opinion is nearly ripe for the adopting of legislation that will show that in religious freedom, they are ahead of some nations of Europe.

He wrote:

"The great and glorious event of the day is that, about a week ago, the edicts prohibiting the introduction of foreign religions have been removed by command of the government from the public law-boards throughout the country! It is equivalent to granting toleration! The Lord be praised!

"Hoping for the approach of this good time, I handed it to his Excellency, the Minister of Religious Affairs—quite privately, as I usually manage such business with my native friends—a 'Rough Sketch of Laws and Regulations for the Better Control of Church Affairs in Japan,' a few days before the removal of the edicts. My object was to show what might, rather than what ought to be done in this direction. My sketch was drawn up under eighteen heads, with eighty-one articles in all. The heads were as follows: The congregation, churches, church property, creeds, the priesthood, clerical jurisdiction, religious meetings, rites, ceremonies, feasts and holidays, religious notices, religious societies, and orders, seminaries, the priesthood, religious connection of children, cemeteries, charitable institutions, religious publications, miscellaneous, penalties and punishments. When I come to Europe and America, I intend to take a copy with me, to submit to good and learned men for advice and criticism.

"I wish I could send you something to print (which the above is not); but I find it quite impossible at present. I fear it is not my gift to write for publication, and I must beg of you and the respected board of directors to let me do things in my own silent way, for a while at least."

And they did. Wise, generous, charitable, liberal-minded "Calvinists," as they were, they shamed the "Liberals" who often made merry over "orthodoxy" and "narrowness." How empty are names, and how often must "He who sitteth in the heavens" laugh at men who without light or knowledge judge each other. Mr. Verbeck also wrote:

"I inclose a small photograph of myself bowing to the emperor, when he visited our college

The Great Embassy to Christendom

last year. The ornamentation of the hall is my work."

The occasion referred to was when the emperor named of old the Mikado, "Son of Heaven," "Tenno," Dairi, and "Possessor of the Dragon Countenance" acted like a delightful human being and visited the University. To make a fitting hall and seat Mr. Verbeck spent anxious hours, and enwrapping one of his best parlor chairs with his wife's India shawl, furnished a temporary throne for the most interesting of Asia's monarchs. The scene absurdly idealized to suit reactionary and imperial Prussian notions was duly set forth in an illustrated paper. It resembled the actual scene at which I was present during several hours as do certain German works in history, theology, and biography may be supposed to resemble reality, useful as they are.

It was time now for the weary worker who had toiled during fourteen years, in a way to shame bees or beavers, to rest. He had lived to see a nation moved, toleration won, fanaticism receive its deathblow, a Christian church organized, persecution abandoned, priest-craft rebuked, Buddhism disestablished, and civilization in its thousand forms adopted, by the Japanese.

His proposal to leave Japan for recuperation was duly carried out as we see by his letter dated Zeist, July 10, 1873.

"You will be surprised to receive a letter from me at this time, or rather not ere this time, and from this place, the place of my birth. The simple fact is, the past six years of actually uninterrupted labor has brought me to such a state of nervous weakness that I could hardly write connectedly. It was therefore necessary that I should leave Japan, for a short time to recover my health. So I obtained six months' leave of absence, and sailed from Yokohama for England (by Suez) on the 16th April. I had to tear myself away, to flee, as it were, from my post and numerous friends. On the 14th June I arrived in London. Thence I made a hasty trip to Switzerland to see his Excellency Iwakura, who was on the point of returning to Japan. Then I came here, where I have been since the second instant. Soon after leaving Yokohama, I found that I could not well travel without my dear wife. I therefore wrote her to come on by the next mail, if she possibly could. To-morrow I go to Southampton to see if she has come. Then, after attending to some school business in London, I return to the continent for a trip on the Rhine and perhaps to Vienna, in such a way that (D. v.) I reach New York early in September, when I hope to have the great pleasure of seeing you."

Sailing from Liverpool August 28, Mr. Verbeck arrived at Jersey City September 7, and spent some days in New York, seeing a few friends. He crossed the continent and sailed for Japan from San Francisco, October 1.

His first experiences on arriving upon his old

field of labor were not particularly happy and for reasons which are best revealed in the summary of the situation, which I proceed herewith to give.

I remember how early in the year 1874, a great change came over the administration of education in Tokio and especially in the management of the Imperial University. It was as though the demons of partisan politics, nepotism, and spoils had broken loose in a city where formerly the oversight of education had been kept free from such wasting forces. At first I could not understand it, notwithstanding that I knew that the government was practically administered by the men of one clan. In the rapacity for office, they had put in men who were evidently better acquainted with machine politics than with modern education and culture. The whole social climate seemed to have changed. Instead of courtesy and appreciation I found myself with many others receiving treatment far from courteous.

One of the first things attempted to be done was to abolish Sunday as a day of rest to the foreign teachers. This was in direct violation of solemn promises made them and of the stipulations in the written contract. Evidently it seemed to the politicians in charge and to the men of the Department of Education who were behind them, that they could arbitrarily break faith in order to carry out their plans. As there were more Japanese holidays than Sundays in each month, it was doubtless expected by them that the foreigners would yield. In this they reckoned without their quest. At least one man was determined not to stand such treachery.

At the first opportunity, after notice of intentions to violate contracts had been served, I went to see the English-speaking teachers and professors, both British and American. All agreed to protest against the changing of rest days from Sunday to the "Ichiroku" or the one-and-six days in each month, viz, the first, sixth, eleventh, sixteenth, and twenty-sixth days of each Japanese lunar month. We based our protest and refusal not only upon contracts already made, but upon the fact that the rest day of al' Christian nations, and especially of the countries from whence we came, was on Sunday, and we did not wish to expatriate ourselves while serving in a foreign land, though perfectly willing to teach as we had always done, on Saturdays, though that too is a holiday with most schools at home.

This action on the part of the American in Japan, though done with all courtesy, so far as known, immediately aroused the wrath of the gentleman then in control who stands in memory as the typical Japanese politician and spoilsman, about as closely resembling the American "boss" as any creature ever met with. The subsequent proceedings of this specimen politician show the closeness of the comparison; for, very soon afterward, notice was served upon the American teacher that his contract would not be renewed. As the American had no idea of remaining in the country beyond his first engagement, this caused no inconvenience, but to receive this sort of treatment from a petty underling was neither fair nor honorable, nor calculated to raise the character or reputation of the Japanese government or its contracts.

Without further communication with the lower authorities, I dropped a note to Mr. Iwakura, the junior prime minister, simply stating the case. The matter was very quickly settled to my satisfaction. Another position of equal honor and emolument for three years was offered me, which I declined with thanks. The department of education, with courteous consideration, desired to know my wants. I expressed them and received at once a new engagement of six months which enabled me to return home at a convenient period, in the summer, and after finishing my travels and journeys in Central and Northern Japan.

It was not very long after this, that the Japanese government and department of education found that the favorites of men in high office were less valuable than trained educators, and the passionate instinct of clanship less useful for the administration of a great university, than men of intellect and scholarship. A new head of the university was chosen, who filled his position with honor and ability.

The next matter that loomed upon the horizon was the Formosan affair, of which Mr. Verbeck writes as follows:

Verbeck of Japan

"The country is in quite a turmoil on account of the presumed nearness of a war with China. Early in the spring an expedition of about 3,000 landing troops was sent to Formosa. The object of the expedition was to punish some barbarous tribes for the wanton murder of a number of Loo-chooans, and the objective point was on the eastern coasts, which part of the island was supposed not to be under Chinese jurisdiction. In fact, according to Japanese accounts, Japan has previously negotiated with China about this matter, and China had then disclaimed sovereignty over the coasts in question; yet now she not only claims sovereignty there, but strenuously insists that the Japanese must forthwith evacuate these parts.

"In the immediate objects of the expedition, the Japanese were completely successful. If then they had immediately withdrawn their troops, the effect on China would doubtless have been very salutary, in teaching her to respect her active valorous neighbor. But unfortunately the Japanese are thought to have been allured probably by their prompt success, to enter on plans of colonization, and these China very naturally cannot brook on an island, at least two-thirds of which is under her rightful sway. So the matter now stands: both nations preparing for a struggle, but neither having declared war as yet. A Japanese ambassador is at Peking now; but it is supposed that he can achieve little while the Japanese occupation of Formosa continues. A

IMPERIAL UNIVERSITY IN TOKIO, 1874.

large indemnity paid by China to Japan is one of the possible solutions of the difficulty spoken of. The alternative is war, and in that case, it might not be difficult to prognosticate the issue. If the war is a short and decisive one, Japan will probably carry her point, whatever that be ; in a protracted war the immense size and resources of China will probably carry the day. In either case, our hope is that the apparently unfortunate affair will be overruled for the good of either one of these nations or of both together.

" In the meantime, progress is visible in all departments. The educational system is developing; the native churches are unmolested; various modern improvements are introduced; and altogether long promise seems at last to ripen into execution and substantial results.

" We have had an unusually short, but an unusually hot summer, though we can hardly be said to be past it yet,—Dr. Talmage and family gave us a very pleasant call on their way to Amoy."

It was just about this time, besides enjoying at our home in Tokio a visit from the two daughters of Iwakura, my sister and I were invited to a dinner at the premier's house. I shall never forget how, when an American lady, wife of Dr. David Murray, asked of Mr. Iwakura what had most impressed him during his travels round the world, the premier answered without a moment's hesitation: " The strength of the central government at Washington. In a monarchy I could

understand it.   How it could be so in a republic,
I could not."

It was mainly by the firmness of Iwakura that
the Korean war project had been crushed.   The
Formosan affair also ended peacefully.   Mr. Verbeck wrote:

" The country is overflowing with rejoicings
at the successful termination of the Formosan
question.   War, with all its horrors, has been
happily avoided, the Japanese having carried all
the main points: the savages of Formosa have
been chastised; China pays an indemnity; the
peculiar dangers of the Formosan coasts are removed for the future.   By this last, Japan has
placed all seafaring nations in these parts under
obligation."

The only comment the biographer need make
is, that it is at least probable that had war come
at that time, Japan with her closer unity would
have won, for it is even yet doubtful whether
the Chinese are a nation or only a race.   However, it was left in the course of Providence
that twenty years should elapse until Japan had
developed and consolidated her material and
naval resources.   Then with amazing celerity,
quiet, secrecy, order, and precision, she sent
armies across the sea, wiped out the naval
power of China, and annihilated in one battle
almost every one of the disciplined troops of
China.   After that the Mikado's soldiers fought
chiefly mobs of soldiery gathered under the
yellow dragon flag, and conquered a space of

territory in Manchuria, larger than her own empire.

After the interference of Russia, Germany, and France in armed intervention which checked her development on the continent, she received Formosa and the Pescadore Islands and enough money in indemnity to buy a fleet of new battleships, not one of which she had ever before possessed, for all her men of war were cruisers and gunboats only. Yet the victories of war and diplomacy saddled her with terrible burdens. Japan has been obliged to enter upon a program of military expansion that will tax her people to the utmost of tolerable limits, for a decade and perhaps for time indefinite, crippling her educational and other lines of development.

Yet in all the operations by sea and land in 1894-95, there was, we must remember, no war between China and Japan, but between Japan and three or four maritime provinces of China. China has never had a national army or navy. In spite of all her resources the Chinese have not unity and perhaps not even the potency of unity such as Japan possesses.

Yet even in the matter of national defence, of military development, resources, and education, no real history of Japan can leave out the name of Guido F. Verbeck. It is no exaggeration to say that his advice was a potent factor, like leaven unseen, indeed, but none the less efficient, in making that Japan militant which, in 1894, surprised the world. As far back as 1870, at a critical moment in the nation's history, as Mr. Verbeck himself told me, he was asked by Iwakura and his fellow-statesmen whether Japan should seriously begin the formation of a national army and navy and the defence of her coasts, and also to give his reasons why this should be done. The interview was in the nature of a conclave which lasted several hours.

Mr. Verbeck believing that Japan, then weak and divided, was in the presence of the continually growing power of the great aggressive European nations, Russia, France, and Great Britain, advised military and naval development and defence of the coast. For this he gave two reasons, first and greatest of all, to secure national unity and the development of the resources of the empire, and second to preserve the very existence and integrity of the Japanese nation. He gave his advice as a man of affairs and of this world, and in the sincere belief that he was doing the right thing in the sight of God, as well as for that which was ever his desire and end in view, the good of the Japanese people.

XIV

IT was from the beginning and has been throughout, the aim and purpose of the biographer to set forth with some detail, only that part of Mr. Verbeck's life which is but slightly known to the public, or even to his missionary brethren. From the time he entered upon direct missionary work, about 1875, until his change of worlds in 1898, his life and influence have been patent to all. There seems less need to show with any minute detail what he did in these years, for it is known. We need, therefore, only outline his labors in that latter part of his life, for which previous years had been a preparation. After the removal of the ban on Christianity, and the organization of Christian churches, he could bring all his superb powers to the building up of Christian Japan, and this he did. He lived to see hundreds of churches organized and many tens of thousands of members enrolled, to rejoice over the flood and to sorrow over the ebb of spritual life.

Although he had accepted a five years' contract with the government, as attache to the Genro-In or Senate from 1873 to 1878, by which he could support himself, he was yet as busy as a preacher, as if he were also a settled pastor. For his sermons, one or two every Sunday, he made elaborate preparations, soon in unction and effect on his hearers reaching a height and power to which they could find no equal among alien speakers of the vernacular of Japan.

His feelings are mirrored in the letter of August 26, 1874:

"By last mail's papers I was agreeably surprised in finding that Rutgers college had done me the honor to confer upon me the honorary degree of D. D. I must confess that it was an unexpected favor—in fact quite a surprise—and that I feel it to be an undeserved one. I wish I knew whom, next to the faculty of Rutgers, I have to thank for this kindness. Whoever he be—and you are apt to know best—I should wish him to know that, highly as I may value the gift and gratefully as I accept it, I value still higher and acknowledge more gratefully the kind intentions of him who suggested the bestowal of it. God grant me grace to bear the title humbly and honorably.

"In my present position matters are somewhat improving, I mean in the way of congeniality and usefulness of subjects in hand. But I have not as yet been able to see my way clear so as to decide on the proper course to take in the future. The government very kindly offered me a contract for five (5) years from the 1st of December, last, which is a longer term than is generally offered to foreigners in the government service. Two or three years is the usual term, and four years the longest I have heard of. In fact, at the time of making my contract I was told that this long term of five years was offered me because they knew me well, and there need be no question of probation. Still I am not considered so bound, but that I can withdraw at any time from my engagements on due notice and for good and sufficient reasons. The only difficulty, then, in the case would be to decide on the goodness and sufficiency of the reasons, and there Providence will help."

The work upon which Dr. Verbeck now entered was in continuity of that which he had already been doing for years. He was still an educator of the Japanese nation. We have seen him at Nagasaki training young men to read and understand the New Testament and the Constitution of the United States. Now in 1874 the Genro-In, or Senate, the preparatory step to the National Constitution and Imperial Diet, formed in 1889, we see him as the direct adviser of the highest officers of the progressive government, not a few of whom had been his pupils. To sum up, as I have already written in *The Nation:* "During the decade of his Tokio service as unofficial attache of the Cabinet, his multifarious services were those which only a cosmopolitan linguist and scholar, absolutely trusted by a naturally suspicious and sensitive people, could perform. He translated into Japanese the Code

Napoleon, Bluntschli's 'Staatsrecht,' Two Thousand Legal Maxims, with commentary, the constitutions of the states of Europe and America, forest laws, compendiums of forms, and hundreds of other legal and political documents."

It is not necessary to speak in detail of these great works, nor of Dr. Verbeck's part in rendering them into Japanese. It may be said that the translator's whole life had been a preparation for this work, long and tedious as it was in detail. "He had four mother-tongues," for work, and he could be "silent in six languages" when called to patience and waiting. His mighty power of silence as well as of speech enabled him to be a true educator of a nation and its leaders helping to prepare them for constitutional, safeguarded freedom.

A glimpse into the manner of life of this busy man is given in the letter of May 21, 1877:

"If pardonable, I ask you—not once, but seven times—to pardon my long silence. It is true, I might assign various reasons of more or less weightiness, but unsupported by lengthy arguments, they could all and each be readily shown to be insufficient. I might for instance plead long seasons of dejection of spirits—probably it would have been relieved by writing to sympathizing friends; or multiplicity and urgency of engagements; others are similarly situated and yet find time to write; or hereditary aversion to writing generally,—it is a vice that ought to be heroically overcome; or dislike of minute explanations, without which accounts from this distance are hardly intelligible,—but this is proving too much, as it makes concise writing from distant parts a well-nigh useless labor; or want of interesting matter,—but what may seem commonplace on the spot is often deemed to be very interesting abroad; or a large family and consequent heavy family cares,—so much the more reason for keeping up social connections at home; or any number of other reasons, but all, if unsupported by details, equally capable of being answered off-hand. I am obliged, therefore, to come back to my first position, and simply and sincerely to beg of you to excuse my protracted neglect of one part of duty. This I now beg of you again, and further take the liberty to say a few words, not in full justification, but in extenuation of my long silence.

"Now, to revert to the extenuating matters above referred to, in the first place, my peculiar position obliges me continually to disregard the teacher's precept 'to attempt to teach nothing but what you have mastered fully yourself.' Almost daily, questions occur that oblige me to undertake much research and extensive reading. The wisdom or folly of continuing so long in a position of this kind is another question; but what is certain is that it involves a perhaps quite disproportionate expenditure of time. One good thing in connection with the whole matter is that, so far from requiring the least relinquishment of principles, all these inquiries rather favor, nay necessitate the unvarying maintenance of the highest principles.

"Besides the above, my official work, I endeavor to carry on at least some purely missionary work, which consists in preaching once every Lord's Day morning, with sometimes an afternoon sermon in addition. But of this part of my work I prefer that others, especially the Rev. David Thompson, with whom I cooperate, should speak. Another consideration to be referred to is that all this work has to be performed in a language that none of us can find sufficient time to devote to; but this is perhaps again proving too much, because common to all foreign missionary work and workers."

That the seriousness and multifariousness of Dr. Verbeck's labors, during his years of service to the Dai Jo Kan or Supreme Government Council and the Genro-In, or Senate, may be understood, we need only remember that Dr. Verbeck for years stood to the new government in place of the great corps of expert advisers which were afterward assembled. Hence, he had to supplement the routine toil of the day by long and hard reading at night. As the business of the government became more fully reduced to system, distributed in departments and bureaus, and as able men of special abilities from abroad and at home were sought and found, there was less need of Dr. Verbeck remaining in government service. In his work of translation, he was nobly assisted by such native scholars as Mitsukuri,

Decorated by the Emperor

Kato, Hosokawa and others. He looked joyfully forward to the hour of release.

"As to the Lord's cause throughout the country, it is a joyful fact that the times of mere hope and expectancy, that used to keep up the courage of us older hands, have under a gracious Providence been changed into times of real fruition and ingathering.

"One piece of real news I have to communicate is that my long connection with the government is at last to come to an end, namely, on the 1st of July next." [1877.]

As an appropriate conclusion to his long services to the government, the emperor of Japan bestowed upon him the decoration of the third class of the Order of the Rising Sun. This was, as he wrote, the first piece of jewelry that Mr. Verbeck ever owned. The central circle contains a fine large ruby and is surrounded by pointed rays in gold filled in with white enamel, the colors being those of Japan and the symbol that of the sun shining in its strength. Above the symbol is the three-leaved blossom of the kiri tree, the Paulownia Imperialis, the three flowers surmounting the leaves, all in gold, the leaves being in green and the flowers in purple enamel. The Paulownia flower is the emperor's family crest, the tree never growing in groves, but in each case by itself alone. At the very top of the emblem, there is a golden clasp through which passes a heavy white silk ribbon with deep red borders, and by this ribbon the decoration is worn around the neck so as to hang upon the shirt bosom. The ceremony on presentation of the decoration was the same as that observed in the emperor's presence, but as he was at the time of its bestowal in Kioto, his deputy the Honorable Ogiu acted at court as the imperial deputy, conducting the prescribed ceremonies. The decoration was put up in a fine lacquered casket accompanied by a patent to which were affixed the emperor's signature and the great seal of the empire.

In writing of it to the Mission secretary, Mr. Verbeck said: "Indirectly it is a tribute to the cause of missions." To his sister he wrote: "Of course the chief pleasure in receiving such a distinguished honor is not, for a servant of the Master, in the beautiful jewel or in the worldly honor it confers, but in the kind intentions of the kind donors. My 'D. D.' I hold in a similar estimation."

In the scientific name of the imperial flower of Japan are blended also associations with Russia and with Holland, and to the student of history the words call up the precedent of the introduction of western civilization into Russia by Dutchmen, scholars, engineers, and teachers in the seventeenth, as in the nineteenth century, foreigners introduced the more improved forms into Japan. "Present Japan—this beautiful Japan came from beyond the sea." The Princess Paulownia, after whom in science and in compliment, this lordly tree of Japan is named, was the bride

JEWEL OF THE ORDER OF THE RISING SUN.

JAPANESE BIBLE WITH ITS CASE.

Decorated by the Emperor

of King William II. of Holland. He it was who sent men-of-war to Japan in the early forties, bearing the olive branch and urging the Japanese to open their country to the world. After the Russian princess Paulownia, mother of King William III. and grandmother of Queen Wilhelmina, one of the finest polders (or lands reclaimed from the waters) in the Netherlands takes its name. Since Verbeck of Japan was born under her rule, the associations were doubtless pleasant. Verbeck, estimating the gift at its real value, rarely showed it to any of his friends, and then usually with apologies, though appropriately doing honor to the giver by wearing it on the state occasions, to which he refers in his letters. To the last years of his life he was, on account of his decoration, a guest at the imperial audiences.

To show how differently a genuine Christian, as compared with a mere seeker of earthly honors, looked upon a bauble made of gold and jewels, Verbeck sternly reproved any and all well-meaning persons, native or foreign, who tried to "make capital" even for Christianity out of a decorated missionary. "My kingdom is not of this world," said the Master, and Verbeck, His loyal servant, knew it too well to allow any trifling even by friends. We shall read how his actions spoke louder than words, even though his words were as thunder. The lightning of his firm resolve struck withering all plea of furthering the gospel by material show. Rev. E. Rothesay Miller writes:

" I recall an incident that occurred in Shinano, as related to me by himself. He was expected to lecture in one of the large towns in that prefecture, and the lecture had been advertised as widely as possible. The doctor, according to his wont, was taking a morning walk, about the only kind of exercise he indulged in, and of which he was very fond. During these walks he would arrange his thoughts for the discourse he was about to deliver. While wandering about, he came to the centre of the town and saw there a large poster with the notice of the lecture. Almost unconsciously he stopped to read it, when, to his surprise and chagrin, he saw, in very large characters, that 'Berubeki Hakase,' (Doctor Verbeck) who had been decorated by the emperor with the third class of the order of the Rising Sun, was to deliver such a lecture at such a time, etc. He went back immediately to the hotel and, looking up the young Japanese who was making all the arrangements for the meeting, told him that, if those posters were not all taken down immediately, he would absolutely refuse to speak: that the fact of his being decorated by the emperor had nothing to do with his speaking as a Christian missionary; and that, although he considered the decoration a great honor and appreciated it greatly, still it was not given because he was a missionary, and he did not speak of Christianity because he had been decorated by the emperor; that he was there that day to preach because he was a minister of

Jesus Christ, and those who came to hear him must come with that understanding. At first there was some demur, on account of the posters having been already put up, but as the doctor re-mained firm, men were sent out and all the obnoxious bills were taken down and others posted in their stead.

"The only reason why I came to be informed of this incident was because Dr. Verbeck was apprehensive lest it be repeated when he was to lecture in Morioka, and so asked that the leader of the meeting be told not to mention the fact of his having been decorated. It was well he had mentioned the incident, because the leader of one of the meetings had fully intended to make very prominent the fact of the decoration, and was much disappointed when he found that he could not allude to the matter in any way whatever."

On one occasion he found his possession of the jewel of great practical value. Being at the wrong end of Tokio, in Tsukiji, when time was short and he had an important engagement in the city at the other end, while also, owing to a conflagration, the streets were impassable because of the people, he put the silken button representing his decoration to a novel use. He had but to show the lapel of his coat to a policeman, when presto—so excellent are the guardians of the peace—a way was made for him and he filled his engagement.

Hoping to get free from engagements, in order to have six months' rest in America, and then to enter again upon the full work as missionary, Dr. Verbeck was nevertheless kept on from month to month as attache to the Senate. Then several offers having been made him for service to the Japanese, he finally accepted for one year, a position, (not knowing whether or not the Mission Board at that time would require his full services or could support him) in the Nobles' School, at which we must look.

It must be remembered that some years after the restoration of 1868 the classes of society, formerly four in number, with many subdivisions and varieties, were reduced to three,—nobles, gentry, and commons. In the new nomenclature, the beautiful and august word Samurai was dropped, and the awkward Chinese term shizoku substituted; while for the terms kuge, or court noble, and buke or landed nobility, the general term kuazoku, meaning flowery nobility, was in 1886 substituted. At this writing in June, 1900, with the augmentation consequent upon the marriage of the crown prince of Japan, there are no fewer than 776 peers, or 243 more than there were originally, these with their families numbering 4,523 persons. Japanese patriots begin already to think that a bad imitation of European customs has been made and that it would be wise to limit the transmission of certain titles to two or at most three generations. Fortunately for Japan, over against this unseemly lust for honors and titles, so out of harmony with the spirit of the age, is the noble desire of many natives who,

Decorated by the Emperor

in character and abilities, are higher than decoration or honors can make them and who prefer to remain commoners. There are even honorable men of Samurai blood who have voluntarily stepped down, or rather risen higher into simple manhood by becoming heimin or commoners.

To educate this class into greater efficiency for national service, Kuazoku Gakko or Nobles' School was formed. To give it the right momentum and direction, who better than Guido Verbeck? So thought the projectors.

This year of unexpected labors, for during this time he gave his services freely to the young churches also, brought Mr. Verbeck into a condition of weakness and nervousness which required immediate rest, so he prepared to leave Tokio with his family July 31, 1878. For about a month before his departure, he was overwhelmed with tokens of affection from nobility, gentry, and commons, from official and private parties, from high and the low, from the Christian and, as this son of hope wrote, "*as yet* un-Christian." He left Japan uncertain as to whether he should be able to see his dear people again. His first purpose was to restore his own health and to settle his children in school in California. Hear what Mr. E. H. House, editor of *The Tokio Times*, a most excellent journal conducted by a trained journalist, wrote of Verbeck:

"The steamer which sails for San Francisco next Wednesday, will carry from Japan a gentleman whose name has been identified with the educational development of this country from the earliest days of foreign intercourse to the present moment, who has enjoyed during the successive years of his career an unexampled degree of confidence throughout his large circle of social and official connections, and who stands almost alone in the possession of an esteem which has never been dimmed by distrust and which the Japanese of all ranks and conditions have united in according to him with a singular abandonment of the reserve that commonly characterizes their closest association with strangers. His long residence has been an unceasing benefit to alien dwellers of all nations, in ways of which he can never have been conscious; for the unexerted influence of such men goes far to counteract, in time of need, the impulses of anger inspired by the more frequent examples of selfishness and prejudice which the people of this country have had to encounter. To the Japanese themselves, in numbers extending indefinitely beyond the region of his personal contact, it has also been an advantage which they recognize with a promptness and a fullness alike just to their friend and honorable to themselves. His absence will be a real loss,—not so serious as if his departure had been determined upon during the unsettled days of the government change, domestic disorder, and undefined external relationship, but still one that will be lamented with a sense of obligation that words can only imperfectly acknowledge and acts cannot wholly requite."

Decorated by the Emperor

Dr. Verbeck tells the story of his old and his new work in his letter of July 24, 1877:

"As I believe, I intimated to you in my last, my long connection with the government service is about to be severed. According to present appearances, I shall leave my attacheship to the Senate by the middle of September.

"A fair and honorable offer was made me some time ago, but I declined it. The Nobles of Japan have formed themselves into an organized society, and under its auspices carry on various enterprises, among which there is a so-called Nobles' School (Kazokii Sakka). This is a large institution, chiefly intended for the education of the descendants and relatives of the 'kuazoku' or nobles. It was in this school that a place was rather urgently offered me. The chief reason of my excusing myself is that, though much good might be done in that institution, I think that in the present progressed state of the country I could be more useful than in teaching the mere rudiments of an English education, unless it were in a distinctively missionary school. There are many others as well or better qualified for the work in question. It is true, it was intimated to me that from time to time I would be called upon to lecture in Japanese to some of the nobles themselves; but if that be a desideratum, it might be accomplished without the drudgery of teaching spelling and grammar. At such a time as the present when preaching and educating for the ministry can be effectively carried on, I think that we may leave mere secular teaching to secular teachers.

" As in many respects an appropriate and gratifying conclusion to my long connection with the government, the emperor did me the distinguished honor of conferring on me the decoration of the third-class of his Order of the Rising Sun. As I have ever borne the title of the missionary and have always stood forth in and for the mission cause, and as I have always been, under grace, a champion of those good things that Paul commends in Phil. iv. 8, this honor bestowed on me may properly be regarded as an indirect tribute to the cause of missions. Certainly, if the government cherished hostile feelings toward Protestant missions, it would not have taken such a step. As to the honor itself, I hope that as a Christian and a minister I may know how to bear it. The decoration is a pretty piece of jewelry, the first I have ever owned. The central circle is a fine ruby; this is surrounded by pointed rays of gold, filled in with white enamel. The symbol of the sun is surmounted by the emperor's family crest; the three-leaved 'paulownia imperialis,' with a cluster of blossoms on the tip of each of the leaves, also all of gold, the leaves filled in with green and the blossoms with purple enamel. At the very top there is attached a golden clasp, through which passes a heavy white silk ribbon (one and one-half inches wide) with deep red borders. By this ribbon the decoration is to be suspended around the neck, so as to

Decorated by the Emperor

lie on the shirt bosom. The ceremony on the occasion was the same as that observed in the emperor's presence; but as the emperor is at present at Miako, the Hon. Ogin had been appointed to act at court as his deputy. The decoration is put up in a fine lacquered casket and accompanied by a patent, to which are affixed the emperor's signature and the state seal."

His first letter from San Francisco is dated 18th of September, in which he says, "What amidst all the novelty and advantages of this great city we miss most in our daily dealings are the docile and kind-hearted Japanese."

On arriving in America the reaction came. He was taken with an illness which lasted some weeks. After his recovery, to rest his mind by change of occupation, he gave himself to a new method of literary investigations, by which he "hoped to ascertain more scientifically and positively than had hitherto been possible the real authorship of any composition."

During this stay on the Pacific Coast he improved every opportunity to hear good preaching. Abundant proofs that he succeeded are found in his commonplace books, crowded as they are with notes, comments, analyses, sermon plans, hints, suggestions, seed thoughts, excerpts, and scraps of all kinds. It would be interesting to open the wealth of scholarly accumulation, or even to show the chips in the workshop of this scholar, man of affairs, and consecrated servant of God and man, but space forbids. Returning to Japan, he wrote on the 9th of January, 1878:

"Under date of the 21st May last, I wrote you, giving a full statement of my case; chiefly of the prospect of my leaving the government service for good, of my intention of taking about six months of rest and home duty; and of my readiness, at the end of this or early next year to rejoin the active ranks of the mission, if agreeable to the Board."

Meanwhile he made a new engagement as his letters show:

"I did not feel myself at liberty to refuse some of the offers most kindly made me and I entered on a contract for a year, from the 20th November with the Kuazoku gakko and with one of the departments of the government. The latter is, however, a mere private arrangement between me and the officers of the department in question and not with the government itself. My contracts, too, do not bind me so that in an emergency I cannot make myself free. Moreover, in making the above arrangements, I have reserved sufficient time (with a proportionate loss of salary, of course) to enable me to continue my usual missionary labors and my lectures on the Christian evidences and homiletics in the Union Theological School."

A year of severe, constant, and multifarious labors again wrought adversely upon his health and strength and he took a vacation in California. He writes June 18, 1879:

Decorated by the Emperor

"I am interested to hear what progress is made in regard to the proposed high school or college for Japan. If it can be brought about without diminishing the regular mission contributions, much may be said in favor of the plan, and I for one am ready to take an active part in it, if desired. Though, on the whole, it might be better in a country like Japan, if all or nearly all the men connected with the college were new men, who had never been in Japan before. I should prefer to work with new men. All who have been there any length of time have their specific gravity fixed upon them by the natives, and their usefulness in an educational career will depend largely on the rate thus assigned them. As to the influence of skeptics, I do not dread it much, and think that the purity of truth and morality is in itself a sufficient defence against its effects.

"The most important thing in Japan to-day is the gospel faithfully preached, and if this should be at all interfered with by the new college, as far as the contribution of means is concerned, I think it had better be left alone. The government does so much for secular education and its institutions are so complete in their various appointments, that if an independent college is to be gotten up, it had needs be a very good and superior one.

"During my prolonged recess here, it was necessary for me to be occupied in some quiet way, on the principle that a change of occupation amounts very nearly to rest, as well as in the hope of perhaps producing something that might go to aid in supporting myself and family. For some years past I had had in my mind a new means of literary criticism. The working out of this idea supplied just the kind of unexciting work my case needed, though it has thus far failed to yield the more substantial benefits hoped for. Since recovering from my first illness which I was taken with soon after my arrival here, I have worked at it more or less, and for some time past worked hard. But with the best of wills, though I have many pages ready for the press, I find I cannot at once finish the work so as to make a complete whole of it now. In the prosecution of the work I am, however, encouraged to hope that I have fallen upon an important discovery and have made some useful inventions in the way of the application of means to the end in view.

"My scheme consists chiefly in a new method of literary investigation, by which I shall be able to ascertain, more scientifically and positively than seems to have been hitherto possible, the real authorship of any composition. Though my tests are applicable to styles of all ages and in all languages, they would be peculiarly so to the Scriptures of the Old and New Testaments. I have analyzed the whole of Romans and tabulated every one of its 9,337 words. For mere qualities of use numerically recorded quantities, thus arriving at positive, scientific results. Fleay, in his 'Shakespeare Manual' (1876), comes very near the idea I had in mind; in some late numbers of the transactions of the American Philological Association, I find some faint attempts in the same direction; but nowhere do I find anything like an elaboration such as I have achieved. The Sermon on the Mount, some papers of Addison, etc., I have also subjected to my process, as I fancy, with satisfactory results. I should like very much to confer with a trustworthy and able philologist on my work before proceeding further with it."

Right here we may glance at Dr. Verbeck's family. His firstborn baby daughter, Emma Japonica, and Guido, who lived to be sixteen, are no more on earth, but at this writing, June, 1900, there survive, five sons and two daughters. William, Channing, Gustavus, Arthur, Bernard, Emma and Eleanor. The grandson, son of William, bears the honored name Guido Fridolin Verbeck. Emma is married to Professor Terry and dwells in Japan. Two sons in the army of the United States follow the flag in the far east, and one, Gustavus, the illustrator is well known to all who love jolly pictures.

The vacation in California restored him to complete health and we find him back in Tokio, writing September 19, 1879, telling of the warm welcome he had received and later giving a statement of his routine work, especially his preaching at the Koji Machi Church.

"As regards work, I find there is plenty of it. For the present I am assigned homiletics and

Verbeck of Japan

evidences in the theological school. This will leave me time enough to do a good deal of preaching besides. If after this there are still found to be unoccupied spaces there are several translations to be done which are urgently wanted. In the course of my regular work, too, I hope to meet with materials for longer letters and more frequent letters than has been my wont of sending you heretofore."

On the 12th of May, 1880, he wrote:

"It may be presumptuous to say I am very busy, for who is not? In laying out my plan of work for the past winter (teaching in the theological school and preaching) I did not think of making allowance for a variety of extras; yet they have turned up so plentifully that they sometimes sorely try the camel's back. And very often I feel as if the extras are not a whit less important than the stock work. For instance, copying from my diary: ' 1st day, lecture at the Nobles' School, 2 to 4 o'clock P. M. 2d day, preaching at Koji-machi church (communion) 9:30 A. M.; Do. at Shitaya church, 2 P. M. 3d day, moved from Miss Gamble's school to my present house; 4th day, address before the alumni and officers of the old Kaiseijo of 1869 and '70 (my wife will send you a newspaper slip about this); 6th day, sermon at the dedication of the new Koji-machi chapel, 2 P. M. 8th day, an address at the inauguration of the Japanese Young Men's Christian Association in the Kyo Bashi church, 2 P. M.'

"The dedication of Koji-machi chapel was an

298

interesting occasion. It took place on the 6th instance, Rev. Mr. Ibuka, the pastor, presiding. The services were opened with a hymn, after which Rev. Mr. Okuno read the Scriptures and offered up the dedicatory prayer. My sermon which followed next, was on Ps. cxxvii. 1, 'Except the Lord build the house, etc.' After another hymn Rev. Mr. Waddell of the Scotch Presbyterian Mission, made some excellent remarks on the name of the church, 'Koji-machi church' meaning 'Leaven Street church.' Rev. Mr. Ogawa followed with some striking exhortations to the church, and the services were concluded with prayer by Rev. Mr. Kozaki, minister of the Congregational church, the doxology and the benediction by Rev. Mr. Soper of the Methodist Mission."

To this Koji-machi church, Dr. Verbeck gave much time, thought, prayer, love, and labor.

Of Dr. Verbeck's nature and habits of generosity—and it made little or no difference what his salary was—we learn from what Dr. David Thompson wrote in 1898, when "he who never rested rests."

"Afterwards he (Dr. Verbeck) came to Tokio to help lay the foundation of the present Imperial University. While thus engaged, the first church of Tokio—the Shinsakai, was organized with eight original members. This number rapidly grew, and in a short time for various reasons it became imperatively necessary to erect a house of worship. Dr. Verbeck was one of the first to see this necessity, and the first to suggest the possibility of securing one. He called at our house one evening and spoke to me, then acting pastor of the church, of a plan that he had thought of for raising funds. A few days after this he had set his plan to work. He brought me a sub- scription paper headed: 'G. F. Verbeck, $50.' Then followed, 'A friend, $50.' A third fifty was put down under another device, so that every one who saw the paper thought that Dr. Verbeck had given fifty instead of one hundred and fifty dollars. Such was his modesty. Thus headed, and at his suggestion, I took this paper to a considerable number of foreigners, principally professors in the university. A number gave liberally. This help, with the contributions of the native church, enabled us to put up a build- ing at a cost of nearly one thousand dollars, free of debt. Both before and after this building was erected Dr. Verbeck taught the whole church as one large Bible class for a long time, from Sab- bath to Sabbath."

XV

THAT decade of years, the ninth of the nineteenth century was with Dr. Verbeck, then in the
fullness of his powers, the era of Bible translation. Arrangements were made by which three
Bible societies, American, British, and Scottish,
and the missionaries of the various evangelical
societies in Japan cooperated in the production of
a Japanese version of the Holy Scripture. Re-
ducing his other engagements to a minimum, he
spent for many months and years five out of
every six days exclusively in the work of rendering the holy Scriptures into the tongue of the
Japanese people. With this work so delightful
to his soul, he made alternation and variety by
going on preaching tours into near and distant
parts of the empire. For either work, both oc-
cupations made mutual enrichment. Coming
fresh from the mastery of the thoughts of men
moved by the Holy Spirit and the work of expressing these thoughts into Japanese, the man
of God was in a sense complete, furnished unto
every good word and work. In June, 1900, asking one native preacher of many years' experience
in the pulpit the secret of Mr. Verbeck's power
over the hearts of the Japanese, he told me that

he thought it was marvellous skill in using passages from native authors to defend, illuminate, and enforce Scripture truth, and show that God "in these last days hath spoken unto us."

During the month of May, 1882, with the young preachers Komoro, Uyeda, and Naomi Tamura, author of "The Japanese Bride," Dr. Verbeck made a preaching tour in Kiushiu of twenty-four days, preaching or lecturing twenty-one times to large gatherings in eight places.

In writing, December 22, 1880, he gives in detail a most interesting incident of a soldier, who secured for himself and his comrades and friends liberty of conscience and freedom from unfair assessment in the interest of paganism.

On September 7, 1881, the household was completed by the birth of a son and Dr. Verbeck had now three sons and a daughter on either side of the Pacific. Like so many missionaries, also, he owned a grave in other than the home land. In the same soil in which his own body was to lie, but at Nagasaki, lay precious dust to which memory often turned.

He wrote September 9, 1881:

"By this time I have fairly started on Old Testament translation. My work hitherto was very various; Sunday preaching (on an average twice a week); teaching at the Union Theological School (evidences and homiletics); a weekly Bible class at home; three lectures a month at the Nobles' School; translations for our Presbytery; besides a goodly number of attendances at occasional or periodical meetings, and occasional missionary tours into the country. Under these circumstances it could not be expected that I should make much progress in Bible translation."

He also kept up his connection with the Nobles' School, giving chiefly moral lectures. Already this institution, under Mr. Verbeck's magic name, had become the gateway through which not a few men had entered high government positions.

" What induced the political students to ask for an increase of my instruction, I am quite sure was chiefly this. Quite recently the emperor issued a proclamation setting forth that in the twenty-third year of Meiji (1890), he would grant the empire a constitution, a parliament. However well or ill-founded it may be, there is a general expectation among the nobles (daimios, large and small), that their body, or a large portion of it, will then (in 1890), be formed into something like an Upper House. I think it was a good deal with a view to this that an increase of the political lectures was desired. If I had been in these peoples' service and supported by them, nothing would have been more reasonable; but to ask that I should give one-fifth of my time for their secular interests, while being supported by two large religious societies, who would expect adequate returns at my hands, was certainly beside all reason and right.

" Two of my earliest political students, Okuma and Soyeshima, of Nagasaki times, rose very quickly to the highest offices in the empire, ministers and councillors of state, and a great number of my greater pupils are now in various ranks in all the home and foreign departments of the government. Hence there was sprung up a vague notion among a certain class of people that the being under my tuition for a length of time is pretty sure to lead to official position or promotion. I have often been told so, and it may seem and sound very fine; in its time and place, too, it has had and still has the effect, more or less, of liberalizing the minds of some officials, of recommending Christianity to them in a general way and disposing them favorably toward it. But all this has under the Divine blessing been effected already by the sacrifice of precious years and long continued patient labor and any other good effects in the same line, now that the country has been so far opened and advanced, are, as far as I am aware, very small indeed. Our work has to change with the times."

In declining to continue further connection with the Nobles' School, beyond that of giving lectures on ethics, Dr. Verbeck wrote to the Japanese director as follows:

"When I was in the service of the Japanese government and Japanese friends, and was entirely supported by them, I always considered it my duty to give all my time and strength to them. Now I am entirely supported by two American societies, and hence it is my duty to give all my time and strength to their work. It

Preacher and Translator

is a happy circumstance that the work I have to do for these societies is at the same time altogether for the benefit of your countrymen. I love your people and like to work for them. But you will perceive that the above agreement in regard to my work will make it impossible for me to continue my lectures at the Kuazoku gakko."

He wrote home:

" To this letter I received the Director's reply of 8th November, herewith inclosed, marked No. 1. I accepted the invitation to the anniversary on the 17th, stating the subject of my address, ' Reasons for the Students' Diligence,' and on the 12th received another answer, herewith inclosed, marked No. 2.

"Accordingly on the 17th, accompanied by Mr. and Mrs. Miller, whom I had invited, and my wife, I went to the institution, which had a very festive appearance. The scholars, male and female, and a large number of guests were assembled in a spacious hall. The exercises lasted from 1:30 o'clock P. M. till 4:30 o'clock, after which we were ushered into another large hall, where we partook of some fine Japanese refreshments. I had the honor, during the anniversary exercises, to address an immense audience, among whom were two imperial princes, (one of them the representative of the emperor), His Excellency Iwakura, and a great member of daimios. Mr. and Mrs. Miller seemed to be much pleased with the company and the exercises. The musical pieces under the superintendency of Mr. Mason made a pleasant variety in the exercises. Mr. Mason, the Millers, my wife and self were the only foreigners present among the aristocracy of the capital. But the most gratifying features of the whole was that after I had stated so frankly my missionary character and the purely Christian nature of the work, on account of which I declined lecturing in their school, yet I was expressly invited to address them in public on a highly festive occasion. I stood before the people, nobles, and princes as the pronounced representative of Christianity in Japan. Few things could show more strikingly that there is not a shadow of dislike or contempt for our Protestant Christianity. Thanks be to God!

"I said above that it would seem a pity to throw up the Nobles' School too rashly, and this is chiefly because we cannot tell what this work may result in, as in the course of time all classes of the people become more liberally minded with reference to Christianity. I value the souls of the poor as highly as those of the high and mighty, and love them more; yet at the same time, the higher classes here are so very inaccessible to missionaries generally that it would seem a great pity to sever a tie of considerable confidence and intimacy except for the weightiest reasons."

The time had now come, however, when Mr. Verbeck was to leave his comparative isolation among the missionaries and enter into coopera-

Preacher and Translator

tion with them in direct missionary work, while continuing also several years of daily toil at the translation of the Bible, a work at which we can but glance.

Let him open his heart to us and tell how he felt in October, 1882. Increasing honors only made this servant of God and man more modest in human society, more humble before God and Christ's cross. There was not a trace of snobbery in this admirer and countryman of William the Silent and George Washington. As for the malignant envy of the missionary-haters in the seaports, or the slanders of globe-trotters or lecturers on "science," these were to Dr. Verbeck, "like pouring water on the frog's face" of Japanese, or the "duck's back" of our own homely proverb. He wrote:

"But perhaps few know so well as you the differences between the 'then' and 'now' in my particular case. Now as regards the comparatively low estimate in which missionaries are held by the world, as well as the quite unmerited opprobrium often cast upon them by very worldly people (both foreigners and natives), I care very little for it, nay, sometimes rather enjoy it. Besides, in my case, there are pleasant exceptions to this general rule. Once a year, at least, I am admitted to audience, before the emperor; several times a year I am invited to state entertainments; the authorities of the University (grown out of the former Kaisei Gakko) never omit to give me an honorable place on occasion of the annual public exercises (such an invitation for next Saturday, herewith inclosed); the Nobles' School so likewise; all, without exception, of my former acquaintance and connections treat me with the highest consideration and respect when and wherever I meet them, etc.; yet with all this, as you justly surmise, I am only a 'missionary,' and joyfully accept the situation. That the work is congenial to me and that my heart is in it, I need not mention.

"But where I feel the difference between formerly and now most of all is in this: from 1859 to '79, for twenty years, I worked and stood alone, decided all matters large and small according to the best of my judgment: there was little or no occasion for collisions with brethren having life ideals and aspirations, though founded virtually on the same foundations and with the same hopes in view, yet so totally different that mutual understanding becomes at times exceedingly difficult. The fault lies probably largely with myself; those twenty years of solitary action have unfortunately made a kind of Leatherstocking or Crusoe of me, and I sometimes feel like a kind of rough pioneer among regular settlers. With the Japanese, I am happy to say, there exists not a shadow of this feeling; for if there is one sense strong in me, it is that my mission is to the Japanese, that I am here to benefit them.

"For years past I have been urged again and again to join the Asiatic Society (foreign), but I

have never felt a call to do so; I have actually
been a member of the Seismological Society (on
special invitation, but paying the ten-dollar entrance fee), and yet, though I am acknowledged
to be one of the earliest, if not the earliest, ex-
perimenters here, measuring the direction of the
earthquakes by means of variously constructed
pendulums, I have never had the pluck to attend
the platform before a Japanese audience and feel
perfectly at home and in my proper element. I
do not say any or all of this by way of complaint
(except against myself), but only to answer your
friendly inquiry. I often wish, not that things
around me were different in these respects, but
that I might have more capacity to adapt myself
to these things and to changed times and circumstances; for I feel that I sometimes sorely try the
patience of younger men than myself. I repeat
that I consider very lightly the aversion of the
upper grades of society here toward missions
and missionaries, or rather toward Christianity,
for I am convinced it will pass away and is passing away. I rather look upon the present time
of labor as a preparation and qualifying of one's
self for worthily and suitably proclaiming to
these very upper grades the unsearchable riches
of Christ. The Lord grant it in His time."

Feeling the need of such a work, a movement
among the missionaries was made to secure a
history of Protestant missions in Japan. By
unanimous consent, Dr. Verbeck was urged to
attempt this task. He reluctantly accepted the

Verbeck of Japan

responsibility. He first prepared a carefully printed circular, dated November 20, 1882, in which he made request and presented a scheme of topics, historical, educational, medical, and literary. He spent some months in digesting the mass of matter received, finishing the work which, besides a general history and an abundant collection of historical sketches, gave the statistics also of the churches of the three forms of the faith, Greek, Roman, and Reformed. Part of the historical matter was read at the Osaka Conference of Missionaries, a famous gathering held in the year 1883. The work as printed contains one hundred and eighty-three pages including statistics. The annual summary of statistics is happily continued yearly by the Rev. Henry Loomis, of Yokohama, making an extremely valuable annual.

Hard work in the study was alternated not only by preaching tours but also by attendance upon councils or conferences for the organization of churches. Wonderful to relate and a very rare thing in his epistolary experience, Dr. Verbeck wrote home a long letter of thirty pages about the work in Takasaki, a city in the centre of the silk district. Many of the old veterans and the new Japanese Christian leaders were present at this conference of organization and recognition. The incidents connected with the formation of this Takasaki Independent Church led to much searching of heart, exuberant correspondence, and ultimately to the proposed

310

"plan of union" between the Congregationalists and Presbyterians, which however failed to mature. After several intervening years of experience, which did *not* work hope, Dr. Verbeck put on paper his ideas about the formation of churches and how the true independence of the native Christian churches could be secured. We need only summarize his opinions and views. Perhaps these are quite accurately reflected in his paper entitled "An Extraordinary Episode."

Sure signs of the working of the gospel leaven to the transforming of the nation were showing themselves. In 1874, we had called together on Mr. Fukuzawa, the head founder of a college begun on the day of the battle of Uyeno, in 1869, when instead of going to the battle, he sat down with some pupils to study Wayland's Moral Science. From Tokio, July 10, 1884, Mr. Verbeck wrote:

"I send you a copy of the Japan *Mail* that has a rather remarkable article in it. The author, Mr. Fukuzawa, who has hitherto shown himself extremely hostile to the introduction of Christianity into Japan and has now so completely changed his mind, is a kind of opportunist and has a large following among what may well be called 'young Japan.' Although, humanly speaking, there seems to be little hope of his ever embracing our faith himself, there can be no doubt that his article will exert a very extensive influence in favor of Christianity."

Of Fukuzawa, "the grand old man of Japan,"

Verbeck of Japan

Mr. Basil Hall Chamberlain in 1891, thus draws a portrait, "this eminent private schoolmaster who might be minister of education, but who has consistently refused all office, is the intellectual father of one-half the young men who now fill the middle and lower ports in the government of Japan." At the opening of the twentieth century, being even more pro-Christian, he is vigorously opposed by reactionaries as the preacher of "Occidental," that is, Christian morals.

One of the preaching tours taken in 1885, was through Tosa, in Shikoku, the Island of the Four Provinces, which Mr. Verbeck declared was "by far the most lively and interesting trip I made since I came to Japan." In the large towns and cities the theatre was becoming more and more the usual place of large gatherings. Let us look at the situation of the modern apostles and their occasional experiences with the "sweet reasonableness" of Japanese audiences. In one instance,

"After the opening prayer and brief introductory remarks, a remarkable altercation occurred between a youthful ringleader of the boisterous portion of the assembly and the local evangelist. The occasion of this was that the introducer had ventured to request the audience to listen quietly and to reserve any possible dissent for inquiry and discussion at the close of the meeting. Upon this the young champion wished to be informed whether the present addresses were to be lectures or sermons; if the latter, he

Preacher and Translator

and his mates would of course abstain from noisy demonstrations, but if lectures, they claimed an inalienable right of expressing their assent or dissent by all the customary means,—which customary means are often sufficiently disturbing. Our interpellant was informed that, although lecturing had perhaps been mentioned in the public notices, Christian lecturing amounted really to about the same thing that he would call preaching. He was quite satisfied and promised that in this case his party would willingly listen in silence. And they kept the promise, except once or twice in the case of one of the Japanese speakers, when they objected loudly that he was wandering from his text and lapsing from preaching into lecturing! The whole thing may seem rather trivial, and yet it is significant and encouraging. The concession in favor of preaching on the part of these young hotheads who have very little respect for anybody or anything, as well as the restraint they must have laid upon themselves to keep their part of the voluntary compact, was a surprise to all of us, as agreeable as it was novel."

In primitive Christianity, throughout the Roman empire, the synagogue was the cradle of the faith. It furnished always to the peripatetic apostles a place in which to proclaim their new theology, that is, to show the fulfillment of the old kingdom, priesthood, and prophecy in Christ. Whether welcomed or abused and expelled, the disciples could at least find initiative in the syna-

313

gogue, which also and not the temple, furnished out of its own life the organization of the Christian church. In Catholic Europe the theatre grew out of the church. In new Japan, the churches for the most part were either born in the theatre or found their cradle in its edifice. The players' home furnished the church clothing, so to speak, before she could walk for herself. An audience room ever ready, was the theatre, with its stage and auditorium, its aisles and its facilities of entrance, exit, and with its ready-made regular organization for the easy sitting of auditors and the platform for the speakers, with the personnel of advertisers and janitors and the material— pretty much everything convenient for a public gathering.

Yet let no Occidental fall victim to his mental associations. Any one accustomed to the luxury of metropolitan theatres in America or Europe may be led astray by the word alone. One must not think of upholstery, or easy chairs, or gilded and decorated ceilings, walls, or luxurious loges, or of electric lights, or of carpets. Let one imagine rather enormous barns with no intermediary between flesh and floor. Indeed often mother earth herself furnished not " standing room only," but even reserved seats, the actual cushions being what one's own bones may be clothed with. With some modern exceptions in the large cities, no signs of luxury or comfort, in our sense of the word are to be seen in Japanese playhouses. One must think rather of great wooden tents under roof, unwarmed and very poorly lighted. Often the kurombo, or men with blackened visage, held candles fixed at the end of long poles close up to faces of the actors, in order to show the play of simulated emotion. In winter these barn-like structures were intensely cold. To the average missionary, accustomed to the atmosphere of air-tight houses, theatre-preaching was a great trial to health. Prolonged exposure both in travelling over rough roads and in places out of the way, with alternate freezings and heatings in the theatre-barns, helped powerfully to break down all too soon Dr. Verbeck s constitution.

Nor were the audiences always tractable or polite. Often it required a good deal of skill to subdue the unruly element in the form of "lewd fellows of the baser sort," egged on or in the pay of Buddhist priests or fanatical Shintoists, or young ruffians who had lost the courtesy which was supposed to be so characteristic of Japan. Furthermore, a new character had risen in the form of the Soshi, who was a sort of a malignant ghost of the ronin of earlier days. The word Soshi may be roughly translated, "stalwart." These political radicals, or fire-eaters, to decent citizens and genuine patriots and even to ministers of state and the emperor's own servants, were even more troublesome than they were to Christian missionaries. Besides being bullies, ruffians, and often cowards of the meanest stripe, they served as "heelers" to turbulent politicians, or were ready to do any dirty work in the name of "patriotism." They so pestered the emperor's lawful servants with their impudent deputations, remonstrances, and advice, that it was necessary occasionally for the government to issue proclamations to disarm and to deport them from Tokio,—sweeping them out as housemaid would the vermin from her closets and kitchen. Indeed it was these fellows who, by their unwisdom and brutality, imperiled the very existence of that constantly increasing measure of liberty which was being given to the people. Good men in honorable political opposition had to suffer with the bad. It sometimes seemed that in order to smoke out the rats, the government was in danger of injuring the foundations of a noble structure.

Later on, Mr. Verbeck in company with his friend and colleague, Rev. Henry Stout of Nagasaki, went through Kiushiu and among other places visited Sago, the home of his first convert, Wakasa. Dr. Stout wrote from memory in 1898:

"How different the circumstances on the occasion of our visit! Now we could preach the gospel openly. We held a great preaching service in an old theatre, with thousands in attendance and officials on the platform to guarantee order. Another night we had a service in a house in a remote portion of the city. Part of the floor gave way—not a serious matter—but a disturbance arose. On our way to the hotel some lads of the 'baser sort' followed us with taunts and derisive shouts. Finding that this produced no effect, they began pelting us with sand and gravel. Finally, the doctor was struck square in the back with an old sandal. It was a cruel blow. He turned upon the boys and administered a reprimand, in which something of temper was not wanting. However, the effect was not unfavorable. The good man did feel the indignity keenly, and it was a long time before he could dismiss the occurrence from his mind."

Another course of preaching (in 1885) was at Mishima in the Hakone mountains. Here the militant pagans tried to interfere with the propagation of Christian truth, by getting the policemen to come and break up the meeting. Their design was frustrated by Mr. Verbeck's thorough knowledge of human nature, whether priestly, official, or commonplace, and of the law, and his firmness demanding its enforcement. Rev. Mr. Yasukawa was especially useful in checkmating the reactionaries.

The "upper" classes in Japan who looked down on the religion of Jesus and the "uppish" folks at the seaports who opposed aggressive Christianity, were chaining themselves to a corpse, just as the old Latins of the decadent Roman empire did. The new life of New Japan is linked with Him who came that men might have life more abundantly. As opposed to the reactionaries, both native and foreign, Christianity had begun to win the respect of the leading thinkers of the nation headed in popularity by

Verbeck of Japan

Fukuzawa, whose remarkable articles in his own and other newspapers attracted great attention. To his multifarious labors, Fukuzawa—the great apostle of western civilization in Japan, adds that of editor. He is one of the most voluminous of writers, his pen touching every subject with grace and force. Hosts of his friends on either side of the Pacific rejoice in the recognition of his work for the good of his countrymen in the gift from the emperor in connection with the crown prince's wedding, in May, 1900, of 50,000 yen, in lieu of a patent of nobility, which would have been gladly conferred, only that Fukuzawa preferred to remain a commoner.

Heart sorrows were happily not frequent in the case of this earnest missionary, but sometimes they came with crushing force. On January 26, 1885, he wrote: "I have but just time to let you know that last night we received the very sad news from California, that early in December last we lost our darling boy, Guido, age sixteen." The incident turned his mind to Eastern America which he longed to visit with leisure.

He wrote February 1, 1885, of his longings, but he could not go as yet, for there was just below the horizon the sun of constitutional Japan. Already in the refraction of faith, Guido Verbeck saw the full glory and rejoiced. He saw the long bright day already dawning. Not in vain had he a generation before taught his young pupils, now statesmen high in office, the New

Testament and the Constitution of the United States.

"There is another consideration which has a good deal of weight with me. The year 1890, which is to witness the establishment of the new constitution of this empire, and promises to be a period of immense importance to the Master's great cause and to the church and mission work, is gradually drawing near. In that year (1890), and the year preceding it, I should be very loath to be absent from the field and work."

This time he must go home at the mission's charges, for Guido Verbeck never saved anything. Whether his salary were a thousand or seven thousand dollars, they were all winged, in some way, or put to flight by his constant generosity, his self-forgetfulness, and lack of worldly mindedness and business skill.

"Since I was first sent to Japan in 1859, this will be the first time that I leave it at the mission's expense. In 1873 I travelled at my own expense; and in 1878 I returned home with my family and lived a year with them in California, altogether at my own charges. It was only since my leaving California, in August, 1879, that I became again chargeable to the mission both for myself and family."

Two years passed away in steady toil at Bible translation, evangelistic tours, on the work of hymnology, in teaching in the theological school, and in manifold labors connected with the organization and maintenance of Christian Churches.

Verbeck of Japan

His special work amid many was the translation of the Psalms, a happy task, which on the 19th of July, 1887, he completed, finishing on that day, as usual, five hours' toil in the study.

Another long tour was made in Kiushiu in 1888. When he wrote about this he was hoping to come to America to spend a year in one of the intellectual and religious centres, New York or Philadelphia, for his own and his family's sake. For nearly two years past he had suffered an impediment of his right hand, brought on by a sprain made in his daily gymnastics. This second Kiushiu tour was taken, leaving Tokio October 9th, and returning December 7th. Two weeks of his time were spent at Kagoshima in Satsuma. Everywhere he found Japanese hearers, as in the days of the Reformation, when Bible exposition was new and the message was fresh, ready to listen by the hour. On one occasion he wrote:

"This endurance on the part of Japanese audiences (especially rural audiences), at preaching and lecturing assemblies, while it taxes to the utmost the powers and resources of the speaker, especially when he is unassisted, on the other hand also helps him not a little; for he need have no fear of exhausting the patience of his hearers. When there is a number of speakers, there is nothing in the way of having, with due notice beforehand, a well attended meeting from two o'clock in the afternoon till ten o'clock at night, with a pause of an hour or an hour and a-half for supper intervening.

"In the evening we again found the same excessively cold theatre well filled, the audience being even more attentive and well behaved than on the previous day. Mr. Hayashi gave a spirited address on the Superiority of Christian Ethics; Mr. Miura lectured on the Person and Character of Christ; and finally I treated of the Survival of the Fittest from a Christian point of view, explaining the fittest to be whatever is most nearly conformed to God's will; and inferring thence the survival of Christianity after the downfall of idolatry, Buddhism, and all false religions and philosophies. The lectures, though fewer in number, being longer than those of the night before, we again retired at a late hour."

The inevitable change comes when the gospel message is less of a novelty. A Japanese pastor in June, 1900, tells me that everywhere in the cities the native Christians increasingly like short sermons.

The biographer feels that he would hardly be forgiven if his work should not show some familiarity with Dr. Verbeck's commonplace books—"Varia," he labelled them—and sermon notes. In his system, pencil marks of various colors meant much to his own eye when preaching. The same system of mnemonics and association helped him in reading. Dr. Verbeck was an omnivorous reader, with a memory of wonderfully retentive power. Below are a very few anecdotes, notes, incidents, and illustrations jotted down in his thesauros.

NOT NUMBERS ONLY!!!

Do not rely on the number of adherents to any religious faith, in order to recommend it as superior to others; but rather on present vitality (not activity only); on recent growth (in the presence of modern science and politics); on its predominance as a force in building up useful and beneficent institutions; on its spiritual faithfulness; on its spiritual and material sacrifices; on its being a power for good in society; on its shining lights in the past, and especially present; on its history and historical development; on its accord with reason; on its nearness to God's will and word.

"ACCUSING GOD AND PROVIDENCE"

A man, having spent his money riotously, comes to a town, and having nothing special to do, walked about the streets sight-seeing. At last he begins to feel hungry, and passing a baker shop, he puts his hand into his pocket for money to buy some bread. Finding none, he bursts out in anger: "Bah, this is a miserable town; I have not even a penny to buy a little loaf of bread! A curse upon it!!!"

People having no intellectual coin in their heads, take it out in vilifying Zion, and the Kingdom!

Preacher and Translator

SIMILARITY OF "THINKING YOU HAVE" AND "REALLY HAVING"

Mrs. D. B. McCartee sent a relation a sum of money to buy herself some "Satsuma ware" in New York city. After a time Mrs. McCartee received a letter from New York stating that the "Satsuma ware" had been bought and that her friend was exceedingly happy with its possession. A year or two later, the relation in New York died, and when another year later Mrs. McCartee went home and called at the relation's house, she was shown the "Satsuma ware" which had given so much satisfaction, and, lo and behold! the ware was only a homemade imitation of Satsuma!!!

THE BEST PLOUGH

There is no "best plough." Different soils require very different ploughs! So with methods of teaching and preaching; and hence the use and usefulness of denominational differences! Plough well, plough deep,—this is the great thing!

CROW IN DARK AND UNBORN BABY

At a country meeting a man got up and left the hall saying, "Why, this is like seeing a crow fly on a dark night and hearing an unborn baby cry."

WHEN MEN FALL FOUL OF EACH OTHER IN PERSONALITIES

An owl perched on a high roof. Two men were to kill or knock it down. To make sure,

323

one of them was to shoot an arrow from one side of the house, while the other was to throw a big stone from the opposite side. Result: The stone killed the archer and the arrow killed the stone thrower; but the owl sat still and winked her eyes.

MEMORY

The perspective of memory is in many cases the reverse of ocular perspective:—the farther back in the past, the bigger things appear, as in the events and experiences of youth recalled.

"THE WORD IS EVERLASTING"

In posts and sign boards in Japan, upon which the legend is written with China ink containing charcoal powder, it is often seen that the wood between the writing is worn away by time and weather of years, while the writing abides intact, slightly in relief above the surrounding wood. So the Word of God upon the tablets of the ages.

ANECDOTE

Dr. Thompson preached on the sinfulness of all men, "none righteous, no not one," before a large Japanese audience, when a "soshi" sprang to his feet, bawling out: "What! do you mean to say that our emperor too is a sinner?" The doctor was startled and did not know, on the spur of the moment, what to say, or how to deal with this unexpected interruption, when he was as unexpectedly helped out of the difficulty as it

had been sprung upon him. A lawyer (once a believer himself, somewhat under the influence of liquor) also sprang up and with the air of saying something quite incontrovertible (of course) declared that the soshi (interlocutor) was quite wrong, since Christianity and the emperor had no relation whatever with each other.

PREPARING SERMONS TO LAST

I know a preacher who says that he dislikes to preach any of his sermons over again. The fact I believe to be, that his sermons are not prepared to last; they all are of a more or less "occasional" character,—have no original permanency in them. There are, of course, and there must be "occasional" addresses and sermons. But generally sermons should be, from the first, prepared so as to be fit for repeated use;—not indeed, verbally throughout the same, but substantially. This rule will hold good especially in circuit and in evangelistic preaching. Care and time bestowed upon the first preparation of sermons will save much time and labor in the future.

The year 1889 Dr. Verbeck carried out his plan of going to America, visiting a great many of the Reformed churches both East and West, speaking in Dutch and English. He remained in the United States until July 16th, sailing from Manhattan Island in the steamer City of New York, with his two daughters, staying at Zeist, but visiting in one great tour the principal cities of the Netherlands and speaking in many of the churches great and small. He enjoyed intensely this visit to the fatherland and especially that made to Delft, where is the Westminster Abbey of Japan, containing the tombs of the princes of the House of Orange, and of Hugo Grotius. On August 16th, he was taken ill with a light paralytic attack on his right side, but quickly recovering he fulfilled his engagements, which had been carefully arranged in the tour by the minister of the great orphanage at Neerbosch. He returned to Japan via America and sailed at three P. M. January 13th, 1891, by steamer Oceania, having among his fellow-passengers to Japan, Dr. and Mrs. Nitobe. His letter of February 23d, 1891, says: "Here I am at work again almost as if I had not been away at all,—four lectures a week, requiring about six hours of preparation each, and preaching on Sundays—and I can assure you it is pleasant to have regular work again."

XVI

A MAN WITHOUT A COUNTRY

AFTER correspondence with the State Department at Washington, Mr. Verbeck found from Secretary of State, James G. Blaine, that he could not get citizenship from the United States government, so on arriving in Japan in 1891, he wrote to the Japanese Department of Foreign Affairs. The correspondence explains all and needs no comment from the biographer. Secretary Awoki was formerly Minister to Germany, an Enomoto student in Holland in the early sixties and the same whom we heard in 1868, later Minister to Russia and a statesman of great ability.

While in the United States, Dr. Verbeck had endeavored to secure American citizenship, but there were found to be insuperable obstacles and Secretary James G. Blaine referred the matter to the American Minister in Japan to see what could be done. The issue is best set forth by showing the correspondence. Mr. Verbeck trusted the Japanese even to willingness to become a citizen of the empire and his faith was rewarded according to his works.

Tokio, March 3, 1891.
"TO HIS EXCELLENCY THE VISCOUNT AWOKI,
"Minister of Foreign Affairs.
"SIR:—Having recently returned to this empire after a temporary absence, I find that, having

327

left the Netherlands, my native country, about forty years ago to come to the United States of America, I have legally lost my original nationality, and although I took the necessary steps in order to be naturalized in the United States, my residence there was not of sufficient duration to mature my naturalization in that country.

"If there existed in this empire laws for the naturalization of foreigners, I should under these circumstances gladly avail myself of them. But in the absence of such laws, I take the great liberty to request of your Excellency to be so very kind, if possible, to use such means as your Excellency may deem proper and suitable to have me placed under the protection of the Supreme Government of this empire.

"I have but little to recommend myself to your Excellency's favor, unless I be allowed to state, for the benefit of those who may perhaps not know it, that I have resided and labored in this empire for more than thirty years and spent one-half of this long period in the service of both the former and the present government of Japan.

"Hoping that your Excellency will very kindly consider my request, I have the honor to be, sir, your Excellency's most obedient servant,

"G. F. VERBECK."

" *Tokio, July* 4, 1891.

"TO THE HON. GUIDO F. VERBECK,

"SIR:—In consequence of your having lost your original status as a subject of Holland without having acquired the rights and privileges of a citizen of the United States of America, you are left without any national status; and desiring to live under the protection of our Imperial Government, you did—in the month of March of the present year—make an application for this purpose to the former Minister of Foreign Affairs, which was endorsed by him.

"You have resided in our empire for several tens of years, the ways in which you have exerted yourself for the benefit of our empire are by no means few, and you have been always beloved and respected by our officials and people. It is therefore with great pleasure that I send you, on a separate sheet, the special passport which is desired and which I trust will duly reach you. Furthermore, the special passport above referred to will be of force and effect for one year dating from this day, and permission is granted you to renew and exchange the same annually.

"Respectfully,

"ENOMOTO TAKEAKI,

"Minister of Foreign Affairs."

(Translated from the original
  by Dr. D. B. McCartee.)

SPECIAL PASSPORT (Translation)

"G. F. Verbeck, Order of Merit 3d class; Maria Verbeck; (here follows a list of seven children);—the persons above named being under obligation, while in this empire, to obey the imperial laws, and regulations in the same manner as the subjects of the empire, shall be permitted from July 4th, 1891, until July 3d, 1892, to travel freely throughout the empire in the same manner as the subjects of the same, and to sojourn and reside in any locality."

(Seal of the Department of Foreign Affairs).

'*Tokio, July* 6, 1891.
" To his EXCELLENCY VISCOUNT ENOMOTO,
      " Minister of Foreign Affairs.

"SIR:—This is simply to express my most sincere thanks to your Excellency and the Viscount Awoki for your great kindness in assisting me out of the peculiar difficulty of my political status (or rather want of status) by sending me your Excellency's very kind letter of the 4th instant and a special passport, which places me—in gracious compliance with my somewhat bold request of the month of March last past—under the powerful protection of the empire of Japan. I assure your Excellency that I cannot express sufficiently my obligation for this special favor and honor of which I shall avail myself always with the utmost care and prudence. I have the honor to be, sir, your Excellency's most obedient servant,   G. F. VERBECK."

The honor thus conferred upon an alien is absolutely unique in the modern history of Japan. Dr. Verbeck wrote home:

" This solution of my great difficulty has given me much rest. In fact, I could not well have

特許状

外國人

結婚
無シ

妻

長男

二男

三男

四男

五男

長女

二女

右者帝國内ヲ旅行スルコトヲ許ス
各地方官ハ本國法律規則ヲ遵守シ
帝國ノ臣民ト同様ニシテ帝國臣民ノ義務ヲ擔當スル者ニ付
外國人ヲシテ帝國臣民ノ義務ヲ

明治二十五年七月四日
外務

明治二十四年自三月三日由三月三日至
許ス 旅行
明治二十四年七月四日
準

PASSPORT FOR DR. VERBECK AND FAMILY.

A Man Without a Country

continued in this country, unless it had been solved in some such way as now adopted. If anything I have obtained much more than was absolutely necessary in the case. I assure you I am very thankful to the divine Disposer of all these matters. Doubts have been finely cleared up and faith has been confirmed."

The Japan *Mail*, the ablest newspaper published in Japan, thus commented upon this transaction:

"His case is also well worth the consideration of those who so strenuously object to the idea of submitting to Japanese jurisdiction. Dr. Verbeck, one of the leading sinologues in Japan, has had exceptional opportunities, during his thirty years' residence, of judging the disposition of the people and estimating the nature of their institutions. Yet we find him unhesitatingly placing himself, his wife, and his family under Japanese jurisdiction. The act of such a man seems to us more eloquent than the talk of a hundred cavillers who raise a barrier of imaginary perils in the path of free intercourse."

Even at the risk of repetition, it is well to know fully of Dr. Verbeck's manner among a people to whom etiquette is almost a religion, and with many of whom it is a substitute for faith and worship. One who knew him well wrote in 1900:

"There is no doubt that Dr. Verbeck exercised great tact when forced into association with a certain class of Japanese men—the official class— who are to this day, afraid of other missionaries

—afraid even now, because most of these think they *must* force religion upon every Japanese they meet, regardless of time, place, and circumstance. I am wrong to say 'most of them'—but I am sorry to say there are some others of the —— type, though he is the most notorious in reputation among the foreigners. Dr. Verbeck employed the reserve and courtesy that men of the world, who have *savoir-faire*, show in their intercourse with other gentlemen. This attracted the sincere respect and confidence of the Japanese. They were not frightened off by dread of insidious and too personal attacks. At the same time Dr. Verbeck never flattered the natives; he was always direct in his truthfulness; being polite too, always. This is admitted by all who knew him—natives and foreigners. It has been, and still is, almost impossible to reach with Christianity a certain class of Japanese men, but to gain their respect and confidence, as a Christian gentleman, and to be sought for advice, are great victories."

Another secret of his power with a people naturally suspicious and distrustful is revealed in a letter to a friend in 1871. Declining his request in one way, Dr. Verbeck gratified it in another by assuming the trouble, responsibility and expense himself.

"One of my principles in dealing with the Japanese, and one to which I attribute a large part of the confidence reposed in me by them, is 'never to ask personal favors of them.' I do for

A Man Without a Country

them what under the circumstances I can, and am content with what they consider as my due in return. This principle, which by long use has become almost a second nature with me, I feel reluctant to lay aside. They have learned to trust me as a safe man, as regards asking personal favors, and I should not like to see their confidence shaken."

For about ten years, on and off, Dr. Verbeck taught in the Meiji Gaku-in or the College and Theological School supported by the churches of Reformed Christianity holding the Presbyterial system of government and doctrine. He wrote in 1891:

"I shall mention my branches of study in the school. They are (or were, I hope): Introduction to the Old Testament; D° to the New Testament; Old Testament exegesis; Pastoral Theology and Homiletics. I taught all these in Japanese, although for the Old and New Testament Introduction the students had English text-books. But all of these studies, except Homiletics, could be taught in English and with English text-books, the best English student in the class acting as professor's interpreter."

It cannot be said that Dr. Verbeck greatly enjoyed this sort of indoor work. Furthermore this was a period of doctrinal change, of the ever new theology fulfilling the old, and it is not certain that the grand veteran could see eye to eye with the younger and possibly less wise men. The ebb and flow of opinion in the native churches troubled him. He was as much disturbed at the new development of thought as was Washington with Jefferson and Hamilton in his cabinet, pitted like game cocks against each other. How he looked at the situation may be best shown by his comments on a typical gathering of aliens and natives, as found in a document written in 1898, just before his death, and left among his papers, no names being recognizable. He heads the article as follows:

AN EXTRAORDINARY EPISODE

In the History of the Church of Christ in Japan

(After rough notes of the time—1888)

The thing happened at the time of the calamitous courtship between the Union Church of Christ in Japan and the native Congregational Church, with the view to bring about a union of these two churches. In fact, it was at about the time that the lengthy negotiations seemed to draw toward a culmination, but when it was yet uncertain whether it would be "on" or "off." . . .

At that critical time, the leaders in this movement . . . became aware that many of the pastors, evangelists, elders, deacons, and of the laity of the Itchi-Kyokwai were still strongly opposed to the proposed union with the Congregational Church. One chief reason of this aversion was known to lie in the fact that the proposed union would necessitate the relinquishment,

in large part at least, of their church standards.
These people had been sedulously taught that the
Westminster Confession and Shorter Catechism
and the Heidelberg Catechism contained a statement of sound Christian doctrine; they had
adopted these as their church standards many
years before (1879) and, as a church, had prospered by them; they had learned to regard these
documents as indispensable instruments for the
upbuilding and maintenance of their church, and
many of their best men had become warmly attached to them. On these accounts it might
easily happen that a majority could not be gotten,
when the Union scheme should be submitted to
these good people for a final vote.

In this state of things, the so-called leaders
conceived the bright idea that a special but in-
formal meeting should be called, for the sole purpose of instructing the deluded conservatives in
this case, so as to show them the futility of their
own or any other extensive church standards.
. . . A large gathering of pastors, evangelists,
elders, deacons, and laymen was expected. The
meeting was to be held in the centrally situated
Nihon-Bashi Church. Not being in sympathy
with the object of the meeting, I at first did not
intend to go, but at the last moment I made up
my mind to attend. When I arrived at the
church, I found it quite full of a respectable lot of
people and all in readiness to open the meeting.
Before I had taken a seat, Mr. Iroha moved that I
should take the chair, which I could not well help

doing. The chief, in fact, the only speaker was Mr. Nihohe. . . .

I did not note down at the time all the arguments used to show the futility of extensive Creeds and Catechisms in Japan; but they were such as one often hears from those who do not like full statements of doctrine such as are usually found in these documents. The general trend and tenor of the address covered most, if not all, of the following arguments, although perhaps quite differently or not so fully stated as here set down:

THAT Creeds and Catechisms are not Christianity—(who says that they are?);—THAT all that is in them is already supplied in the Bible—(true, but generally how difficult for unlearned neophytes out of heathenism to find, rightly collate and comprehend!);—THAT after all the final appeal in matters of doctrine and ecclesiastical practice is to the Bible—(nobody maintains that it is not);—THAT they are the outcome of the ancient and post-reformation history of the church, of which the Japanese know nothing and with which they have nothing to do—(much of their value lies in the fact that they are of historical origin and not merely theoretically concocted affairs);—THAT a large part of them is intended to guard against various errors and heresies of those distant ages, quite unknown in Japan, this large part of them being therefore quite inapplicable and valueless here, in fact, perhaps rather suggestive and dangerous—(not so

A Man Without a Country

unknown as Mr. Nihohe imagines, and sure to
spring up here too, from the perversity of the
same human nature!);—THAT too detailed Catechisms and Creeds are rather calculated to keep
people out of the church—(it is not desirable, nay
rather dangerous to have people in the church
who are not pretty well grounded in the faith;
besides, denominations with the most pronounced
tenets) . . . the Episcopalians with their
prayer-book, the Baptists with their immersion,
the Methodists with their organic connection
with a foreign church (that bugbear of Mr.
Nihohe, Tochiri, Nuruwo, Wakayo & Co.), these
denominations have in recent years prospered
better in Japan than the Union Church of Christ,
(comprising the Presbyterian and Reformed
Churches) with its little skeleton of a confession.
THAT there is much in them not essential to salvation—(the same may be said of the Old Testament, and besides, what is not essential to salvation may be essential to the education, harmoniza-
tion, and the keeping together of a well ordered
church);—THAT full church standards are very
good things for those that like them, but that it
would not be right to force them upon every-
body—(are they forced upon anybody in the
United States?);—THAT a man might be well up
in Creeds and yet not be a Christian, and on the
other hand, a man might not know any Creed or
Catechism and yet be an exemplary Christian—
(one might say the same of the Old Testament
saints);—THAT a simple faith in Jesus Christ is all

that is requisite in order to personal salvation—
(that is what our Catechisms teach: Shorter Catechism, question 38 and Heidelberg Catechism,
question 21).

As I said before, I was called to take the chair.
Again and again, I felt like jumping up and beg
Mr. Nihohe to stop; for I knew that incalculable
harm was being done all the time. This I could
clearly see in the faces of the native Christians
present, some on one side of the question under
discussion and some on the other, some trium-
phant and some despondent,—one elder actually
shedding bitter tears. I contained myself, but
was filled with amazement, sitting on thorns, as
it were, all the time. . . .

More than once have I listened to injudicious
remarks from platform or pulpit, but never to
any so much as these of Mr. Nihohe's at that
memorable meeting in the Nihon-Bashi Church,
now about ten years ago, addressed to a gathering of weak believers but just emerged—if quite
emerged—from the darkness, the uncleanness
and the delusion of heathenism. These people
had as yet but little knowledge of Christianity
and of the Church of Christ, beyond what they
had at one time gratefully gathered from those
very church standards which were now to
be taken away from them. It was a pitiable
case! . . .

How silly to judge of the educational and
spiritual wants of Japanese proselytes by his
own highly privileged case! Here Mr. Tsunera

A Man Without a Country

was far ahead of Mr. Nihohe. Mr. Tsunera had the gift (it almost amounts to that), very useful to a missionary, of placing himself in the mental condition of a heathen and then dealing with the natives somewhat from their own blank and obscure standpoint. This gift seems to be totally lacking in Mr. Nihohe. And then out of the forty millions of this nation, Mr. Nihohe knows only one man, a superior specimen, Mr. Tochiri —and him he does not know thoroughly. To judge of all Japanese converts by a man like Mr. Tochiri is foolish and can only lead to the most mistaken conclusions.

A highly privileged person like Mr. Nihohe, the son of a godly minister, brought up in a pious family, educated in one of the foremost colleges in America, graduated from a celebrated theological seminary, ordained to the ministry, proficient in teaching and preaching, may well say for himself: "I don't take much stock in Creeds." But when he goes on to infer that therefore Creeds are equally dispensable to Japanese converts, most of them pretty full yet of all kinds of heathen notions, having as yet a very limited knowledge of the Scriptures, impatient of all mental and moral restraint or discipline, even in church matters, fond of a loose happy-go-lucky sort of way,—THIS is, according to my experience, the height of injudiciousness and very bad logic withal.

The fluent reader may laugh at spelling-books; the advanced mathematician may speak scornfully of the multiplication-table; the clever author and orator may well dispense with common school grammars, a native or old resident of New York has no need of a map to find his way, and he who plays Beethoven and Gounod's music may well poke fun at piano instruction books. So likewise Mr. Nihohe, if he feels in the mood of it, may say: "Creeds are of no use to me." But when he further reasons that because he can do very well without fully detailed church standards, therefore Japanese neophytes can do so too, he makes a most egregious blunder!

Dr. Verbeck spent many months with his fellow church-builders upon the constitution of the Union Church in Japan, giving much time also to preaching tours in various parts of the empire. In one of these tours he traversed the ultramontaine region of Buddhism on the west coast, his itinerary passing through Fukui in Echizen. Vastly changed from the romantic picturesque capital of a feudal principality, it is now the centre of the new *habutai* or light silk industry.

Again in 1893, he found the need of surcease from exhausting labors. Crossing the Pacific, he wrote from Alameda, Cal., August 18, 1893:

"I was glad, how glad I cannot say, at last to be with wife and children once more and have enjoyed myself exceedingly since my arrival. And yet, strange to say, there are a few things I seem to miss here. Chief among these is the moisture and consequent verdure of Japan. Here, at this season, all is draught and dust, and what to me is real cold. At night the thermometer down to 50° and in the daytime seldom over 70°."

We find him back at work again, writing from Tokio, November 13, 1893. His letter shows that the Japanese, passing through their over-conscious period of unripeness, Chauvinism, and self-conceit, were extremely, even ridiculously, sensitive to criticism. The Japanese never decorate their critics who criticise publicly. None more than the thoroughly genuine Japanese, who love truth and righteousness, even more than wealth, offices, honors, or decorations laugh at this over-sensitiveness of their countrymen. It vividly reminds Americans also of our own "green apple" stage, when our grandfathers and grandmothers took the criticisms of trans-Atlantic travellers and book-makers so very painfully.

Dr. Verbeck wrote:

"Although, of course, in many respects I regret not having been able to see the Columbian Fair,—this regret I share with tens of thousands, —yet if I had been present at the 'Parliament,' I can now see that I should have been much embarrassed. The difficulty that would have beset me there is one that sufficiently troubles and hampers all of us here in our regular work. It lies in the fact that one cannot freely and frankly express one's real opinion in public about the Japanese without giving offence to them, and without more or less impairing one's usefulness among them. Everything said as well as written, about the Japanese in Europe or America, is sure to come back here in print. Under these circumstances it would have been very hazardous to correct or contradict in public the many mistaken and some utterly false statements made at the 'Parliament'; whereas, on the other hand, silence might and probably would have been construed as assent or approval. All this I escaped by not being present."

None of the glib statements of elegantly-dressed Japanese gentlemen, or priests in picturesque garb at Chicago or elsewhere, could blind this profound student of human nature as to the reality of morals and religion in Japan, and as to their need of repentance, faith, and a righteousness exceeding that even of " living Buddhas " and Shinto gods, and "divinely descended" rulers. Of the general situation he wrote:

" While there is not a little to regret in the present state of the Japanese churches, there is a good deal of activity shown just now. The autumn is always a good time for holding all kinds of meetings; but this fall there is an unusual number of so-called series of preaching and Christian lecture meetings in all the denominations in Tokio. Some of these are held every night for a week together, others for three or four nights, and so forth. Usually one foreigner and two Japanese speak at these meetings. I have attended a few, and last Saturday a church dedication, and am sure that the Divine blessing attended us."

Of the less felicitous phases of church life and growth, and of the personal peculiarities of missionary men and women, we need not here speak, except to say that Dr. Verbeck's experience of them led him to formulate the following, which I find among his papers:

THE SCIENCE OF MISSIONS

The Science of Missions is (should be), based upon the Holy Scriptures, church history, mission practice, and human nature (?)

MISSIONARY CODE

(Based upon the Science of Missions)

1. A mission in the foreign field should be, as nearly as possible, a homogeneous body, and should, in all matters of missionary policy and methods, as well as of doctrine, act as one body and in perfect harmony.

("United we stand, divided we fall." "Eendracht maakt macht." "Every kingdom divided against itself is brought to desolation, and every city or house divided against itself shall not stand." Numerous and calamitous difficulties have arisen between the native church and missions solely on account of a want of unanimity in some or another of the missions.)

2. In order to this end, the Home Boards should ascertain of every applicant or candidate for the foreign field, whether he is disposed at

all time to submit to a majority of the mission to which he is to be sent, on all questions of mission policy, methods and work, and whether he is resolved to teach and preach nothing at variance or in conflict with the standards of the Church which commissions him.

3. All matters that cannot be satisfactorily arranged or settled by the mission in the field, shall be referred and submitted to the Home Board for its assent or decision.

4. In all cases where a missionary shall feel himself wronged or aggrieved by the action or decision of his mission, he shall have the right of appealing (with the knowledge of his mission), to the Home Board, in reference to the matter in question.

On the subject of the necessity of creeds and confessions of faith, Dr. Verbeck's convictions were strong. He wrote in 1898:

"My opinion on this point is that, in a community or nation generally and from of old permeated by Christianity and full of Churches, the Bible alone might perhaps be safely made a Church's sole rule of faith and life. But on heathen soil to endeavor to organize and build up with safety a Christian church without, or next to without, binding church symbols, seems to me about as wise and feasible a proceeding, as for a mariner to undertake to cross the Pacific ocean with a valuable cargo and a hundred human lives in his charge, and safely to enter the Golden Gate without compass, chart and nautical almanac,

—simply by the guidance of 'that marvellous curtain of blue and gold,' the starry heaven overhead!"

On July 23, 1894, he again surveys the situation.

"The general results of the recent meetings of the Dai-Kwai [General Synod], as well as of the Council of the Cooperating Missions, you have been informed of by the usual channels. As regards the so-called 'Plan,' it was more than once loudly called for in the Council, but it never came under serious discussion. Of this I was glad, because there was no occasion for its being introduced at this time. The 'Plan' has already done much of its intended work indirectly and silently. When first gotten up, it was not done 'in a corner'; it was widely distributed among the foreign missionaries and the native pastors of all denominations, especially of the Congregationalists. The comparatively happy tone that prevailed at the last General Conference of the Kumi-ai Church, the three resolutions above referred to, and much of the action at the recent meetings of Dai-Kwai and Council are all more or less traceable to the 'Plan.' By means of the 'Plan,' the eyes of those hot-headed brethren who used to talk of sending home the missionaries as no more needed, were unexpectedly opened. They now saw what had never occurred to them before,—namely, that if they carried things beyond all reason and endurance, the despised foreign missionaries might themselves solve the difficulty in a very practical though un-looked for way.

"But I must stop this, for I find myself drift-ing into matter that should not be touched upon without time and space to substantiate it, and this would lead me back to my rejected sixteen pages of foolscap."

Two or three more quotations from Dr. Ver-beck's letters, showing his evangelistic zeal must close this "record of foundation work," and then shall be told the story of his last days on earth.

Under date of June 4, 1895, he wrote:

"As doubtless you have heard ere this, Mr. Ballagh left Yokohama for a home furlough on the 17th May. At a regular meeting sometime previous to his departure, the mission agreed that I should, during his absence, take the charge and oversight of his evangelistic work in the country districts. The main part of this work lies in the province of Shinshu, where there are six stations, each of which is occupied by a Japanese evangel-ist. Each of these stations has its out-stations worked from the centre to which they belong. Three of the six stations (Komoro, Uyeda, and Nagano) lie on a railroad line and are accessible from Tokio at small expense. The other three stations, situated from thirty to forty miles south of the railroad line, are reached by pretty rough roads and mountain passes. The whole of the Shinshu field is geographically well defined, but capable of considerable extension within its own limits.

A Man Without a Country

"The other parts of our country work lie scattered in various directions. A couple of stations across the bay, opposite Yokohama; some around the base of Mt. Fuji; a few more near Yokohama; and one station (Seto) a dozen miles from Nagoya, make up the list.

"At Uyeda I had the pleasure of meeting Miss Brokaw and Miss Deyo, whom I found toiling away zealously at their promising work among the women of this town and neighborhood.

"Silk culture, like time and tide, waits for no man. Shinshu is one of Japan's chief silk districts, and its people are exceedingly busy at certain seasons and almost quite disengaged at others. Hence we have to conform the times of our work here to this state of things. At the next propitious season, I hope to do some good work at all of the stations in a less hurried way than I was obliged to follow on this tour. I was absent from home just a fortnight and preached nine or ten times. May this labor, light and easy though it be, be not in vain in the Lord."

XVII

"WEARY WITH THE MARCH OF LIFE"

DR. VERBECK aged visibly during the last year of his life. He had lived out two-thirds of a century, years of intense activity. From the first, his constitution had been none of the strongest; and his wonderful life is another proof of the fact that what one accomplishes depends more on temperance and intelligent care of the health than on natural vigor.

In October, 1897, the physician forbade evangelistic tours, and it was a great disappointment to the doctor that he dared not undertake a proposed trip to Kiushiu. The day after Christmas a complication of chronic ailments prostrated him, and from that time on he was never quite himself. Gradually, however, he seemed to improve; only there were new pains in the chest that were supposed to be caused by indigestion. He was seized with terrible paroxysms at times, but would not go to bed and took his regular exercise whenever possible. In Tokio he still continued to preach, the last time on the night of February 26th.

One of the last works upon which Dr. Verbeck was engaged was the preparation of an address in English to the emperor of Japan, on the occasion of the presentation of a handsome copy of the Bible in Japanese, the result of many years of the united labors of Verbeck, Hepburn, Fyson and many others.

The other work, which filled heart and hand within a few hours of his call to higher service, was his reply to the fourteen questions submitted in writing to him, by Mr. Robert E. Speer, on the present state of Christianity in Japan.

In this paper, one of the last of his utterances, this unflattering truth-teller, ever loving and kind, gives his impressions of the Japanese man, uttering his faith also in the coming better man of Japan, " created anew in Christ Jesus."

Probably one of the last, if not the very last of his letters, is the following:

" *Tokio, 3 Aoi-cho*, Feb. 24, 1898.
"DEAR DR. COBB:

"I am exceedingly obliged to you for your very kind assurances of sympathy with me in my poor state of health. Never having been sick in bed for a week together during thirty-five years in this country, I may be somewhat over-cowardly in being now seriously 'under the weather'; at all events, I probably feel it more than those who are more frequently ailing. At the bottom of my ailments is hypertrophy of the prostatic gland, consequently impending inflammation of the bladder and the like. I think that I should be for at least some months under a specialist or in a sanitarium,—very much as a watch out of order is put in the hands of a watch-maker. But this is difficult to carry into effect here.

" For two things I am particularly thankful. I never suffer from headache. If I did, this would be likely to knock me up sooner than almost any other common ailment. My head is in good and clear condition. And the other good thing is that warm weather is coming near. This last winter I have suffered more from the cold than in any former year that I remember. I am already bene-fited by the somewhat milder air of these last weeks. In fact, I feel I am now able to lay out plans for some near country work. The fresh air and exercise on country touring always bene-fit me much. And a little later I hope to be blessed with strength enough to respond to two calls to more distant fields: Kochi and our large field in Kiushiu. These two calls came to me within the last ten days. And then there is our own Shinshiu field which is never off my mind.

" As to requesting Mr. Speer to keep my an-swers to his fourteen questions ' private,' it was and is almost a necessity. If some of the things in these answers were to be quoted in print and under my name, it would draw upon me a host of foes, Christian as well as non-Christian. I suppose you have seen my old friend Dr. Martin's book on China (A Cycle of Cathay) ? If a man should undertake to write a similar book on Japan and the Japanese, with but one-tenth, nay, one-twentieth, of its critical and personal reflections in it, he had better not think of ever coming again to this country. It might not be safe to do so.

"As regards writing on the inner history of the work of missions in Japan from the beginning, the difficulty is that it cannot well be done without becoming more or less "personal." But I shall bear your kind suggestion in mind, especially if I should be still further laid up at home.

"One important episode in the history of the Church of Christ (viz, the 'proofs' I referred to in my fourteen answers) I have ready and all typewritten to be sent off. But since . . . figures as the chief agent in it, I should have to let him see it before sending off, so as to enable him to defend his peculiar position in this matter, if he should deem it fit to do so. I could not do such a thing behind a man's back.

"By this same mail I send a letter to Mr. Speer. I requested him to let you see it 'as opportunity serves,' because there are some things in that letter I should like you to know.

"Once more thanking you for your friendly sympathy, I remain,

"Sincerely yours,

"G. F. VERBECK."

"Please to give my kindest regards to Dr. Amerman."

The machinery of physical life seemed to wear out very rapidly as the spring of 1898 approached, the heart and kidneys being especially weak.

Verbeck of Japan

On the 27th of February, with his daughter Emma, who for months had been his ministering angel, he was able to take a long ramble of about six miles. He went to Yokohama on the 3d of March to arrange with Mr. Ballagh a preaching tour in Idzu. On March 6th, the walk together of father and daughter was very short, and it was his last. On the 9th he sat up to dinner and played a game of chess with his daughter. He had marked ahead, in his diary, under date of Friday, March 18th, " Yoko. Lit. Soc. Personal Reminiscences," and was to have given this lecture in English before the ladies and gentlemen of the great seaport. How they would have so enjoyed hearing about a Japan now utterly vanished and a part of very ancient history.

It was not to be. At noon on the tenth, sitting in his study chair, attended by his body servant, he was just about to eat his usual light " tiffin " or noon meal, when the call to change worlds came and the machinery of life stopped. Verbeck of Japan was dead.

Of the last offices of affection, of " dust to dust," none has written so vividly as the Rev. James H. Ballagh, so long friend and fellow-worker.

" The death of our dear brother was as simple and as beautiful as his life. The weakness of the past few months developed some angina pectoris and his medical advisers counselled care and freedom from exposure. Growing restless

352

to be again in the work of visiting the field, he came to me a week ago to-day, with a little map carefully made, seeking light on the Idzu field, which he was desirous of visiting to make trial of strength for larger undertakings. In my study he met Dr. Fest, whose name he had down on his list for the purpose of consultation, if occasion offered. He narrated how that in coming up the bluff he had to stop several times owing to the sharp pain he felt in the region of his heart. He alluded to the fact that Dr. Brown died of that disease. Little did he or any of us think this was to be our last conference in the flesh, and a week later, at about the same hour, his body would be borne by devout men to his burial-place in Awoyama.

"All this occurred on the 26th anniversary of the organization of the Kaigan Church [The First Reformed Church organized in Japan, the edifice standing on Commodore Perry's treaty ground] when two important and largely attended meetings were in progress, one in P. M. in Van Schaick Hall, and the other at night in the Kaigan Church. Both full, if not crowded, with most blessed signs following.

"It was so sudden, and now that the interment and all is over, it appears more like a dream than a reality. We will come to realize our loss at our regular meetings, and in all counsels concerning mission work and in the more general inter-relations of all the missions, at which times he was looked upon as the Guiding Authority. That is well illustrated in the proceedings of the last Karuizawa Council Conference where, although he took hardly an observable part, his counsels are fully reflected in the council's action on cooperation of missions with the Church of Christ in Japan, and are so faithfully reflected in Mr. Speer's report ; a report I think that gave Dr. Verbeck more complete satisfaction than anything of the kind yet written."

Much of the preparation for the funeral and memorial services at the Shiba Church devolved upon Mr. Ballagh, who went at once to Tokio on receipt of the telegram announcing the sad news :

"Miss Verbeck I found very composed and receiving Japanese and all visitors, and attending to a host of calls regarding invitation to officials and friends of the Doctor. Some one or two hundred such were sent out. In consequence we had to request the schools, and 'bodies of people' not to come, inasmuch as a large foreign audience would gather together who could not be refused.

"Notice had been given to the foreign communities of 'No flowers,' but still a number of most beautiful wreaths and palm branches were sent in. These added much to the beauty of the casket and hearse en route to the Shiba Church, and to the cemetery at Awoyama. There were several carriages kindly furnished by friends. Bishop McKim taking Miss Verbeck and Rev. and Mrs. Wolfe, Dr. Verbeck's cousins—whose presence was a great comfort to Miss Verbeck and assistance in many ways.   One thing of importance was the bearing of the Imperial Order of the Third Class, on a velvet cushion.   This was placed on the casket in the church, and in consequence of the deceased being a decorated man, a company of soldiers escorted the body two whole miles to the cemetery and afterward saluted the grave with presentation of arms, etc.

"The church was filled below with officials and foreigners, or invited Japanese guests, and the galleries with ministers, workers, and a women's side with Bible women.   Rev. Wada, the pastor, read the ninetieth Psalm in Japanese, and was followed by prayer in English, by Dr. David Thompson.   It was inspired with reverence, awe, faith, and hope.   It was most helpful.   A Japanese hymn, tune Ward, a version of the forty-sixth Psalm followed, and then the address in Japanese by President Ibuka.   The latter was strong, succinct, and satisfactory; giving all the main facts of his life.   I followed in English, with a short appeal in Japanese at its close to the Japanese to follow him as he followed Christ. Then Father Okuno[1] poured out one of his touching, sympathetic, and glowing prayers.   The ninetieth Psalm 'Our God, our help in ages past, etc.,' sung in English, with a tribute in Japanese by the president of the Japanese Evangelical Alliance, Rev. T. Honda, also president of the

[1] One of the earliest converts, a fluent and forceful preacher, poet and hymn writer, the Nestor of the Reformed Church in Japan.

Verbeck of Japan

Awoyama College, one of our original church members, read in solemn tone, together with the benediction pronounced by the Rt. Rev. Bishop McKim brought the church services to an end.

"The master of ceremonies of the Imperial Court had sent a representative, Mr. Yamada, to attend to carrying the famous decoration, which was laid on a cushion and placed on the casket during the services.

"The procession was then formed and wended its way to the cemetery, two miles distant, led by a company of infantry marching four abreast with arms reversed.

"At the grave, Rev. Mr. Booth read impressively the burial service, Rev. Y. Ogawa, our first ordained elder and minister offered prayer in Japanese. After the hymn, 'Asleep in Jesus,' in Japanese, the benediction was pronounced by the Rev. Hugh Waddell of the United Presbyterian Scotch Mission. The evening was growing chilly and turning away in sadness and yet in a sense of gladness at his triumph and the great mercies of God experienced this day, I reached my home about 8 P. M.

"I found the rumor of 500 yen having graciously been given by His Majesty, the Emperor, was true. It came per master of ceremonies of the court, Mr. Sannomiya, who has taken so lively and fatherly interest in Miss Verbeck in all this affliction. The day I first visited her, he was there, kindly advising her about her father's decoration and that it was right to retain it. On go-

Monument of Dr. Verbeck, erected by the grateful Japanese.

ing out he was introduced to me, and said with tears in his eyes, ' I am so sorry.' I replied, 'Not for Dr. Verbeck, but for those who are left.' I am informed he attended the services at the church, though I did not observe him.

" I felt happy to have had two short prayers over my dear brother's body; one with my wife and Mrs. Wolfe yesterday ; and the other in Japanese with a number of Japanese brethren ere the cover was to be fastened over his noble and peaceful form forever, nay! till lighted up at the resurrection word.

"The city government of Tokio sent the late Dr. Verbeck's family a receipt for a perpetual lease of the little plot in which he lies buried. Claimed by three nations, but a citizen of none, he has found for his weary body a final resting-place in Japan; and Japan has not failed to show due appreciation of the honor.

" Dr. Whitney and others propose a memorial service for Dr. Verbeck should be held, owing to the fact many were not apprized of the death, and bodies of people had been requested not to come to the church service. It is therefore truly necessary to give an opportunity for expression of the popular and Christian grief. Miss Verbeck does not object under the circumstances. So we propose to hold it Saturday 19th, 2 P. M. at the Y. M. C. A. Hall, Kanda, Tokio. It is possible Sir Ernest Satow may consent to preside as he is an excellent Japanese scholar, and that would be suitable if the services be in Japanese.

Verbeck of Japan

" A very striking fact comes with peculiar power to me now in connection with the long delayed presentation of the copy of the Bible to H. M. the emperor. Dr. Verbeck at the request of the Bible Societies' committee wrote the address to the emperor, and it has been beautifully engrossed in German text on Vellum. Now it strikes me it will prove a most welcome and prized gift by H. M. coming from one so honored by H. M. and all his people. Is not this a fitting sequel to a life so singular in humility and devotion to be able not only to disarm prejudice from the minds of the Government of Japan, but to present to H. M. a copy of that Blessed Word of God upon which all his own hopes were founded for eternity ?

"Several points of interest not dwelt upon in account of Dr. Verbeck's funeral service in my notes of Saturday night may now be added. One is that the seating of the persons invited to be present was very successfully accomplished owing to the Rev. Thos. McNair of the Presbyterian Mission, and Mr. Miller, Secretary of the United States Legation, having kindly consented to act as ushers, in which they were also assisted by a Japanese gentleman of the Imperial Household Department. This was the more needful, as several high officials of that department were expected to be present. They were assigned seats in the central aisle immediately behind the family, as the next chief mourners. The representatives of foreign governments, of whom several were present, including Hon. Mr. Buck, United States minister, were assigned seats in the same and adjoining aisle, missionary ladies and gentlemen also filled up these aisles. The pall-bearers, twelve or more in number, comprised representatives of the missions, two Hollanders, and a number of Japanese gentlemen, friends of the family, one of whom was Barrister Masujima, occupied seats at the right of the pulpit, and the choir, under direction of Miss Moulton, the opposite side of the pulpit.

" The intermixture, or alternation of Japanese and English in the service was a happy circumstance. Indeed nationality faded away under the solemnity and sublimity, we may say, of the universality of the grief at the loss of one whom, without a distinct right of citizenship, three countries claimed an equal interest in as their representative; and, as President Ibuka put it, if to be judged by time of residence, and extent of labor and influence he was more of a Japanese than an American. It is a beautiful exemplification of the lives of the ancient patriarchs that having the promise of the whole land, they owned nought in it save a burial-place, because his true citizenship was in heaven. Another circumstance, small though it be, was happily suggestive of our Heavenly Father's care for His loved ones— even for His dear son's interment with suitable honors, that the request that no flowers should be sent, which went forth to the foreign community, was disregarded by the Imperial Household department, for the half dozen or more of beautiful wreaths sent by the Kunaisho added much beauty to the casket and decorated the hearse during the procession. They seemed too beautiful to be left upon the tomb to perish under the snow mantle and the storm that has since fallen upon them. Nor is this all the kindness, His Imperial Japanese Majesty's Government has shown, for an intimation that a largess of five hundred yen were sent to Miss Verbeck, to defray her reverend father's funeral expenses, has reached us. If this be so, or not, it is evident the Japanese rulers and their people are susceptible of the highest and kindest sentiments of gratitude and sympathy toward any whom they can love and respect."

As the fitting conclusion of our story of Verbeck of Japan, we reproduce some of the tributes of the native Japanese press, both secular and Buddhist, as translated for The Japan *Evangelist*, with a word or two from those who knew him best.

The first is from the *Yorodʒu Cho* published in Tokio.

"Brown, Hepburn, Verbeck—these are the three names which shall ever be remembered in connection with Japan's new civilization. They were young men of twenty-five or thereabout, when they together rode into the harbor of Nagasaki early in 1858. The first said he would teach, the second that he would heal, and the third that he would preach. Dr. S. R. Brown

opened a school at Yokohama, and with no os-
tentation of a Doshisha, he quietly applied
himself to his work until he died. Such eminent
men as Mr. Shimada Saburo, Revs. Uyemura,
Oshikawa and Honda, are the fruits of his labor.
Dr. Hepburn healed ; famous Mr. Kishida Ginko
made his name and fortune through him ; while
the Doctor's dictionary will ever remain as a
monument of patient philological work, not to be
surpassed for many years to come. The two
of the devoted triumvirate have joined the ' choir
invisible' now for several years.[1] The third has
now passed away, full of honors and good
works. All three by their silent labors have left
Japan better than they had found it.

"Forty years of continued, unstinted service
for the people not of one's own race and nation!
Let our readers think of it. Is there any one of
our countrymen who is thus spending and being
spent for our immediate neighbors, the Koreans?
Forty years of continued unostentatious work,
not to get money, or praise, but with an aim
known only to himself and his Maker! Apart
from the doctrines he came here to preach, there
was a sustained energy in the man such that we
might well envy and seek to possess. Perhaps
he had in him the Dutch doggedness of his native
land. But the joy, the contentedness, the sweet
submission in his work seemed to imply some
other source of strength not wholly explicable by
physics and physiology."

[1] Dr. J. C. Hepburn is still (Oct. 1, 1900) living.

Verbeck of Japan

The *Kokumin no Tomo* [The Nation's Friend] said :

"By the death of Doctor Verbeck, the Japanese people have lost a benefactor, teacher, and friend. He was born in Holland, was educated in America, and taught in Japan. The present civilization of Japan owes much to his services. Of the distinguished statesmen and scholars of the present, many are those who studied under his guidance. That during his forty years' residence in this land he could witness the germ, the flower, and the fruit of his labor, must have been gratifying to him. It should be remembered by our people that this benefactor, teacher, and friend of Japan prayed for the welfare of this empire until he breathed his last."

Even the Buddhists knew who was the friend of Japan. *The Hanzei Zasshi* said:

"Dr. Verbeck was a missionary, who came to Japan before the Meiji Restoration, and rendered great services both to evangelization and education, through the long course of over thirty years. The doctor is surely one of those who rejoice in being the friends of Japan. We Buddhists who have no conspicuous success in foreign mission-work should be shamed by the example of this venerable missionary."

Here is the tribute of a true Christian woman, Miss Leila Winn, who, in the Master's name, toils in northern Japan:

"Though for many years a member of the same mission with Dr. Verbeck, I never felt that

"Weary with the March of Life"

I really knew him until the autumn of 1897, when he came to Aomori to give us a ten days' series of lectures and sermons. The first thing that impressed me was what a student he was. He never preached at random. One could see at once that there had been thorough preparation beforehand. He called the little park at Aomori his 'study room.' As soon as breakfast was over he would go off to the park and not be seen again till noon. After dinner he did the same till evening. It was no wonder then that, evening after evening, he held his audiences spellbound.

"His self-effacement was another thing that impressed me. A compliment seemed to give him pain rather than pleasure. He always changed the subject. He wanted people to think of Jesus Christ, not about himself.

"Dr. Verbeck swayed and governed those about him by his gentleness, rather than by words of fault-finding and criticism. His visit here made me wish to be a nobler, better woman, and to overcome all that was petty and belittling in my nature.

"One evening after one of his lectures I remember finding my Bible woman in a brown study. When I asked what she was thinking about, she replied, 'I am thinking of that great man, Dr. Verbeck—and to think that after all he is human like the rest of us, and some day will die and be buried like any one else.'

"Neither she nor I realized that his end was so

near,—when to use his own words, he would 'go home to heaven, to his good father and mother.'"

Among the many notices in the newspapers of the United States, we reproduce that from *The Independent*, New York:

"We have here an illustration of what a man of strong nature and fine culture can do when he has the courage to use his concentrated powers. Dr. Verbeck has impressed his stamp on the whole future history of renovated Japan. The country which will give impulse and direction to all Eastern Asia will feel his influence and will hold his name in reverence through all the centuries of its future history. This plain, modest, forceful, learned, devoted missionary will be remembered as are St. Augustine in England, St. Patrick in Ireland, and Ulfilas, the missionary to the Goths. The race of Christian heroes does not yet fail, nor the opportunity to serve the world."

Let this final word close our story:

"When all is said, his life is best summed up in the words: 'I determined not to know anything among you, save Jesus Christ, and Him crucified.' Untiring consecration to his Master's work ruled in all he did. His first pleasure was preaching, for which he had talents that would have made him notable in any land. I should say that his chief powers were the graphic vividness with which he could portray a scene, being richly gifted in voice and gesture; then the resistless logic with which he forced truth home. His sermons abounded in illustrations, and were the delight of Japanese audiences. Wherever he went, the people came in crowds to see and hear.

"Without him, Japan will not seem like itself. Because of him Japan will grow less like itself, and more like the kingdom of heaven."

Index

Index

Index

Enomoto, 195, 329, 330.

Epidemics, 98.

Europe, 52, 60, 144, 185, 188, 213, 231, 232, 234.

Europeans, 54, 119, 146, 163, 246.

Evil Sect, 149.

FERRIS, ISAAC, 63.

Ferris, Rev. John M., 154, 155, 200, 213.

Fest, Dr., 353.

Foreign Languages, School of, 220, 234.

Formosa, 72, 271, 272, 274.

Fort Howard, 49.

France, 115–120.

French, 44, 112, 132, 135, 162, 193, 203, 204, 218, 233, 234.

Fuji Yama, 21, 27, 218, 250.

Fukui, 171, 208, 214, 217, 250, 252, 253.

Fukuzawa, 194, 252, 311, 318.

Fushimi, 152, 165, 181, 275.

GASKELL, Mrs., 39.

Ga Kinosuke, 163, 168

Genahr, Rev., 66.

Gen Ro In, 277, 282.

German, 39, 46, 59, 64, 66, 203, 210, 211, 212, 23

Germanic, 60, 136.

Germany, 29, 41, 42, 234, 275.

Gingko Kishida, 361.

Goble, Rev. Mr., 163.

Gojingahara, 230.

Gokuraku, 167.

Goto Shojiro, 163, 170.

Government, Imperial, 50, 138, 182–186.

Green Bay, 38, 48, 52, 55, 57.

Greene, Dr. D. C., 252.

Griffis, Miss M. C., 222.

Grotius, Hugo, 151, 326.

Gutzlaff, 42, 142.

HAGUE, THE, 177.

Hakase, 26.

Hakodaté, 53.

Hakone Pass, 107, 194.

Hale, Rev. E. E., 28.

Harris, Townsend, 77, 87, 92, 104, 106.

Hartley, Mr., 164.

Haruko, Empress, 195.

Hasègawa, 211.

Hayashi, 321.

Hebrew, 192.

Helena, Ark., 51, 52.

Hepburn, Dr. J. C., 87, 108, 208, 360.

Heusken, 92.

Hideyoshi, 25, 59.

Higo, Daimio of, 117, 212, 213, 223.

Hikone, 106.

Hiogo, 158.

Hirado, 60, 157.

Hirozawa, 225.

Historical Summary, 233.

Hitosubashi, 107, 143, 146, 230, 245.

Hizen, 59, 99, 124, 131, 132, 152–160, 171, 175, 197.

Index

Index

371

Index

Index

Index

Index

Index

Made in the USA
Coppell, TX
18 August 2021